ARCHIVES
ALIVE

ALA Editions purchases fund advocacy, awareness, and accreditation programs for library professionals worldwide.

ARCHIVES
ALIVE

Expanding Engagement with Public
Library Archives and Special Collections

DIANTHA DOW SCHULL

ala
editions

An imprint of the American Library Association
Chicago | 2015

DIANTHA DOW SCHULL, principal and founder of DDSchull Associates, is an advisor to libraries, museums, and foundations. She was formerly president of Libraries for the Future (LFF). Prior to joining LFF, Schull was executive director of the French-American Foundation, director of exhibitions at the New York Public Library, and director of interpretive programs at the Library of Congress. Schull is the author of *50+ Library Services: Innovation in Action* (2013), co-editor of *Boomers and Beyond: Reconsidering the Role of Libraries* (2010), the author of numerous articles on cultural institutions, and a frequent presenter at professional conferences. For more information see www.ddschull.com.

© 2015 by the American Library Association

Extensive effort has gone into ensuring the reliability of the information in this book; however, the publisher makes no warranty, express or implied, with respect to the material contained herein.

ISBN: 978-0-8389-1335-2 (paper)

Library of Congress Cataloging-in-Publication Data

Schull, Diantha Dow.
    Archives alive : expanding engagement with public library archives and special collections / Diantha Dow Schull.
        pages cm
    Includes bibliographical references and index.
        ISBN 978-0-8389-1335-2 (print : alk. paper) 1. Public libraries—United States—Special collections. 2. Public libraries—Cultural programs—United States—Case studies. 3. Archives—Cultural programs—United States—Case studies. I. Title.
    Z688.A3U66 2015
    027.473—dc23   2014049140

Cover design by Kimberly Thornton.
Cover images from *Cool + Collected: Treasures of the Boston Public Library*. Licensed under a Creative Commons Attribution 2.0 Generic License. They are attributed to the Boston Public Library, and the original versions can be found at: https://www.flickr.com/photos/boston_public_library. Clockwise from upper left: *Birds of America*, "Snowy Owl," by John James Audubon, 1829; *Fuge for Three Strings*, by Wolfgang Amadeus Mozart, 1780; *Novus Planiglobii Terrestris per Utrumque Polum Conspectus*, by Gerard Valck, 1672; *First Anniversary of the Kidnapping of Thomas Sims*, broadside, 1852.

Text composition by Alejandra Diaz in the Minion Pro, and Proxima Nova typefaces.

♾ This paper meets the requirements of ANSI/NISO Z39.48–1992 (Permanence of Paper).

Printed in the United States of America
19 18 17 16 15   5 4 3 2 1

CONTENTS

2 COMMUNITY ARCHIVES 31

3 EDUCATIONAL INITIATIVES 55

4 EMERGING INSTITUTIONAL MODELS 85

5   EXHIBITIONS AND RELATED PROGRAMS   131

6 INTERACTIVE ARCHIVES 175

7 LECTURES, CONFERENCES, AND BROADCAST PROGRAMS 213

8 NATIONAL AND INTERNATIONAL PROGRAMS

235

9 ORAL HISTORY AND COMMUNITY DOCUMENTATION PROJECTS   247

10 TOURS, COMMEMORATIONS, AND SPECIAL EVENTS

ACKNOWLEDGMENTS

This book reveals the experiences and insights of public library archivists and special collections librarians. Over the course of eighteen months I had the privilege of interviewing, and learning from, some of the most innovative and dedicated professionals in the library and archival professions. They have willingly shared their stories and their plans for expanding access to archives and special collections in the public library setting. They are the true authors of this publication, without whose expertise and inspiration the study would not have been possible. I extend to each and every one of them my sincere gratitude.

I especially want to acknowledge the contributions of the following individuals: Donna Bachowski, Jim Baggett, Stephanie Bayliss, Susan Becker, Ingrid Betancourt, Andrea Blackman, Tom Blake, Tim Blevins, Debra Bloom, Larry Borowski, Ani Boyadjian, Jennifer Brannock, Scott Brouwer, Nicholas Butler, Jim Carmin, Marguerite Cheman, Dan Chuzmir, Esther Chung, Joy Testa Cinquino, Nicole Cloutier, Brian Collins, George Combs, Beverly Cook, William Cook, Richard Crawford, Maria Benn Cunningham, Amy Dawson, Rose Dawson, Patricia DeFrain, Todd DeGarmo, Renee DesRoberts, Anita Doering, Lisa Dowd, Wayne Dowdy, Lisa Dunseth, Abigial Elder, Pamela Eyerdam, Jodie Fenton, Laura Fletcher, Henry Fortunato, Stephen G. Fullwood, Gary Galvan, Sean Garvey, Steven Geise, Timothy Gleisner, Jordan Goffin, Susan Goldstein, Amanda Graham, Andrea Grimes, Gregg Grunow, Ted Hathaway,

Jonathan Hiam, Deidre Lynn Hollman, Sandy Horrocks, Glen Humphreys, Mary Jean Jakubowski, Judy James, Michael Johnson, Ladi'Sasha Jones, Judy Kamilhor, Richard Kaplan, Tavis Kimball, Judy Knudsen, Matt Knutzen, Stephen Landstreet, Rosemary Lavery, Yesenia Lopez, Julie Lynch, Nora Lyons, Ivy Marvel, Laura McCarty, Renee McClendon, ShannonMcDonough, Natalie Milbrodt, Mary Milinkovich, Brenda Miller, Mike Miller, Romie Minor, Danelle Moon, Christina Moretta, Annie Nelson, Terry Nelson, Mary Beth Newbill, Jane Newell, Donna Nicely, Lynne O'Hara, Angela O'Neal, Lisa Opeenheim, Alyssa Pacy, Emilie Parker, Peter Pearson, Gina Perille, Dawn Peters, Ben Peterson, Amy Pickard, Janine Pollock, Eva Poole, Beth Prindle, Gregory Priore, Susan Rabbiner, Christina Rice, David Riordan, Wright Rix, Brian Robertson, James Rogers, Pauline Rothstein, Jane Salisbury, Elizabeth Sargent, Abraham Schecter, Jan Schmidt, Jamie Seemiller, Karen Shafts, Betty Shankle, Elly Shodell, Steve Smith, Todd Stephens, David Stricklin, Monique Sugimoto, Patricia Van Skaik, Mona Vance, Irene Wainwright, Danny Walker, Kate Wells, Heidi Wigler, Beth Willauer, Tom Wilsbach, Stuart Wilson, Curt Witcher, and Kim Zablud. Final thanks go to the staff of ALA Editions, especially Rob Christopher, Angela Gwizdala, and Jamie Santoro, and to the members of my family, who have patiently endured my preoccupation with the wonders of public libraries and their special collections.

DECEMBER 5, 2014

INTRODUCTION

> As an archivist it is a fabulous time to be working in Special
> Collections in a public library. Archives are the core of a library . . .
> they make that library different from every other facility.
> They also help people recognize what is special about their own
> lives and neighborhoods.
>
> —Elizabeth Sargent, Assistant Director for Special Collections and Director,
> Houston Metropolitan Research Center, Houston Public Library

All across the United States public library archivists and special collections librarians are experimenting with programs that raise public awareness of and promote engagement with special collections. Through interpretive programs, community archives, crowdsourcing, digital access projects, educational outreach, commemorative events, exhibitions, collection development initiatives, and broadcast programs archivists and librarians are developing new approaches to connecting patrons with rare, fragile, and historically or culturally significant collections. The programs take multiple formats, engage diverse audiences, sometimes involve partners, and, more and more often, use digital technologies and social media to extend their visibility and enable remote participation. Programs range from Denver Public Library's Creating Your Community Project, an online social media archive, and Houston Public Library's Student History Internship Project, to Hartford Public Library's Arts and Archives Classes, Newark Public Library's Puerto Rican Community Archive, and San Francisco Public Library's OldSF project that involved experts and enthusiasts in geocoding the library's historical photographs.

The new programs are significant for their potential to reframe public and professional consciousness about public library special collections. They are significant as vehicles for access and as catalysts for collections management and digitization. And, they are especially significant in the context of current professional discussions regarding the meaning of "access," the value of archives and special collections, and the evolving roles of special collections professionals. Despite their significance, there has been relatively little attention to public library archival and special collections programming at professional meetings or in library literature. It was not until 2010 that the Society of American Archivists approved formation of a roundtable on public library archives, now known as the Public Library Archives/Special Collections Roundtable (PLASC).

Archives Alive aims to shine a light on archival and special collections programming in American public libraries at a time when libraries and archives everywhere are undergoing profound change. By examining current programming trends, and profiling 117 programs, projects, and archival departments, *Archives Alive* documents the scope and variety of collection-based programming—programming that has the potential to help change perception and use of special collections. It is a resource for library leaders and archivists, special collections librarians, reference librarians, library and archives educators, state archivists and state librarians, students in library studies and archival and rare books programs, and other members of the library and archival professions concerned with the relationship between special collections and public audiences. Focused on public libraries, the book offers examples and lessons that can be applied in academic, museum, or special libraries as well.

Beyond the library and archives communities there are stakeholders for whom the following examples of innovative archival and special collections programming are relevant: historians, especially public historians; curators and educators in museums and historical societies; community and oral history specialists; students of book arts and material culture; and leaders of humanities councils and digital humanities projects associated with cultural heritage organizations. In fact, the relationship between these stakeholders and public library special collections is itself shifting, and is an aspect of the changes taking place in programming.

BACKGROUND

Three trends in the recent evolution of American libraries influence current developments in public library archives and special collections:

- the changing identity of the public library, from a static repository of print materials to an open, networked, user-centered destination for inquiry, interaction, and creativity;
- the evolution of digital technologies that are transforming approaches to collection management, services, and communications; and

- changing definitions of "access" and purpose in the realm of special collections, with prominent archivists calling for streamlined approaches to cataloging and digitization, a greater emphasis on visibility and access, and more focus on the use of collections for education and community-building.

These trends converge in the phenomenon of increased public programming, both analog and digital, based on public library archives and special collections. Responding to the new library environment, new user expectations, and calls for new approaches to documentation and community engagement, archivists and librarians are moving beyond traditional exhibitions and scholarly lectures to offer an array of new programs from social archives and history symposia to community scan-ins. These activities are reshaping internal and external perceptions of archives and special collections. Ivy Marvel, manager of the Brooklyn Public Library's Brooklyn Collection, explains this phenomenon in relation to the library's first experiment with an Artist-in-Residence:

> An archive is typically deemed a repository of the past, compiled for the sake of posterity, the future; this public conversation, which is grounded in the collaborative relationship between photographer and archivist that has developed during Felicella's time as Artist-in-Residence at the Brooklyn Public Library, presents an opportunity to consider the archive in the present tense and as an open, active endeavor.

While some programs profiled in this book build on prior efforts to create finding aids for scholars or display special items for public viewing, most current programs reflect new goals: increased exposure to archives and special collections and direct engagement with aspects of these collections by members of the general public. Some projects even invite members of the public to contribute information about collections, thereby enhancing the overall institutional record. According to David Riordan, Product Manager for NYPL Labs:

> We often think about the public library as a public platform . . . While archivists are essential for building collections, members of the public can add information that enriches the collections. By creating a context for public involvement we enable them to participate in the future of humanities research.

Many of the new programs enhance digitization projects or result in digital initiatives. Beyond basic digitization, however, they use new technologies for communications with audiences, for community-based collection development, and, even, to enable individuals to create their own programs or personal collections. The combination of digital access with online communications and face-to-face programming is powerful, enabling public library archivists to make their collections more visible, more accessible, *and* more meaningful for multiple audiences.

Despite the clear evidence of a movement toward public access through programming, there are barriers to change: a lack of consensus about the value of increased public engagement with special collections within the community of archivists and special collections professionals—what the president of the Society of American Archivists has called the profession's "resistance to change" (*Strengthening Our Identities, Fighting Our Foibles.* Inaugural Address, Society of American Archivists, September 1, 2007); the lack of a forum to connect and support those carrying out new programming; minimal training in interpretive activities or public programming, other than exhibitions, in most archival and rare book studies programs; and the lack of visibility within the professional library and archival communities for the experimental activities that are beginning to transform the identity and use of special collections.

Beyond these barriers there are two other major and interrelated challenges, one a matter of perception and one a matter of resources. With respect to the former, there is a lingering perception of archives and special collections as insular, static, and associated with the library's past rather than its future. This perception is evident even within the library profession. One of the most recent studies of library futures, for instance, by the Aspen Institute Dialogue on Public Libraries titled "The Challenge: Re-envisioning the Public Library" (November 2014) includes relatively few specific references to archives or special collections. This, despite the report's lucid discussions of public libraries as "trusted community hubs and repositories of knowledge and information," "interactive entities that can facilitate people operating individually or in groups," and "platforms for the learning needs and goals of the community." Ironically, these descriptors could have been used in connection with many of the institutions and programs profiled in the following chapters.

Somehow, in the rush toward the library of the future, the collections that are the foundation of most libraries, the programming that is occurring around these collections, and their value in the digital age have been overlooked. It would behoove library leaders to confront this oversight, and to reframe the value and position of archives and special collections as they plan for library futures.

The relative lack of attention to archives and special collections in library planning is especially ironic in light of the high levels of professional interest in the Digital Public Library of America (DPLA). This extraordinary initiative is laying the groundwork for a new digital network of cultural heritage collections made up, in part, of public library archives and special collections. As local collections are digitized and integrated with other collections, the individual and collective value of these special collections—their social, historical, pedagogical, aesthetic, and civic value—will become more and more apparent, along with the value of their source institutions. The DPLA network will provide public library special collections with new visibility, a new platform for service and a new rationale for sustained support as a part of a larger national whole.

Beyond the issue of perception there is an additional challenge, one that was voiced over and over by the professionals interviewed for this publication—namely, the need to improve the balance between routine archival functions and the new forms of public programming and digital communications. Many professionals, such as Janine Pollock, manager of the Rare Books Department at the Free Library of Philadelphia, welcome and, indeed, believe in the need for increased public engagement with collections.

> As part of a public library we have a two-sided mission, on the one hand to safeguard
> our collections and make them available to scholars, and on the other hand to inspire
> people's curiosity and help get them interested in arts and culture.

However, these same professionals, including the "lone arrangers" in smaller departments, find themselves caught between the possibilities for doing more education and interpretation, both online and on-site, while also carrying out traditional archival practices. Despite their dedication to outreach and their capacity for program development many archivists and librarians simply do not have the requisite support to operate on all fronts simultaneously. Jordan Goffin of the Providence Public Library explains: "With only two professionals for the entire department, it is difficult to realize the potential for creative, collections-based programming."

For this author, the very real dilemma confronting those who are motivated to experiment, to reach out, to engage with their publics, raises questions that merit exploration in archival and library forums. How can special collections librarians continue to carry out their traditional duties while also creating new opportunities for public participation, discovery, and learning? What routine functions can be discarded? How can new tools streamline archival processes? What additional skills and supports in special collections departments would free up creative archivists and librarians who are keen to develop the interpretive and educational potential of their collections?

GOALS

Archives Alive is intended to help address these questions and barriers. By highlighting examples of proven programs and cutting-edge experiments, *Archives Alive* aims to stimulate librarians, archivists, and key stakeholders at all levels to reenvision and revitalize special collections programming—and, indeed, the position of archives and special collections—in the public library setting.

Designed as a report to the field, or a scan of the landscape, *Archives Alive* brings together a range of programs that represent changing practices at a certain point in time: 2014, just over a decade into the twenty-first century. It shines a light on the many programs, projects, and departments that are, individually and collectively, helping reshape the image, functions, and content of public library special collections. In so doing *Archives Alive* aims to raise their visibility across the library and archival professions and create a base of information for future analyses and reports.

Archives Alive also seeks to raise the visibility of the professionals who are managing special collections departments and/or carrying out the projects that are profiled. Relatively invisible within the public library hierarchy or outside the library sphere, these professionals are dedicated to ensuring the preservation of their collections *and* finding ways to share them meaningfully with the general public. Their voices provide texture and values to the reports on specific programs and authenticity to the overall landscape scan.

A final and related goal is to foster professional exchange around public library archival and special collections programming. Again and again over the course of the research for *Archives Alive* individuals at one institution would express surprise and curiosity about the work of peers in other locations. Public library archivists and special collections librarians are relatively isolated, few have the time to report on what they are doing or exchange information with colleagues about public programming, and even fewer have the personal or institutional means to attend national conferences of archivists or librarians. By creating a resource for the profession, *Archives Alive* seeks to stimulate increased recognition for and contacts between the professionals carrying out the new programming.

CONTENT AND ORGANIZATION

Archives Alive consists of 117 profiles—104 programs and 13 institutions or departments—organized into ten topical categories. The profiles reflect the extraordinary variety of subject matter and collection formats found in public library special collections, from illuminated manuscripts, iconic photographs, landmark poems, and presidential letters to restaurant menus, diaries, plans for ships, railroads, planes and parks, yearbooks, and records of local unions, clubs, businesses, schools and public agencies. Creative archivists in public libraries across the country are reexamining these collections and finding new ways to make them meaningful for diverse audiences. Some are focusing on whole collections, such as Kansas City Public Library's exhibition Greetings from Kansas City: Postcard Views of a Midwestern Metropolis, 1900–1950, that presented 200 postcards as forms of instant messaging and indicators of popular cultural developments over time. Others are using a single item to engage residents in rediscovering a key period in local history, such as the Cincinnati Panorama project of the Public Library of Cincinnati and Hamilton County. And some, such as the Cleveland Public Library and the Providence Public Library, are encouraging new artwork inspired by their collections.

Whatever the scope or topic of a particular program, it takes a particular form. *Archives Alive* identifies nine programming categories that demonstrate the range of ways that librarians are using collections to inform, inspire, educate, and entertain. These categories provide the organizational framework for the book. From broadcast programs and community archives to interactive projects and commemorations, the projects and programs profiled suggest the scope of the national landscape. Traditional program formats, such as tours and exhibitions, are important parts of the landscape—and are often the subjects of experimentation and transformation—along with nontraditional formats such as virtual scrapbooks and geocaching events. Trends within these categories are summarized in the introduction to each chapter.

In addition to the nine programming categories, one chapter examines the full array of programs being offered by thirteen special collections departments. These "Emerging Institutional Models" reflect organizational as well as programmatic trends. Some of the institutional models also offer excellent examples of specific program types, in which case the latter are profiled with like programs in the appropriate chapter. Together, the ten categories demonstrate the vitality and variety of programming in archives today.

With respect to content, it is important to point out that *Archives Alive* does not document programs based on genealogical collections. Although many of the public libraries referenced here include or even feature genealogical collections and provide extensive services and programs on genealogical research and family history, they are so extensive as to require a book in and of themselves.

It is also important to point out that *Archives Alive* is not comprehensive. Such a report would be impossible to compile given the number and variety of public libraries and library systems and the scope of programming taking place in and through their archival departments. For each program example included here there are many others that could have been included. *Archives Alive* uses the examples to suggest the larger universe of activities, to present potential models, and to trace current trends.

METHODOLOGY

Archives Alive is not based on a rigorous survey nor does it reference established criteria for selection of program examples. In fact, no such criteria exist. The programs, projects and institutions described in this volume do not have a collective identity, nor do they, yet, have the professional recognition necessary for formal codification. In reporting on the scope, variety and significance of current public library archival programs, *Archives Alive* aims to prompt professional recognition and, eventually, more rigorous assessment and evaluation.

The projects and institutions profiled in *Archives Alive* were originally selected for inclusion based on the author's deep knowledge of libraries and of interpretive programming in libraries, museums, and other cultural institutions. A list of nearly 175 projects was drawn up for further exploration, along with the following informal set of criteria for further program selection:

1. What is the program or project format and how effective is it in illuminating an aspect of the collections?
2. To what extent does the program reflect new programming approaches or a reshaping of prior program approaches?
3. How does the program contrast or align with others of its type?
4. To what extent does the program reflect the archives/special collections department's commitment to public programming?
5. Is there something distinctive about the program that makes it stand out from others of its type?
6. Is the project replicable in other libraries?

Using these criteria and the initial list of projects, the author then interviewed 77 library directors, archivists, special collections librarians, and communications specialists regarding their overall approaches to public programming and the specific program or project under consideration. Based on these interviews the number of examples was reduced to 117. These represent 62 institutions, with some institutions represented in multiple programming categories.

As a national scan, *Archives Alive* does not emphasize rigorous analysis. The programs and projects speak for themselves. Brief comments about each project indicate its value as an exemplar of a particular programming approach. In addition, the author provides a brief analysis of the trends in each program category as part of the chapter introductions. At this stage in the development of public library archival programming, criticism is less important than professional and public recognition and information exchange; at a later stage in the development of these programs deeper analysis and development of evaluative criteria will be beneficial.

In the context of current professional discussions about archives and special collections, particularly in relation to digital projects, *Archives Alive* provides a timely and complementary resource that focuses on the programs, and the people behind the programs, that are transforming special collections. *Archives Alive* reports on the work of many professionals across the country and in so doing gives them visibility and voice. Their work reflects a shift in how archivists and special collections librarians regard the general public and a shift in how they are organizing and reorganizing resources to meet public users' needs. Based on this evidence their work is having a strong impact on their institutions and their constituents. If the vitality and variety shown in these examples are sustained, *Archives Alive* will be the first of many "reports to the field."

ONE

ART AND ARCHIVES

The Providence Public Library is dedicated to ensuring
the continued rebirth, rediscovery and reinterpretation of these
treasures by making them available to artists, students, scholars
and members of the general public.

—Jordan Goffin, Special Collections Librarian, Providence (RI) Public Library

P ublic library archives and special collections have important roles to play
with respect to the arts. These roles are obvious in the case of collections
focused on one or more art forms such as prints, musical scores, literary manuscripts, or book arts. In these collections the very mission is
to preserve, organize, and promote appreciation of the works of art. However, the
connection between art and archives is also relevant to other types of collections,
collections of manuscripts, glass plate negatives, diaries, maps, cuneiform tablets, or
even born-digital documents. No matter the formats of the documentary sources,
artworks, or material culture in their collections, there are myriad ways that public
library archivists and library special collections librarians can use the collections to
strengthen art and art-making in their communities.

The fourteen examples assembled in this chapter reflect the range of possibilities for art-related programming. They can be grouped into four broad categories, each of which suggests a trend in how public library special collections fulfill their roles with respect to the arts.

The first trend has to do with new approaches to interpreting and celebrating the artwork in public library special collections. Beyond straightforward exhibitions that showcase art in their collections, many libraries are developing complementary programs that deepen appreciation of the works on view, place them in historical, social, or artistic context, and, even, stimulate new works. The Los Angeles Public Library's Songs in the Key of L.A. program displayed treasures from the library's sheet music collection, offered public programs exploring their cultural and artistic significance, and sparked new works in the form of musical recordings, contemporary compositions, and performances. Programs such as this augment exhibitions and attract audiences of different types.

Archivists and special collections librarians can play another cultural role by supporting and connecting artists. They can identify and promote local artists through exhibitions and performances, as exemplified by the two-part exhibition of Newark Art and Artists organized by the Special Collections Division of the Newark Public Library. They can also provide opportunities for artists to meet one another and exchange ideas about their work or work in the library's collections. Jan Schmidt of the Jerome Robbins Dance Division at New York's Library of the Performing Arts states that "Community building is an important function for a research collection in a public library." The Division uses projects such as the African Dance Project to encourage networking across the dance community. Similarly, the Los Angeles Public Library's Photography Collection offers a regular lunchtime program, The Photographers Eye, which provides an opportunity for photographers working in Los Angeles to discuss one another's work in an informal setting.

Beyond contextualizing their art collections and promoting dialogue between artists, there is a third role that archives and special collections can play, namely, fostering arts appreciation and arts education. Many archivists and librarians offer lectures, tours, exhibitions, performances, and workshops that illuminate the artwork in their collections. These programs interpret and celebrate the work of particular artists or artistic styles, present work that is generally inaccessible to the public, provide opportunities to examine works at close range, and otherwise help participants make connections that would not otherwise be possible. The Free Library of Philadelphia's Fleisher Collection of Orchestral Music offers broadcast programs that enable remote listeners to hear works from the collection and learn about them from music history specialists. The Cleveland Public Library's Special Collections augmented its 2013 exhibition on Paper Stories: Adventures in Kamishibai, Manga, Graphic Novels and Zines with lectures by book artists and workshops on book-making and paper making.

A final approach to fulfilling special collections' cultural role takes the form of encouraging artists or art students to use special collections as sources for art-making. While artists have always used libraries for education and inspiration, some institutions are extending invitations to artists for residencies or special projects. They are encouraging interpretive activities in different media and featuring the resulting works in performances, exhibitions, or other public celebrations. In this way public library special collections are following the lead of many museums that have discovered the value of engaging artists to generate fresh interpretations of collections.

There is no single approach to special collections' expanded efforts to engage artists with special collections. The Brooklyn Public Library's first Artist-in-Residence program stimulated a photographer to document the library itself and, especially, the Brooklyn Collection—its patrons, staff, functions, and spaces. The Special Collections department of the Providence Public Library works regularly with contemporary artists who use works from the collections to create new art, curate thematic exhibitions, and even organize workshops for members of the public. Chicago Public Library's One Book, Many Interpretations project in 2006 invited book artists from around the world to create and exhibit works inspired by the library's One Book, One Chicago readings. The works were so exceptional that the project was repeated five years later.

The trend to encourage art-making based on special collections also extends to members of the general public. The Hartford Public Library's Hartford History Center uses its collections to inspire participants in workshops on the arts and humanities. The San Diego Public Library's Wangenheim Collection of book arts and illuminated manuscripts invited students in a graduate class in graphic design to create works based on "treasures" such as cuneiform tablets and palm leaf manuscripts. Cleveland Public Library's Special Collections carries out similar projects with students at nearby art colleges.

These trends and activities vary from institution to institution. They reflect the imagination and skill of individual archivists and librarians and the institutional support they receive to carry out their visions. There are not enough such examples, yet, to define best practices or even create a community of interest. However, they do suggest the exciting possibilities for public library archivists and special collections librarians to strengthen the arts in their communities.

AFRICAN DANCE PROJECTS, JEROME ROBBINS DANCE DIVISION

New York (NY) Public Library for the Performing Arts

OVERVIEW: The Jerome Robbins Dance Division (Dance Division) of the New York Public Library for the Performing Arts (Performing Arts Library) organized and recorded a series of programs on African and African American dance in 2013 titled On Fire with African Dance. The programs had a dual purpose: to develop the Dance Division's documentation on African Dance, while also helping to stimulate interaction between African Dance performers, scholars, and students. A related project, The Mertz Gilmore African Dance Interview Project (African Dance Interview Project), complements On Fire with African Dance and preserves the voices and experiences of traditional African Dance teachers and performers in New York City. Both projects reflect the Division's mission to "connect artists, scholars and lovers of dance."

> **The library of the future will continue to have print material, photographs and digital collections, but it will also become more of a community place, for performances, discussions and collaboration. On Fire with African Dance enabled us to bring together, and document, performers and experts on African Dance and establish the basis for ongoing dialogues about African and African American dance forms.**
>
> —Jan Schmidt, Curator, Jerome Robbins Dance Division

The Dance Division contains the world's largest research collection on dance. The rich array of visual, written, aural, and digital sources chronicles the history of dance in all forms: ballet, ethnic, modern, jazz, social, and folk. Building on these sources, the Division organizes exhibitions, lecture-demonstrations, tours of the collection, film screenings, and performances to reach out to both professional and lay audiences.

ON FIRE WITH AFRICAN DANCE. In 2013 the Dance Division undertook a special project designed to expand the Division's documentation of African Dance and African American Dance and to foster dialogue and collaboration among a growing community of African Dance choreographers, dancers and dance students, researchers, and musicians in the New York region and globally. On Fire with African Dance consisted of a series of public programs held in the Bruno Walter Auditorium of the Performing Arts Library, all of which were followed by a reception and informal dialogue between performers and audience members. Programs covered the following topics:

- Staccato Incandescence: The Story of Mambo, a lecture-performance by Robert Farris Thompson.
- Ronald K. Brown/Evidence: Cultural Exchange through Ancestors, Inspiration, and Grace, a presentation and film screening by Brown and members of his troupe regarding a groundbreaking tour of Africa.
- Concepts in African Dance: Choreography versus Authenticity, a lecture-demonstration by dancer, drum innovator, and master teacher Djoniba Mouflet, in which he and members of his company discussed and demonstrated West African dance and drumming.

AFRICAN DANCE INTERVIEW PROJECT. This grant-funded project was a natural progression from the On Fire with African Dance series. The project involved organizing an African Dance Advisory Group, composed of performers and experts who helped staff shape the project and identified potential interviewees. The primary activity was videotaping interviews with African Dance teachers and performers, thereby capturing the experiences and insights of leaders in the New York dance community.

The African Dance projects were funded by the Committee for the Jerome Robbins Dance Division and the Mertz Gilmore Foundation.

◉ CHALLENGES. The Performing Arts Library was not originally designed for groups to meet informally, making it difficult to carry out the Division's goal of fostering connections across the dance community. Despite this problem, Division staff provides conversational events after formal programs to help advance contact between performers and audience members.

◉ FUTURE PLANS. The Dance Division intends to continue the African Dance Interview Project, while the African Dance Advisory Group will continue to advise the Division and promote communications within the community of African and African American dance professionals.

ARTISTS-IN-RESIDENCE PROGRAM
The Rosenbach of the Free Library of Philadelphia

OVERVIEW: The Rosenbach Museum and Library (the Rosenbach), which recently merged with the Free Library of Philadelphia (FLP), was one of the first libraries or museums in the country to offer residencies for artists and to commission new works inspired by the collection. Launched in 1998, the Artists-in-Residence Program has been a signature program resulting in multiple new artistic works ranging from orchestral pieces to dance performances. This approach offers a model for other institutions seeking to generate artistic use and creative interpretation of its collections.

I had an inkling that the Marianne Moore archives would be of interest because her poetry often creates equivalences between humans and wild nature in poems such as "The Octobus," "The Paper Nautilus" and "No Swan So Fine."

—Sue Johnson, Visual Artist and 2009 Artist-in-Residence

The Rosenbach is a formerly private collection, founded in 1954, that includes paintings and sculpture, decorative arts, manuscripts, rare books, presidential letters, and many first editions. As a museum and a library, it offers ample opportunities for artists interested in developing new work based on the collections. The Artists-in-Residence Program, which commissions artists to create new works, is seen as a way of supporting contemporary artists and generating fresh and alternative views of the collections.

The Rosenbach's first commission involved the Headlong Dance Theater, a Philadelphia-based company known for its witty take on contemporary culture. The company created "Ulysses: Sly Uses of a Book by James Joyce," based on the Rosenbach's manuscript of the modernist masterpiece. Since then the Rosenbach has worked with visual artists, musicians, poets, filmmakers, graphic novelists, photographers, and others, commissioning at least one artist a year. Each artist gives Artists Talks during their residency.

In 2009 Bryce Dessner, guitarist for The National and the instrumental group Clogs, was commissioned to create a musical work inspired by the library's Lincoln documents. He created "The Lincoln Shuffle," a series of short compositions related to the music of Lincoln's era featuring brass instruments. In 2010 the Rosenbach invited printmaker Enrique Chagoya to spend time at the Rosenbach. Inspired by the prints of George Cruikshank, he created a limited edition print informed by Cruikshank's *The Head Ache*. In 2012 the Rosenbach commissioned a work of puppet art by Brooklyn-based Drama of Works (DOW). DOW created "Go Ulysses!" a 30-minute theatrical adaptation that captured the wit of *Ulysses* while introducing the novel to a new generation of *Ulysses* readers.

The most recent Artist-in-Residence at the Rosenbach was contemporary composer David Burrell, who was commissioned to interpret the Rosenbach's Civil War documents. During this multiyear project Burrell worked with poet Monika Larsson to select items from the collection that became touchstones for a series of compositions with poems that provides the libretto for Burrell's compositions. Both artists were particularly inspired by the manuscript of Lincoln's Address at Baltimore of April 18, 1864. Their collaboration led to a multipart piece titled *Listening to Lincoln.* A fusion of opera, jazz, and improvisations, the piece includes a *Requiem for the Fallen at Fort Pillow* and concludes with a solo piano piece, *One Nation.* The full composition was performed at the Rosenbach. To highlight *Listening to Lincoln* and its connections to the Civil War collection, the Rosenbach also mounted Four Scores on 150 Years Ago: David Burrell's Civil War Concerts, an exhibition that included Burrell's scores alongside the original documents that inspired his work.

⊙ **CHALLENGES.** Funding for the Artist-in-Resident Program has always depended on grants from private donors and has therefore been somewhat uncertain from year to year. Without sustained support it can be difficult to plan ahead for the Program.

⊙ **FUTURE PLANS.** Rosenbach staff intend to continue developing the Artist-in-Residence Program to ensure that it remains relevant to the community and unique in the museum and library field. They are considering focusing on book arts as a special take on a library collection. One approach may involve inviting multiple artists to respond to a single book in the collection and to create a work based on the item. In addition to a study of the book's content, artists would delve into the journey the book has taken through history, who owned it, how it was used, and what it can tell us about the time in which it was produced.

ARTS AND ARCHIVES
Master Classes in the Arts and Humanities
Hartford History Center, Hartford (CT) Public Library

OVERVIEW: Since 2008 the Hartford Public Library's Hartford History Center (History Center), has offered Arts and Archives: Master Classes in the Arts and Humanities (Arts and Archives), free instructional workshops for older adults. These classes in arts disciplines and heritage subjects incorporate artifacts, images, and personal narratives from the collections of the History Center. Participants in the arts workshops, taught by master artists, often use these sources as inspiration for their artwork. The programs are popular, and, by demand, are now open to adults of all ages. Arts and Archives offers an example of how a public library can use its historical collections as sources of lifelong learning and creativity.

> **By helping people explore creative expression through the lens of community history, the Arts and Archives program offers a dynamic way to involve and educate adults while also connecting them to Hartford's richly diverse heritage.**
>
> —Brenda Miller, Chief Public Affairs and Public Programming Officer

The Hartford History Center, formerly the Hartford Collection, is a multimedia research collection that illuminates 300 years of civic, cultural, and business history in Hartford and the surrounding region. With an active program of exhibitions, lectures, and events the History Center endeavors to engage varied audiences with the social, political, and cultural history of the city. Arts and Archives is a seven-part workshop series that focuses on varied media and heritage-themed topics. The classes are designed to build participants' skills in specific media and to introduce them to the History Center. Each series includes a seminar introducing participants to the archival collections and ways they might be used by artists. Many participants select images, artifacts, or other historical sources as inspiration. As one example, participants in a pen-and-ink workshop drew on photographs of Hartford streetscapes to inform their work.

Since the start of Arts and Archives, there have been series on sculpture, storytelling, mixed media, memoir writing, poetry, and photography. The workshops are taught by professional artists with experience in arts education. They aim to help individuals become comfortable working in their chosen medium, to develop critical thinking skills, and to develop an awareness of the historical and cultural resources at the library that they can take advantage of on an ongoing basis. The programs culminate with a public exhibition of work created by participants.

Hartford has many teaching artists and adult learners who have responded positively to the special hands-on mix of arts and humanities programming. Most workshop series have been filled to capacity. The program has also garnered visibility for the History Center. In October 2010, for instance, WFSB, the CBS affiliate in Hartford, broadcast a detailed report on the series as part of its *Better Connecticut* show.

◉ CHALLENGES. Special programs such as Arts and Archives depend on special funding, and obtaining that funding is the key challenge for the History Center. Arts and Archives was originally supported through an Institute for Museum and Library Services (IMLS) grant administered by the Connecticut State Library; more recently grants were provided by two local foundations.

◉ FUTURE PLANS. Library leaders are committed to sustaining Arts and Archives in the coming years if at all possible. Depending on future levels of support, History Center staff would expand the program to include additional media and to offer workshops for intergenerational audiences.

❯ **RELATED PROGRAM.** Cooking It Up! Hartford, Health and History is one of numerous programs carried out by the History Center that have resulted in new connections between the history collections and diverse audiences. Cooking It Up! featured live cooking demonstrations of traditional recipes at well-known ethnic restaurants in Hartford, combined with discussions of nutrition based on these recipes and the collection of family recipes from project participants that have become part of the History Center's collection.

BROOKLYN PUBLIC LIBRARY
An Open Book
Brooklyn (NY) Public Library

OVERVIEW: The Brooklyn Public Library (BPL) undertook its first artist-in-residence project in 2013, involving a three-way collaboration between the library's Brooklyn Collection, the Programs and Exhibitions Department, and photographer Elizabeth Felicella. The project resulted in a library-wide exhibition on the history of the Central Library, a major architectural and social landmark in the borough of Brooklyn. Brooklyn Public Library: An Open Book (An Open Book) featured photographs of the library and the Brooklyn Collection by Felicella. The exhibition and Felicella's photographs provoked discussion about the past, present, and future of the library as a vital element of community life.

> The (Open Book) exhibit became as much about the photographer's process of exploring and knowing the building as it was about the building itself, and the project came to fruition in a way I don't think we could have planned from the beginning.
>
> —Ivy Marvel, Manager, Brooklyn Collection

BPL's Brooklyn Collection is a rich repository of Brooklyn-related archives, images, and documents, including maps, manuscripts, historic newspapers, prints, and oral histories. It is also the institutional archive for the library, the fifth largest public library system in the country. For the initial artist-in-residence project Felicella was invited to photograph the library, its spaces, patrons, services, staff, and collections, including the Brooklyn Collection. The resulting images were to be a special part of the Open Book exhibition on the history of the library. The residency was approached as an experiment, with the hope that it would help "develop a model for future residencies." It was loosely defined in order to give the photographer "room to develop her vision for the project as the residency evolved."

Ultimately, the artist's photographic interpretations of the library were presented in two phases. The first set of images showing the Central Library's public interiors and environs was displayed after several days of initial shooting. The second series, which was put on display months later, showed more of the behind-the-scenes areas of the library that Felicella came to know by spending time in the building and in the Brooklyn Collection.

An Open Book was more than a routine history of the Central Library. Through images and artifacts it interpreted the routines of daily life in the Central Library. Book plates, program flyers, book lists, staff memos, retired library cards, and posters reflected the evolution of librarianship in the twentieth century and the many ways that Brooklynites have experienced their library over time. Displays also focused on the human side of the Central Library, featuring formal and informal photographs of diverse staff members, from catalogers and audiovisual specialists to security guards and children's librarians.

During the Open Book project, staff of the Brooklyn Collection worked closely with Felicella, who was especially interested in interpreting the library archives. Her photographs depicted "the hidden nooks of the stacks, the behind-the-scenes corners of the archives . . ." In addition, the Brooklyn Collection organized a public program featuring a conversation between archivists and Felicella regarding the social and architectural significance of libraries and her response to the library and its special collections.

❯ **CHALLENGES.** As the first such initiative, many of the details of the artist residency were developed over the course of the project. While the experimental nature of the residency was ultimately beneficial for both the library and the artist, it was a learning experience for all involved. Another issue was the lack of dedicated funding. According to library staff, the Open Book was carried out with minimal funding; a more formal artist-in-residency program would need more dedicated funds for artist compensation, materials, and promotion.

❯ **FUTURE PLANS.** Following Felicella's residency, the Brooklyn Collection has been working to accession and process the hundreds of photographs she captured during her time at the library. Brooklyn Collection Manager Marvel expects to write and present on the project in order to share the work with the larger library community.

● RELATED PROGRAM. In 2014, BPL started a second Artist-in-Residence Program, with a painter who works outside on the library's plaza creating paintings of the library and the immediate environment that are then displayed throughout the library. He uses photographs from the Brooklyn Collection as inspiration. According to Marvel, "He is creating modern day reinterpretations of historic images, all in his very distinctive painting style." As the Artist-in-Residence Program develops, the Brooklyn Collection expects to be involved "when it is appropriate to the artist and medium at hand."

DISCOVERIES FROM THE FLEISHER COLLECTION
Free Library of Philadelphia

OVERVIEW: The Free Library of Philadelphia's (FLP) contains the Edwin A. Fleisher Collection of Orchestral Music (Fleisher Collection), the largest lending library of orchestral performance material in existence. To promote awareness and appreciation of the Fleisher Collection, FLP partners with the local FM radio station to offer a monthly program of recordings—Discoveries from the Fleisher Collection. Reaching a large regional audience, the series demonstrates how a broadcast program can widen awareness and appreciation of special collections that are relatively invisible to all but specialists.

> **In Discoveries from the Fleisher Collection, we uncover the unknown, rediscover the little known, and take a fresh look at some of the remarkable treasures housed in the Fleisher Collection of Orchestral Music.**
>
> —Free Library of Philadelphia website

In 1929, when the Fleisher Collection was deeded to the library, its contents were described as "the music of older masters, strange masters, strange scores from distant parts of the world, concertos and orchestrations which are virtually unprocurable in the present day." Numbering more than 22,000 titles, the Fleisher Collection is the largest of FLP's four special music collections and includes nearly the entire standard musical repertoire along with many rare and out-of-print works. Unlike other Special Collections, the library allows selected items to be loaned to performing organizations in the United States and around the world.

Although the Fleisher Collection is well-known to musicians, conductors, and music aficionados, it is less well known to the general public. To promote awareness and appreciation of the Fleisher Collection, FLP partners with radio station WRTI 90.1 FM to offer a monthly program of recordings—Discoveries from the Fleisher Collection—that are selected and introduced by Kile Smith, former curator of the Fleisher Collection. The program airs on the first Saturday of each month, and is repeated every Wednesday at WRTI-HD2. It is broadcast not only in Philadelphia but is also heard throughout the Delaware Valley and is available online at WRTI.org.

Discoveries from the Fleisher Collection was initiated through contacts between Kile Smith and Jack Moore, program director at WRTI. Both recognized an opportunity to widen public access to the library's musical holdings through radio broadcasts. The resulting programs, offered since 2002, are hosted by Smith who occasionally invites special guest experts and musicologists to participate. Each program includes Smith's commentaries on the items selected for broadcast, in which he discusses the composers, conductors, and orchestras, and their significance in the evolution of orchestral performance. These commentaries are the basis for Radio Essays by Kile Smith, a unique body of performance analyses. The Radio Essays are archived on the library's website.

Selections for the series cover the full spectrum of orchestral music, including well-known composers such as Joseph Haydn, John Philip Sousa, and Benjamin Britten as well as less well-known composers such as John Cage and Jose Rolon. The performing conductors and orchestras are equally varied, from the New Philharmonia Orchestra and the Michigan Symphony Orchestra to the Philadelphia Orchestra.

On occasion, Discoveries from the Fleisher Collection links thematically with other library programs. For instance, as part of the library yearlong celebration of Shakespeare's 450th birthday, a WRTI program in April 2014 was dedicated to music inspired by Shakespeare's work. The Fleisher Collection also developed a special list of Shakespeare-related works in the collection that is online.

In addition to its broadcasts and readings, the library has organized recordings of pieces from the collection, working with the Czech National Symphony Orchestra and Albany Records. Through these recordings pieces by less well-known composers have been brought back to public attention.

◉ **CHALLENGES.** Presentation of a broadcast program depends on having a program host with in-depth knowledge of the material and an effective radio presence. Smith's involvement as host has been a key to the success of the program.

◉ **FUTURE PLANS.** The Fleisher Collection intends to continue Discoveries from the Fleisher Collection and also to continue promoting rare, unusual, and neglected works.

◉ **RELATED PROGRAM.** Readings from the Chamber Music Collection is another program series developed by the Music Collection. The Chamber Music Collection is the largest collection of chamber music in the country and is a resource for performing groups who can borrow sets for performance. Recently, based on interest expressed by performers, the Chamber Music Collection started a monthly series of "Readings" at the library. These programs enable chamber music musicians to perform pieces from the collection in an informal atmosphere that fosters dialogue and experimentation.

LOUISA SOLANO POETRY SERIES
Cambridge (MA) Public Library

OVERVIEW: In 2013, Louisa Solano, the longtime owner of the well-known Grolier Poetry Book Shop in Cambridge (MA), and a great supporter of poets, both national and international, gave an important collection of poetry-related materials to the Cambridge Public Library's Archives and Special Collections (the Cambridge Room). In her honor, the Cambridge Room launched the Louisa Solano Poetry Series (Poetry Series) and mounted a rotating exhibition of key items from the collection. Both events underscored the commitment of the library and the Cambridge Room to offer arts-related programs relevant to special collections. They also demonstrate the value of such programs in building audiences for archives and special collections.

> Unique programming designed by the archives is an excellent way to bring people to repositories and introduce them to collections they may have never known existed. When well-attended programming is developed and managed by the archives, it reinforces the important role repositories play in their larger institutions and the community at-large.
>
> —Alyssa Pacy, Archivist, Archives and Special Collections

The Cambridge Room consists of research materials focusing on the city of Cambridge: maps; books; city directories and reports; photographs; archival documents; and the complete run of the *Cambridge Chronicle,* the city's newspaper of record. The library hired its first archivist in 2010, Alyssa Pacy, who is organizing existing collections to make them publicly available, carrying out digitization initiatives, and developing programs that foster engagement with special collections. She is also responsible for curating new collections.

The Louisa Solano Collection was an important addition to the Cambridge Room holdings, including independent press limited editions and signed first editions by well-known poets and Grolier photographs, records, and ephemera. For decades, the Grolier has been a meeting place and source of support for poets living in or passing through Cambridge. Solano, the former owner, provided assistance and encouragement to many poets who later were recognized nationally and internationally—some of whom are Cambridge residents.

In honor of Solano's donation, Pacy organized a Poetry Series that took place throughout the fall of 2013. Over three evenings, the library hosted readings by the following poets, all of whom had known Solano and wanted to help honor her: Robert Pinsky, Gail Mazur, David Ferry, and Frank Bidart. There was an opening reception in the Cambridge Room, featuring an exhibition based on the Solano donation. Titled "In Admiration and Gratitude," the display featured first editions of major poets' works. The authors' inscriptions conveyed Solano's long-standing influence on Cambridge poets and the greater poetry community. The exhibition was changed each month to highlight the poet who would be reading his or her works.

The Poetry Series, opening reception, and rotating exhibition helped draw attention to Archives and Special Collections as an arts resource and a partner in arts programming. The readings were well attended, bringing new patrons and stimulating donations from poets and poetry collectors in Cambridge.

❯ **CHALLENGES.** As the first professional archivist at the Cambridge Public Library Pacy faces a backlog of processing tasks along with new digital initiatives, outreach, communications, and programming. Finding the appropriate balance among these tasks, while also organizing new programming, can be a challenge.

❯ **FUTURE PLANS.** Although the 2013 Poetry Series was a unique event, coordinated and managed by the Cambridge Room, the success of the series has inspired the library to continue to offer programming around poetry. The library plans to invite poets from Louisa Solano's immediate circle as well as those in the Cambridge poetry community to give readings throughout the year. The Cambridge Room will mount an exhibition, post blogs, and otherwise reinforce the connection between the poetry readings and the rich poetry sources in Special Collections.

MAKE IT NEW
SDSU Book Artists Respond to the Wangenheim Room Collection
San Diego Public Library

OVERVIEW: Make It New: SDSU Book Artists Respond to the Wangenheim Room Collection (Make It New) was an exhibition of artworks inspired by landmark items in San Diego Public Library's (SDPL) Wangenheim Collection on the history of manuscripts and books. Artists studying at San Diego State University (SDSU) with book arts specialist Michele Burgess created new "books" based on a 4,000-year-old Babylonian clay tablet, a miniature Buddhist scroll, and other unique items. The exhibition demonstrated how public libraries' special collections can inspire contemporary art and how public libraries can share artists' interpretations of collections with the general public.

The concept for my project was to make a visual comparison between the handheld modern calculator and the handheld ancient Babylonian clay tablet. The purpose of both is to document business transactions and both were used for receipt making.

—Jill Hollingsworth, book artist, student, and contributor to the Make It New exhibition

SDPL's Special Collections are made up of three distinct components: the California/San Diego History Collection, the Genealogy Collection, and the Rare Books/Wangenheim Collection. The latter, one of the country's landmark collections on book arts, includes 9,000 items ranging from vellum manuscripts and Japanese woodblock prints to books with fore-edge painting and examples of modern independent press publishing. Through exhibitions and lectures Special Collections staff work to expose the collection and attract members of the general public to the Wangenheim Room.

In 2008, Michele Burgess, teacher of the Advanced Art of the Book Class at SDSU, brought her students to visit the Wangenheim Collection, where they were to select an object to inform the creation of a new book. The students represented a variety of creative professions—printmaking, painting, and graphic arts—and nationalities. They selected seven diverse items from the collection to carry out their assignment, including a Chinese silk scroll made in 1651, a thirteenth-century Latin Bible, a Singhalese prayer book on palm leaves, a seventeenth-century dictionary, and a miniature Buddhist scroll of Japanese wooden block print from about 770 A.D., considered to be the earliest piece of block printing. Using these works as inspiration, they were to make something relevant to contemporary life, that is, "make it new."

According to Heidi Wigler, then curator-librarian of the Wangenheim Collection and organizer of Make It New, "It was fascinating to see how these students, who care about art and bookmaking, responded to the Collection. They were so taken with many of the items that it was difficult for them to select one item on which to base their project."

The results of the students' work were so impressive that Wigler and Burgess decided to collaborate on an exhibition that would enable members of the public to view their projects—"a culmination of the students' collective vision." Make It New presented the new books alongside the treasures that had inspired the new works. Each student wrote an explanation about their reasons for selecting the particular inspirational work and their approach to creating the new work. For the opening of Make It New Special Collections staff organized a public event during which each artist spoke briefly about their work.

The Make It New project had impacts on multiple constituencies. It gave the advanced book arts students a rare opportunity to create works based on authentic treasures from past cultures and traditions; it gave members of the public an unusual window into the Wangenheim Collection and contributed to their understanding of the creative process; and, it enabled Special Collections to showcase items in the Wangenheim Collection while generating greater public understanding of how historical works of art, including books, can inspire new art.

❯ **CHALLENGES.** The challenge for Special Collections is having staff to focus on the work involved in organizing exhibitions. Without a full-time staff member dedicated to the Rare Book Room and its collections, it is difficult to do more than maintain the collection and provide reference services for scholars.

❯ **FUTURE PLANS.** SDPL's Special Collections moved to a new facility in 2014, which includes a special Hervey Family Fund Rare Book Room. Department staff hope to be able to expand staffing to carry out exhibitions and programs in the larger space.

NEWARK ART AND ARTISTS
Prints, Photographs, and Other Works on Paper
Newark (NJ) Public Library

OVERVIEW: In October 2012, the Newark (NJ) Public Library (NPL) opened Part I of Newark Art and Artists: Prints, Photographs, and Other Works on Paper (Newark Art and Artists), and in January 2013, the library opened Part II of the exhibition. Both exhibitions were entirely drawn from the library's Special Collections Department (Special Collections). The two-part presentation reflected the library's longtime commitment to collect and interpret Newark Art, and offered insights into the variety and quality of art created in Newark from 1800 to the present day. To complement the exhibitions and to encourage art-making in Newark, NPL also sponsored portfolio reviews and resource fairs for artists. The multipart project demonstrates how a special collections division in a public library can be a singular resource on the history of local art while also supporting living artists.

The Newark Public Library proudly supports our Newark artists, and we encourage residents to come to the opening and the exhibition and be inspired by their work and passion. This year's continuation of our celebration of Newark art and artists reaffirms our commitment to serving as a resource for all.

—Wilma Gray, Library Director

NPL is the largest municipal library in New Jersey, with a collection of more than 1.5 million books, audio and visual materials, and a renowned Special Collections Department that includes prints, posters, rare books, illustrated books, artists' books, cards, and shopping bags. NPL has a tradition of mounting exhibitions, with related programs, that illuminate themes reflected in the Special Collections or provide in-depth examination of certain kinds of art.

The two-part exhibition on Newark Art and Artists offered an overview of works in NPL's collection created by artists who lived, studied, worked, or were born in Newark. The works were created between 1800 and 2012. Part I, from October 2012 to January 2013, focused primarily on nineteenth-and early/middle twentieth-century art; Part II featured one hundred works created between 1937 and 2012 by diverse contemporary, living artists. Some of the works presented were purchased recently by the library, or were donated to the library in the past several years. The exhibition included work by artists frequently associated with Newark, such as Jerry Gant and Chakaia Booker, along with other widely known artists with Newark roots such as Barbara Kruger and George Tice. As a posthumous tribute, the exhibition also included works by the late Will Barnet, who taught in Newark.

The opening reception for the exhibition included a talk by Curator Jared Ash on "Art, Artists, and the Newark Public Library: 110 Years and Counting." In his talk, Ash noted NPL's sustained role in documenting and encouraging Newark artists:

> The Newark Public Library has been providing artists with information and inspiration for more than a century. The Library archives are rich with letters from artists who grew up in Newark between the 1930s and present day, which credit the Library's exhibitions and collections as being definitive influences in their artistic development.

In conjunction with Newark Art and Artists exhibition, in March 2013, NPL hosted its second annual Portfolio Review and Resource Fair Art for Artists. The event offered artists an opportunity to discuss their work with four distinguished curators and the chance to meet representatives from diverse arts organizations and "discover new places to show art, see art, sell art, and create art in Newark." NPL's Special Collections, which maintains Newark artist files, encouraged artists to bring biographical information to the event that could be added to the collection for future reference.

❯ CHALLENGES. Continuing budget shortfalls and short-staffing have made organization of Special Collections exhibitions more challenging in recent years.

❯ FUTURE PLANS. NPL intends to continue to showcase works from Special Collections in the future, but major exhibitions may have to be curtailed for budgetary reasons.

ON AND OFF THE WALL
The Visual Arts Since 2000
Cleveland Public Library

OVERVIEW: On and Off the Wall: The Visual Arts Since 2000 (On and Off the Wall) was a one-day regional art symposium held at the Cleveland Public Library (CPL) in September 2014, in which the Special Collections Department (Special Collections) was a major partner with fellow members of Cleveland's ARTneo. Special Collections helped plan and host the event and also mounted a complementary exhibition of artwork by women artists from Cleveland drawn from its extensive collections of regional art. The symposium and exhibition reflect the many art-related activities carried out by Special Collections, including commissioning public art for the library and presenting exhibitions and programs that explore diverse aspects of creative art, from book arts to poetry. The Department's arts activities demonstrate how public library special collections can be cultural leaders in their communities.

Collaboration with other institutions is one of our most effective methods for heightening awareness of collections. Whether we are working to build public appreciation of our art collections or any other items in Special Collections, we try to focus on collaboration.

—Pamela J. Eyerdam, Fine Arts and Special Collections Manager

C PL's Special Collections includes a wide array of unusual and rare items: the White Chess Collection, Islamic Manuscripts, Orientalia, miniature books, works on tobacco, theater posters, sheet music, architectural publications, works on the history of Cleveland, works by regional artists, and a growing collection of unique examples of classic and contemporary bookbinding. Special Collections has a tradition of exhibiting collection highlights, organizing special events, and offering lectures and other public programs based on the collection. Special Collections also commissions artworks for annual installations in the library's outdoor Eastman Reading Room.

Under the leadership of Pamela Eyerdam, Special Collections is expanding its collaborations with other cultural institutions and carrying out increased arts programming such as the On and Off the Wall symposium. The program was organized jointly by Special Collections in collaboration with the members of Cleveland's ARTNeo, an organization that preserves, documents, and promotes visual art and architecture of the Northeast Ohio region. Other ARTNeo members include the Museum of Northeast Ohio Art and Architecture, the Collective Arts Network Cleveland, and the City Club of Cleveland.

On and Off the Wall was designed to present current developments in the Cleveland area art scene and foster discussion about how the visual arts contribute to the vitality of Cleveland. It was the "first in a series of conversations exploring the growth and impact of the visual arts in Cleveland in the new millennium."

Formal presentations by leaders of the collaborating organizations and other visual arts specialists covered public art, architecture, government and the arts, collecting. and the art of collaboration. The program featured a tour of portions of CPL's rich regional art holdings, including its murals, public sculpture, and recently commissioned pieces.

On the occasion of the On and Off the Wall symposium, the Special Collections Department installed A Great Joy: The Women's Art Club of Cleveland, 1912–2006 (A Great Joy). Co-curated by Eyerdam, the exhibition included work by the Club's members from 1912 through 2006, featuring artists such as Edris Eckhardt, Belle Hoffman, and Elsa Vick Shaw. Some of the artists were commissioned during the WPA program of the 1930s, and some works in the exhibition—prints and ceramics—were commissioned by the library. A Great Joy complemented the symposium while showcasing Special Collections and its multiple roles as a resource for artists, a repository of regional artwork, and an interpreter of art for the public.

● **CHALLENGES**. As Special Collections carries out arts-related programming, the major challenges are funding, marketing, and securing speakers.

● **FUTURE PLANS**. The Special Collections Department expects to build on relationships established through ARTNeo, its own commissioning work, and its association with the Cleveland Institute of Art and with other arts organizations to help foster discussion about the arts in northwest Ohio, while also continuing to collect and support regional artists.

ONE BOOK, MANY INTERPRETATIONS
Chicago Public Library

OVERVIEW: In 2006, to help celebrate the fifth anniversary of Chicago's highly successful One Book, One Chicago program, the Chicago Public Library's (CPL) Special Collections and Preservation Division (Special Collections) invited book binders and book artists to create bindings that expressed their reactions to one of the ten books in the program. Book artists from 23 states and England submitted entries, which were judged by a three-person panel of experts in printing and the book arts and displayed in an exhibition titled One Book, Many Interpretations. In 2012, Special Collections mounted a sequel, in which the books read during the second five years of the program were artistically interpreted through the art of binding. Entries were submitted from all across North America. The two exhibitions focused public attention on bookmaking and the library's role in inspiring and preserving books and book bindings as works of art.

As one of many programs to commemorate this fall's tenth anniversary of Chicago Public Library's One Book, One Chicago, I hope you enjoy the creativity unveiled in the 'One Book, Many Interpretations: Second Edition' exhibition which celebrates not only the art of the book, but also the love of reading.

—Rahm Emanuel, Mayor, City of Chicago

One Book, Many Interpretations was developed by CPL's Special Collections, located at the Harold Washington Library. The Division collects in the areas of Chicago neighborhood history, Chicago arts and culture, Chicago parks, children's books, Chicago's World's Fairs, and Chicago and Illinois in the Civil War. Used heavily by scholars, Special Collections tries to reach beyond specialists to students and members of the general public through exhibitions, the Chicago History Blog, a substantial program of educational activities, and an expanding digital collection.

The One Book, One Chicago program, cosponsored by the City of Chicago and the Chicago Public Library, encourages all young adults and adults in Chicago to read and discuss the same book at the same time. Launched in the fall of 2001 with *To Kill a Mockingbird,* the program has become a model for other cities, counties, and local communities, underscoring the value of literature to spark community conversations.

One Book, Many Interpretations was organized to acknowledge the success of the community reading program and to elicit creative responses to the texts by specialists in the art of binding. Participating artists received one of the program texts and were asked to create a binding expressing their reaction to the work. The entries represented a wide variety of interpretations and binding techniques. Forty-seven were included in the exhibition and a "best binding" designation was awarded for each of the book titles. The winning entries were selected by a three-person jury of experts in the history of printing, book and paper making, and book binding.

According to Lesa Dowd, exhibition curator and a member of the Special Collections and Preservation Division:

The "One Book, Many Interpretations" exhibition exemplifies the effects the (One Book, One Chicago) books had on the artists who created them. They represent a diversity of artistic interpretations in the form of traditional fine bindings as well as sculptural book art.

In 2012, on the occasion of the tenth anniversary of One Book, One Chicago, Special Collections organized a sequel to the earlier exhibition. Bookbinders and book artists across North America submitted entries, again reflecting a wide range of artistic responses to the different texts. Some entries were playful, some serious, some literal, and others more conceptual. Collectively, they offered a unique set of responses to the ideas embedded in the literary works.

⦿ CHALLENGES. In organizing One Book, Many Interpretations, the major challenge was coordinating with the many bookbinders and book artists from across the United States and other countries. Each artist had specific needs and display requirements. Each artist shipped her/his binding, thus no two objects were packed in a similar way. Despite the logistical challenges, Glen Humphreys, manager of Special Collections states, "This variety made for a wonderfully diverse exhibit, ranging from fine bindings to texts made into a large flag."

⦿ FUTURE PLANS. CPL staff report that "Book Arts are always on our radar. We currently have exhibitions planned through 2015 and are actively exploring citizen participation in exhibitions, both high and low tech."

reTHINK INK
25 Years of Mixit Print Studio
Boston Public Library

OVERVIEW: For more than 70 years the Boston Public Library (BPL) has collected works on paper by Boston artists, including printmakers, and collaborated with local print studios on exhibitions and publications. The 2012 exhibition reThink INK: 25 Years of Mixit Print Studio (reThink INK), was an exhibition of more than 150 prints by artists associated with the nearby Mixit Print Studios. The exhibition was organized around four distinct components, including a section of works by Boston printmakers from the library's print collection, and displayed in three locations throughout the library. The exhibition reflected the long-standing connection between the library and local printmakers and the ways in which exhibitions and public programs can help draw public attention to a particular type of artwork or the work of a particular community of artists.

The Boston Public Library continues to build on its tradition of supporting Boston artists and sharing their work with the public.

—Karen Shafts, Assistant Keeper of Prints

B PL has been linked to the Boston printmaking community since the 1940s when Arthur Heintzelman, a renowned American etcher, was appointed the first Keeper of Prints. The connection continued under the second Keeper of Prints, Sinclair Hitchings, who was largely responsible for developing BPL's large collection of works of art on paper by Boston artists. In 2001, Hitchings collaborated with Mixit Print Studio, a venue for much local print production, on an exhibition and catalogue titled Proof in Print: A Community of Printmaking Studios.

Mixit Print Studio was established in 1987 in a soap factory in Somerville, Massachusetts, and has been used by hundreds of printmakers throughout the Boston area, some of whom are represented in BPL's collections. On the occasion of the Studio's 25-year anniversary, Mixit partners aimed to showcase the extent and variety of works by local printmakers whose works the studio had helped to produce. Through collaboration with Karen Shafts, current Assistant Keeper of the library's Print Collection, the reThink INK exhibition was assembled from the library's special collections, as well as newly created, never-before-exhibited prints. For Mixit, the opportunity to present its anniversary exhibition at the library was a strong mark of support for printmakers and printmaking. According to Cathryn Kernan of Mixit:

> The opportunity to mount an exhibition of this scale, ambition, and complexity organized by a group of artists, and supported by an institution such as the Boston Public Library, is unprecedented in the history of printmaking in Boston.

The exhibition was divided into four components: (1) the reThink INK Portfolio, a collaborative project of 66 boxed prints that was donated to the library's Print Collection; (2) 44 prints selected by Shafts from approximately 200 works submitted by Mixit Print Studio artists; (3) 13 installations such as multidimensional print projects or installations that brought prints off the wall; and (4) 32 works selected by Shafts from the Print Collection representing work by artists who used the Mixit Print Studio facilities.

Some of the presenting artists submitted works inspired by aspects of the library's architecture and collections, such as the columns of BPL's Changing Exhibitions Gallery and the maps in the Leventhal Map Center.

For the launch of the exhibition the library presented "ReThink INK: Impact and Innovation in Contemporary Printmaking," a panel discussion on Mixit and regional printmaking. BPL's web page for the exhibition includes digital galleries of selected works, information on the exhibiting artists and related events.

◗ **CHALLENGES.** reThink INK was a large exhibition, encompassing more than one million square feet. It was mounted in three locations in the Central Library: the Johnson building lobby, the Wiggin Gallery, and the Changing Exhibitions Gallery.

◗ **FUTURE PLANS.** BPL's Print Division will continue to collaborate with Mixit Studio and with the many printmakers in the Boston area.

SONGS IN THE KEY OF L.A.

Los Angeles Public Library

OVERVIEW: In 2013, the Los Angeles Public Library (LAPL), its Special Collections, and the Library Foundation of Los Angeles (Library Foundation) collaborated on a multifaceted project—Songs in the Key of L.A.—that showcased treasures from the library's sheet music collection, interpreted their cultural and artistic significance, and sparked new works in the form of musical recordings, contemporary compositions, and performances. The project was the first of several collaborations between the LAPL and the Library Foundation to increase exposure to the library's Special Collections and stimulate increased use by the citizens of Los Angeles.

> In the age of the Internet, simply having an archive or a collection is not enough. We want to bring these songs to life, to make the collections accessible to new audiences.
>
> —Josh Kun, Director, Popular Music Project at the University of Southern California and Curator, Songs in the Key of L.A.

The Songs in the Key of L.A. project was centered on an exhibition of historic sheet music covers from LAPL's Special Collections. The collection of printed sheet music is the largest in existence to document the musical culture of Southern California. LAPL's Special Collections include many other unique collections such as the Map Collection, which represents the development of cartography worldwide, and the Rare Books Collection, with more than 22,000 volumes dating from the fifteenth through the nineteenth centuries. The Sheet Music Collection is part of the Visual Collections that include photographs, fashion plates, travel posters, fruit crate labels, bookplates, autographs, and menus. Many of the historical and visual collections have been digitized and can be searched by remote users.

Items in the Sheet Music Collection range from classical music, folk songs, and jazz to musical theater and popular songs. More than 130,000 different songs are represented in songbooks and individual sheets, spanning the 1850s through the 1950s, covering the years when Los Angeles grew from a remote outpost to a sprawling metropolis. The Songs in the Key of L.A. project was centered around a 2013 exhibition curated by Josh Kun, director of the Popular Music Project at the University of Southern California. The exhibition was the first time that historic sheet music covers from LAPL's large collection had ever been displayed. The 46 covers on view featured richly illustrated cover artwork and represented a mix of genres: jazz, Mexican folk, pop, and blues songs. Titles included "Make Your Mind Up to Wind Up in California," and "Catalina Honeymoon." The exhibition offered a rare window into Southern California musical history, the development of Los Angeles's music industry, and the impact of music on civic and popular culture.

The Songs in the Key of L.A. exhibition provided both a focal point and a documentary backdrop for the many other project components.

NEW RECORDINGS. Simultaneous with the exhibition opening, the Library Foundation released five new recordings of music from the sheet music collection by well-known local artists. The recording sessions were showcased online every two weeks in five short documentaries produced by KCET's transmedia series, Artbound.

ANTHOLOGY. The Angel City Press produced an anthology featuring more than one hundred vintage scores. From California lullabies to West Coast jazz, the anthology complemented and extended the exhibition.

CONVERSATION. The organization Grand Performances presented City Librarian John Szabo and Library Foundation President Ken Brecher discussing the future of LAPL, starting with the Songs in the Key of L.A. project.

ALOUD PROGRAM. The Library Foundation's well-known series ALOUD featured an evening with exhibition curator Kun and musical guests talking about L.A. music history.

CONCERT. The organization Grand Performances, in collaboration with the Library Foundation, presented a free Songs in the Key of L.A. concert. Selections were chosen by Kun and sung by well-known local performers.

The various components of the Songs in the Key of L.A. project reinforced each other and attracted diverse audiences. Media attention was extensive, helping to further the project goals of widening public awareness of the library's Special Collections.

FUNDING. Songs in the Key of L.A. was a collaborative effort involving LAPL and Special Collections, with special support from the Library Foundation.

◉ CHALLENGES. One challenge involved copyright restrictions on the sheet music, which meant that the published *Anthology* focused on the front covers of the musical scores.

◉ FUTURE PLANS. Special Collections is working with the Library Foundation on a major project for 2015 on food traditions and food culture in Los Angeles. It will include at least one exhibition that will draw from the library's large menu collection—including menus recently acquired through a major donation—and material from the library's culinary collections.

THIRD THURSDAY JAZZ SERIES
Fort Worth (TX) Library

OVERVIEW: Each year the Fort Worth Library (FWL) offers the Third Thursday Jazz Series, a major series of jazz concerts that attract on average 450 visitors per event. These concerts help to remind attendees about the city's rich musical heritage and the special collection of jazz recordings in the library's Department of Genealogy, Local History and Archives (Local History and Archives). Many of the works the jazz musicians perform at the concerts can be found in the Jazz Archives.

The Jazz Series offers us a chance to offer free entertainment for residents from all over the city and also talk to them about the Jazz Archives, how it is a reference source for performers today, and what they can do to help build the collection. It is a big boost for the Department.

—Betty Shankle, Manager, Genealogy,
Local History and Archives Department

FWL's Local History and Archives is a long-standing entity that today houses collections reflecting a broad range of topics pertaining to the settlement of Fort Worth, its growth and infrastructure, and its businesses, cultural traditions, buildings, and organizations. Many genealogists use the collections, as do researchers and students working on local history topics. Over the last three years the Department has carried out a digitization program, with multiple collections now available online.

The City of Fort Worth has been home to many jazz legends: Ornette Coleman, Dewey Redman, and John Carter, among others. Working in collaboration with local partners FWL began building a Jazz Archives in 2005. The goal is to build a substantial collection that preserves the legacy of Fort Worth's renowned jazz musicians and provides an opportunity for students, scholars, and jazz enthusiasts to explore their impact on American music.

In 2010, in order to shine a light on the Jazz Archives, the library started an annual summer Third Thursday Jazz Series. Local and national jazz artists perform works from the early years of jazz up to the present day. Often, these works are based on recorded pieces housed in the Jazz Archives. Betty Shankle, Local History and Archives Manager, states that "the Jazz Series offers something for the public and also gives us a chance to talk to them about the jazz collection and how they can use it."

◉ CHALLENGES. Archives staff faces challenges in acquiring new materials for the Jazz Archive. One problem is that jazz artists and musicians tend to travel a lot, making it more difficult to schedule meetings to discuss acquisition or donation of their materials. Another challenge is technical, that of converting different formats of recorded music from physical to digital for preservation purposes.

◉ FUTURE PLANS. Local History and Archives plans to continue the Jazz series as an important means of educating Forth Worth residents about their jazz heritage. Staff also plans a digitization initiative to put the Jazz Archives online.

THE WONDER SHOW, REDISCOVERED, WONDERFUL SURPRISE, AND AT PLAY
Providence (RI) Public Library

OVERVIEW: Special Collections exhibitions at the Providence Public Library (PPL), such as The Wonder Show, Rediscovered, Wonderful Surprise, and At Play reflect fresh curatorial approaches, particularly encouragement of artists to create exhibitions and organize related programs inspired by items or themes in the collections. These approaches result in new interpretations of the collections while also engaging diverse patrons in creative experiences in person and online. The exhibitions complement the Special Collections Department's more traditional displays.

> We have amazing materials for historians, for artists, and for everybody. Programs and online exhibitions give people a chance to see these materials and make the connections with their own lives.
>
> —Jordan Goffin, Special Collections Librarian

PPL's Special Collections exhibitions are drawn from the more than 40,000 items covering topics ranging from Whaling, the History of Printing, and Children's Books to Magic and Irish Culture. The Rhode Island Collection and materials on the Civil War and Slavery are two of the most significant research categories. As the library steadily digitizes components of Special Collections, more and more of these items are becoming accessible online.

PPL's Special Collections has a long tradition of mounting in-library exhibitions of artifacts, manuscripts, and other rare materials. When Jordan Goffin was appointed Special Collections Librarian in 2011, he came with a vision for exhibitions that would not only contribute to formal scholarship but would also engage artists and members of the public with the collections in new ways. His vision has led to a diverse exhibition agenda and new types of programs that stimulate creative responses by visitors to exhibition items or themes. The following projects illustrate how Providence is bringing artists and other patrons into closer contact with Special Collections by encouraging "rediscovery and reinterpretation."

Sympathetic Magic, an exhibition exploring optical technologies, was a component of The Wonder Show, a multifaceted project carried out in 2012 that was based on the library's collection of glass plate negatives depicting Providence people and scenes at the turn of the twentieth century. Two local artists were inspired by the glass plate images as both art and community history. They organized the exhibition of rare books, glass plate negatives, and ephemera to promote interest in the history of optical entertainment and to document their own creative processes in creating The Wonder Show. They then transformed the glass plate images into slides for a "magic lantern" (an early slide projector), and used them as the basis for fiction writing workshops at the library and other community locations. The writing workshops, in turn, led to the creation of a script for a magic lantern show at the library, which was presented by local actors reading the script. The Wonder Show performance had to be repeated twice to accommodate the number of interested visitors. According to the show's organizers:

> The origin and meaning of many of these photographs remains unknown . . . it has been a community process to bring these images to life. Through a series of creative writing workshops at the library, residents have imagined possible scenarios for the images as a way of reconnecting with the past.

Rediscovered: Glass Negatives from the Providence Public Library's Special Collections (2011–2012) was an exhibition based on a collaborative project between Special Collections and the Paul S. Krot Community Darkroom at AS220, a local art organization. Use of the Community Darkroom facilities enabled the library to work with AS220 volunteers to print more than 50 archival black and white silver gelatin prints for an exhibition based on a collection of 1,200 glass plate negatives. The prints depicted "average and extraordinary lives in New England during the late 1800s and early 1900s, the height of wet-plate collodion photography." Following their display at the library, the exhibition was circulated to a nonprofit gallery in Massachusetts and two other Rhode Island venues, thereby extending access far beyond the library's usual audiences.

Wonderful Surprise: The Primers for the Naming and Un-Naming of Things (2014) was an exhibition developed by two artists who were inspired by the Wetmore Collection of Children's Books. The artists created "books that analyze the process of naming the world and deconstruct known object-word relationships in new and wondrous ways." An opening event provided the opportunity for the artists to describe their reactions to the Wetmore Collection and how they led to the creation of new art work.

At Play, an exhibition of whimsical items from the Providence Public Library Special Collections (2012), was drawn primarily from the library's Wetmore Collection of Children's Literature. The exhibition took two forms: a "real-world, physical exhibition" and a companion, online mini-exhibition. The in-library exhibition surveyed trends in children's toys over five centuries as reflected in board games, sheet music, and fairy-tale character puppets. The online exhibition included participatory elements. The online introduction stated: "At Play is an exhibition with a twist; not only can you view images of items from the exhibition, you can bring those items into your own home by creating reproductions of games and entertainment from centuries past."

The digital mini-exhibition included images and instructions for creating replicas of five items from the exhibition. The selection of eighteenth-century French board games, for example, included instructions for creating a chess set, and the historical sheet music samples included instructions for performing a Parlor Song. According to Goffin, the online version of At Play was not so much a digital project or even an online exhibition, as it was a chance for "people to make things themselves."

◉ **CHALLENGES.** The major challenge to the staff members attempting to organize or facilitate creative work based on Special Collections is the lack of time. With only two professionals for the entire department, it is difficult to realize the potential for creative, collections-based programming.

◉ **FUTURE PLANS.** Despite staff limitations, Special Collections staff is committed to continuing their efforts to work with artists and to reach out to diverse audiences through new types of exhibitions and programs.

◉ **RELATED PROGRAM.** Giambatista Bodoni at Providence Public Library was an exhibition to mark the 200th anniversary of the influential typographer's death that showcased the library's collection of Bodoni materials, one of the finest in the United States. To signal the importance of the collection the library invited world famous type designer Matthew Carter to lecture at the exhibition opening on the role of historical research in type design. The library also launched the Updike Prize for Student Type Design, a competition to reward undergraduate and graduate students who use the Updike Collection and then go on to design their own typefaces inspired by their research. The project enabled the library to reach beyond its core research users to a new audience of students, designers and graphic artists.

TWO

COMMUNITY ARCHIVES

In the Age of Information, archives have become increasingly important as repositories of memory. We are engaged in a dialogue about why culture and history matter, and public programming helps to facilitate that conversation.

—Steven G. Fullwood, Assistant Curator, Manuscripts, Archives and Rare Books Division, Schomburg Center for Research on Black Culture, New York (NY) Public Library

O ne of the most visible trends in the national movement to engage diverse audiences with special collections is the trend to reconsider the content and organization of community history. This trend can be seen in the development of community archives and new or revitalized local history centers. The phenomenon is related to the increase in community documentation and oral history projects examined in chapter nine of this volume, but it is also distinguished by a focus on organizational change. Beyond changes in collecting priorities and communications strategies, this trend reflects professional recognition of the need to reimagine the structures for local and community history in the public library setting.

Seven examples are brought together to illustrate the trend. Their size, structure, purpose, and community perspective vary, but they all share an impetus to change institutional approaches to collecting, organizing, interpreting, and sharing historical materials. For the purposes of this publication they are grouped together under the umbrella of community archives.

To better understand this trend the examples can be grouped into two categories, one involving development or redevelopment of centers for local history, the other involving formation of new archival collections. The first encompasses initiatives to rebrand existing history collections or history "rooms," to integrate recently collected materials with existing collections, and to develop programs and services that stimulate new public participation. The Center for Local History at the Arlington (VA) Public Library embodies these elements. Its creation, over several years, involved renaming the library's Virginia Room, reorganizing the local history collections, institutionalizing individual community documentation projects, and using new technologies to engage people of all ages in researching, documenting, and sharing local history.

There are other similar institutional efforts in the planning stages. The Spartanburg County (SC) Public Libraries are planning a new local history center that will be a featured component of the public library. According to Todd Stephens, director of the Todd Spartanburg County Public Libraries:

> One of the primary things the public library has to offer its community is local identity. By creating a structure that will help people feel more connected to their local history, and more historically literate, we are fulfilling a fundamental institutional role.

In addition to the formation of new local history centers there are structural changes taking place in some of the larger public libraries that indicate a new emphasis on local history and community participation. The Special Collections Department of the Seattle Public Library is shifting from a centralized approach to neighborhood history to a system-wide, participatory approach. Similarly, the Brooklyn (NY) Public Library has created community-based oral history projects that "aim to lay the foundation for community-produced local history archives at participating branch libraries . . . eventually the goal is to establish the branch libraries as destinations for people interested in Brooklyn history and outreach sites for the Brooklyn Collection."

Coinciding with the organization of new local history centers there is a move to establish new archival collections within existing institutional collections. Many such efforts could be cited, such as the District of Columbia Public Library's Chuck

Brown Archive, newly created as part of the D.C. Community Archives, or the establishment of the Fort Worth Library's Women's Archive within the Local History and Archives Department. These examples and others described below affirm archival professionals' efforts to ensure that special collections are vital and relevant. They also reflect the extent to which new archival initiatives are often community based, emerging from a conviction on the part of professionals *and* community members regarding the need to create a formal repository, applying the protocols of the archival profession to the records of a particular community. The creation of Newark (NJ) Public Library's Puerto Rican Community Archive (PRCA) is an example of such a joint community–library effort.

It is important to recognize that these efforts reflect varying definitions of "community." In some instances community is defined in terms of place—a neighborhood, town, or county—and in other instances community means a group of people with a common social, ethnic, racial, gender, or cultural identity. Whatever the definition or community of interest, these initiatives go beyond one-time projects to create new archives and new or reorganized centers for historical collecting and programming.

Even as public library special collections librarians and archivists are developing new centers for local history or new archival collections, they are doing so in the context of extreme change in how people document their own lives and the lives of others. Twitter, Facebook, Flickr, Instagram, selfies, and other social media and digital tools are transforming personal and community documentation. The changes pose new questions and imply new roles for community archives in the twenty-first century. Some professionals suggest that it may not be enough to create a collection, that interpretation and programming may be essential to fulfill the potential of that collection. According to Elly Shodell, director of the Port Washington Public Library Local History Center:

> In the past so much of local history research was collecting the history and creating the materials that would otherwise not have existed, such as audiotapes of people's life experiences, photos of their childhoods and work lives. Now people have the tools to document their lives continuously, to record the minutiae of all that they do. Raw material for future research is being created daily by everyone. The task going forward is figuring out how to sort through what is out there and how to give it narrative and meaning.

As libraries grapple with the challenge cited by Shodell, broad public engagement and interpretive programming are parts of the solution to how special collections can give "narrative and meaning" to today's collections. The new community archives and local history centers provide supportive contexts for participation and programming. Together, these organizational changes signal professional reconsideration of the structure and content of local and community history.

CENTER FOR LOCAL HISTORY
Arlington (VA) Public Library

OVERVIEW: In 2013 the Arlington (VA) Public Library (APL) changed the name of its Virginia Room to the Center for Local History and organized the Center around three primary collections: the Virginiana Collections, Community Archives, and Digital Collections. With a combination of oral history, digitization projects, community outreach, and a digital projects lab under development, the Center offers a new model for local archives and community history programming.

> **Our mission has always been to "collect, preserve and share" the history of Arlington and the surrounding region, but we have not done as well as we should have with the "share" part of that mission. With digital technologies and new forms of communication we can now be more visible and active and can help people become more personally engaged with family and community history.**
>
> —Judy Knudsen, Manager, Center for Local History

APL serves Arlington County, located just outside the District of Columbia metropolitan area. For decades the library's special collections were known as, and located in, the "Virginia Room." They consisted of a Virginiana Collection, with documentary material on the history of Arlington County, as well as a growing Community Archives, with family papers, photographs, organizational records, and oral history interviews that "narrate the history of Arlington County, its citizens, organizations and social issues." Programming included occasional lectures, workshops, and oral history projects.

During the period 2000–2011, the library started to develop a more active history program, including additional oral history projects, a photo contest for middle school students, and outreach to organizations seeking to document the history of their neighborhoods. Members of the staff were also building a Digital Collection. As a result, staff realized that "Virginia Room" was no longer appropriate for conveying the scope of services and resources nor did it reflect residents' increasing interest in participatory history projects. They organized a Local History Team to reevaluate how the library "presents its mission and projects to the public" and ultimately agreed to redefine the Virginia Room as a Center for Local History. Simultaneously, the library was undergoing a building-wide redesign and renovation. Staff took advantage of this opportunity to advocate for a larger and more visible location for the Center for Local History, on the main floor of the library, and for the inclusion of a Digital Projects Lab within the Center.

SCOPE AND GOALS. APL's announcement of the new Center included the following statement:

> Our mission has not changed: we are still dedicated to collecting, preserving, and sharing the history of our community. Our rich historical collections and range of projects offer the Arlington community the ability to not only learn about and research their history, but also contribute to its telling . . . By changing our name to the Center for Local History we hope to provide a better explanation of who we are, our many projects and the mission that links them.

The three-part structure of the Center for Local History clarifies the Center's content and communicates the equal importance of the sections, especially Community Archives and Digital Collections, both of which are expanding and account for most programming.

With its new identity, infrastructure, and location on the main floor of the central library, the Center for Local History is seeing greater foot traffic and more diverse users. According to Manager Judy Knudsen:

> We see everybody, from elementary school students to university professors . . . some people are doing academic research with primary sources and some are working on their own personal history projects and using our equipment.

In effect, the Center has transformed the library's history services into a more dynamic program, creating a model for other local libraries interested in vitalizing their special collections and stimulating more public use. The following activities reflect the range of services.

COMMUNITY DOCUMENTATION AND ORAL HISTORY. Arlington Library had carried out oral history projects in the past, including documenting residents' responses to the 9/11 attacks. Until recently the library could not digitize all of its oral history interviews. Now the Center can not only put transcripts of interviews online, but also MP3 files. Among the Center's services are workshops on how to organize and conduct oral history interviews for local organizations that seek to document their own history.

NAUCK NEIGHBORHOOD COMMUNITY ARCHIVE. The Center is working with members of the Green Valley/Nauck Neighborhood, one of several historic African American communities in Arlington, to create a local archive that will be accessible for students and residents at the Drew Model Elementary School. The project reflects residents' interest in re-constructing the history of their community as well as the fact that the State of Virginia's Standards of Learning involve the study of local history. Through community scan-ins at the Drew School, fairs, and other local events, the Center makes its scanning equipment available to digitize photographs, slides, photo negatives, or even personal documents. The Center leaves the originals with their owner, thus gaining digital copies for the Community Archives and making them available online.

EXHIBITIONS. Since the shift to a new name and internal structure, with Digital Collections a prominent component of the Center, staff has focused on digitization and also the creation of digital exhibitions. Staff sees these as entry points into Digital Collections. One recent online exhibition featured 80 postcards of locations across the Commonwealth of Virginia; another, For Greater Good: Edward C. Fleet and African-American Social Societies in Arlington County, documented an important aspect of African American social history. The long-term intent is to mount a new online exhibition theme approximately every six weeks.

PUBLIC PROGRAMS. Author talks, workshops on family history and house history, and special events are part of the Center's curriculum. The Arlington Reunion series, involving moderated panel presentations, provides an opportunity for the community to share its memories of Arlington. Topics are aired on the Arlington County cable TV channel, extending access to remote viewers.

SOCIAL MEDIA AND BLOGS. *UNBOXED, Dispatches from the Center for Local History* is the Center's blog, which has gained numerous followers and helps inform the local community about the scope of the collections and the Center's activities. In addition, the Center uses Facebook, Tumblr, and Twitter, and has mounted a substantial number of images on Flickr.

PARTNERSHIPS. APL's Center for Local History works closely with local organizations to share resources and reach various constituencies. Partners range from George Mason University and local schools to historical associations and civic groups.

The combination of these activities and others makes this Center for Local History, in a library serving a population of only 230,000, stand out for its emphasis on outreach, participation, and public programming.

● **CHALLENGES.** One of the challenges faced by the Center has been the need for staff members who are digital specialists as well as historians and archivists. With the new emphasis on digital collections and virtual services, and increasing donations of items that are "born digital," technical skills are essential.

● **FUTURE PLANS.** Leaders of APL's Center are already looking ahead to determine how to "take the Center to a new level." One likely approach is increased outreach and neighborhood documentation. Another approach is the creation of a Digital Projects Lab, a feature of the Center that results from the library's recognition that many people, of all ages and backgrounds, gravitate toward project work centered on local history. By locating a "Lab" in the Center the library will be offering a place for production work such as copying and scanning, and for group and family projects that take advantage of the Center's historical resources.

THE CHARLESTON ARCHIVE
Charleston County (SC) Public Library

OVERVIEW: Charleston County Public Library's (CCPL) Charleston Archive was established in 2007 to preserve and organize the local history materials held by the library and to develop programs and communications that expand interest in local history. Through lectures, outreach, partnerships, and two blogs, Archives Director Nicholas Butler has successfully engaged Charleston residents with historical topics and events. His work has also led to the creation of a new position: official CCPL Historian. The Charleston Archive offers an example of how a comprehensive approach to local history can stimulate public involvement with archival collections and lead to the establishment of a dedicated position for history programming.

Public programs here at the public library are our customary forum for sharing new discoveries, research, images, and models. They increase foot traffic to the Charleston Archive, to the SC History Room, and into the library in general. Most importantly, they are vehicles for stimulating people's interest in local, regional and national history.

—Nicholas Butler, PhD, Charleston County Library Historian and
Former Director, Charleston Archive

C CPL serves the city of Charleston and Charleston County. Its Special Collections include two units: The South Carolina History Room, which contains primarily printed books and genealogical items, and the Charleston Archive, which includes manuscripts, maps, photographs, a South Carolina Pamphlet Collection, and a Rare Book Collection. With pre-Revolutionary documents and city burial records, as well as early twentieth-century women's rights pamphlets, the new Charleston Archive documents the political, economic, and social history of the city and county of Charleston and the surrounding low country.

The formation of the Charleston Archive was prompted by a 2005 agreement between CCPL and the City of Charleston calling for the library to curate the city's surviving historical records. This trove of historical materials, some dating back to 1790, included manuscript records of city institutions and agencies, hand-drawn maps, photographs, pamphlets, and rare books. The material was almost completely unknown to the public or the academic community. In addition, there were materials in the South Carolina History Room that had been slated for a separate "special collection" but had never been thoroughly processed.

CCPL hired public historian Nicholas Butler to consolidate and organize these materials as a special collection. His first task involved gaining physical and intellectual control over the items, a two-year project that also involved identifying other early documents and rare books held by the library that should be included in the special collection. Butler's second task was to share the historical materials with the public. In order to brand and promote the growing collection as an important community resource, the library coined the name Charleston Archive. In 2007, the Archive was officially named as a separate unit to house rare materials, complement the South Carolina History Room, and promote local history.

A fundamental goal of the new Charleston Archive was to expand Charleston residents' interest in local history and, in particular, the materials in the Archive. Drawing on his background as a public historian, Archives Director Butler employed three strategies to accomplish this goal: online communications, history programming, and outreach.

COMMUNICATIONS/BLOGS. When Butler was first appointed Archivist he started a blog titled *The Charleston History Advocate: Research and News from the Charleston Archive of the Charleston County Public Library.* Through regular collection-related posts, many linked to public programs, the blog has helped to reposition The Charleston Archive *and* CCPL in the Charleston community and beyond. More recently, as the CCPL Historian, Butler has established a new CCPL blog: *The Charleston Timemachine,* where he highlights topics and important events in the evolution of Charleston County and the state of South Carolina.

HISTORY PROGRAMS. Butler instituted a series of programs that used the Charleston Archives to illuminate an issue, event, or local story. Topics have ranged from Early Music in South Carolina to the History of the Charleston Orphan House. Scholars and other subject specialists from the region are program presenters. Each program topic is discussed in a post on *The Charleston History Advocate,* and links are provided to digitized images of related collections.

The blogs and the history programs emphasize stories. According to Butler: "When I do a workshop I don't list the highlights of our collection. Instead, I ask people to 'Listen to this cool story.' I invite them to come to the Archives and discover all the stories that are waiting there."

OUTREACH AND COLLABORATION. Butler and other Charleston Archive staff make themselves available to Charleston civic and volunteer groups interested in learning more about the Charleston Archive. They work with local schools to promote use of the Archives, and conduct tours and workshops for social studies teachers. Butler also collaborates with academic institutions in and around Charleston and helped create the Low Country Digital Initiative, a regional digital collection.

The Charleston Archive partners with the City of Charleston in multiple ways. Butler chairs the Mayor's Committee on the Walled City and he assists city officials when new developments and reconstructions reveal artifacts with value to the local community.

The combination of communications, history programs, educational outreach, and collaboration with other history initiatives has resulted in a larger audience for Charleston history. The success of this work led to establishment of a new position: Charleston County Library Historian. Butler assumed this position in mid-2014, which he defines as "acting as a history advocate within the library system and the community." A professional archivist has been appointed to continue developing the Charleston Archive.

❯ CHALLENGES. Butler states that one of his chief challenges has been finding ways to connect the Charleston Archive more systematically with local schools. Although individual teachers are enthusiastic about using primary materials, curriculum standards and teaching traditions inhibit regular integration of blog content or archival materials in the classroom. According to Butler this is "a missed opportunity for the students, who can benefit from direct contact with the real materials that have shaped local history."

❯ FUTURE PLANS. Having organized the Charleston Archive, promoted it locally and regionally, and established an agenda of local history programming at the library, Butler is now shifting his role from archivist to full-time historian. He expects to be carrying out increased outreach and collaborations, as well as continuing to organize programs that stimulate Charleston residents' involvement with history and historical collections.

COMMUNITY ARCHIVISTS PROGRAM

Austin History Center, Austin (TX) Public Library

OVERVIEW: Austin Public Library's (APL) Austin History Center (AHC) has a Community Archivists Program in which outreach archivists work with members of historically under-documented communities to carry out neighborhood documentation projects and identify potential AHC collections. Currently, archivists are working with three groups: Asian Americans, Mexican Americans, and African Americans. The program results in new relationships between AHC and community members, donations of unique historical materials, and exhibitions and related programs that illuminate the history of the target communities and engage new audiences with AHC.

> This outreach opens up the archive in ways that are important for the future. Our country is changing so much every day in terms of demographics, but even though certain groups represent sizable numbers their culture is marginalized. Young people grow up not valuing older traditions and not realizing how significant stories and documents are for understanding their world.
>
> —Esther Chung, Community Archivist with the
> Asian American Community, Austin History Center

AHC is a primary example of a public library history center, with substantial historical collections, extensive public programming, multiple community partnerships, a separate building, and a separate support group. With a core collection of rare books and manuscripts, AHC has grown to include government records, business records, family history materials, and historic photographs relating to the history of Austin and Travis County.

AHC's holdings, like most public library history collections, tend to reflect the lives and experiences of the more established members of society rather than providing an inclusive view of all residents over time. As newcomers have arrived in Austin, their historical and cultural legacies have not been reflected in AHC's collections in proportion to their numbers. This imbalance in collections content has prompted AHC to undertake more inclusive historical documentation and collection development in recent years, along with efforts to organize exhibitions and interpretive programs representative of all Austin residents.

Recognizing the need to broaden the content and reach of its collections, AHC created the position of Community Liaison to the African American community in 2000. Not long after, a second liaison position was approved by the City Council, this one to build connections with the Mexican American community. In 2006, the City Council approved a third position targeting the rapidly growing Asian American community. Today, AHC describes the Community Archivists Program as a "distinctive" component of the Center, with the goal of "locating, collecting and preserving the history of underrepresented communities in Travis County." The three archivists perform outreach by presenting programs about AHC collections and the history of the community; helping organize community documentation or oral history projects; giving talks on aspects of neighborhood history; and by organizing exhibitions, programs, and special events that illuminate the lives and experiences of community residents. They also function as subject specialists in the history of these communities, creating finding aids for newly acquired collections and providing a *Resource Guide* that lists materials related to their community.

AHC staff report that the outreach initiatives are proving effective in widening awareness and use of AHC by diverse audiences and also in developing AHC collections. Public programs, most organized in collaboration with community groups, have high attendance. Many items have been added to the collections as a direct result of outreach, including letters, records of neighborhood organizations and businesses, and photographs. As funds permit, newly donated collections or portions thereof are also digitized. In addition, with a long-term view to increasing its community documentation, the Community Archivists work with educational institutions to offer internships and study experiences that help ensure that future generations learn about the importance of historical preservation and archival work.

Since 2009, a number of exhibitions and public programs have been organized by the Community Archivists:

- Activism and the Brown Berets of Austin, Texas: 1970s–1980s, was a photo exhibition and four-part program held at the Terrazas Branch Library in October 2013.
- Building a Community: The First Century of African American Life in Travis County (2010), an exhibition with programs that included a talk by a local historian on Black Enterprise: Remembering Austin's Pioneering Entrepreneurs.
- Pioneers from the East: First Chinese Families in Austin (2010), a partnership project with the Texas Asian Chamber of Commerce that

consisted of a photo exhibition and public programs. Research for this project added significant items to AHC's collections, which had heretofore included very little on Austin's growing Chinese community. In addition, an online exhibition was created based on this project.

One of the premises of the Community Archivists Program is that activities should be carried out in collaboration with members of the target communities. As a result, most projects and exhibitions have involved teamwork with neighborhood residents. Community-based organizations have been helpful in publicizing activities.

❯ **CHALLENGES.** One challenge AHC has faced is that for each community group there is an existing cultural center or museum. The Community Archivists do not compete with existing institutions; instead, they share information and exhibition materials and avoid duplication. Another challenge is that in some communities there is long-standing mistrust of "official" institutions, especially in communities that have a long history of institutionalized prejudice and segregation. The Community Archivists try to build trust and working relationships with local residents.

❯ **FUTURE PLANS.** AHC intends to continue the Community Archivists Program and to expand programming developed as the result of the Archivists' outreach. According to Mike Miller, AHC manager, "It is important to develop our collections and programs so that we communicate the separate stories of individuals and communities and also the whole story. The only way to look at our history as a whole is to make sure all these stories are preserved."

IN THE LIFE ARCHIVE
Schomburg Center for Research on Black Culture, New York (NY) Public Library

OVERVIEW: In the Life Archive (ITLA) is one of the most recent archives established at the Schomburg Center for Research on Black Culture (Schomburg Center), a research division of the New York Public Library. Steven G. Fullwood, assistant curator of the Manuscripts, Archives, and Rare Books Division, started the archive in 1999; it is now the largest research collection in existence documenting the history, experiences, and art of lesbians, gays, bisexuals, trans-sexual and transgender, queer, and Same Gender Loving (LGBTQ/SGL) people of African descent. A resource for both a local and global community, the ITLA provides the basis for extensive programming such as readings, conversations, and film screenings that make it a model of an interactive, "living" archive.

> **Currently the In The Life Archive (formerly known as the Black Gay & Lesbian Archive) contains information dating from the mid-1950s to the present, documenting the experiences of non-heterosexual men and women of African descent primarily in the United States, London and several countries in Africa.**
>
> —Steven G. Fullwood, Assistant Curator, Manuscripts, Archives and Rare Books Division, Schomburg Center for Research on Black Culture

The Schomburg Center is one of the world's major centers for research on Black History and Culture. It grew out of the personal collections of Puerto Rican bibliophile and scholar Arturo Alfonso Schomburg, whose collection was purchased in 1926 by the New York Public Library. The Schomburg Center's Manuscripts, Archives and Rare Books Division holds comprehensive collections of works by authors of the Harlem Renaissance, Black women authors of the nineteenth century and monographs by and about Black people from the sixteenth, seventeenth, and eighteenth centuries. Major archival collections focus on Harlem, African American writers, performing arts, women, and civil rights groups and activities in the twentieth century. The collections are widely used by researchers and others from the United States and abroad and are constantly growing as works and personal papers are donated by contemporary authors, scholars, and creative artists.

The Schomburg Center is the first research library in the world to actively collect materials on black LGBTQ/SGL culture. ITLA consists not only of books, magazines, and organizational records but also rarely seen photographs, playbills, programs, letters, journals, posters, newspapers, postcards, pamphlets, newsletters, films, flyers, T-shirts, CDs, albums, and more. The archive documents the accomplishments, challenges, and creative work of poets, playwrights, painters, and LGBTQ/SGL civil rights pioneers of African descent. Numerous small collections of paper-based materials form the bulk of ITLA, which, according to Fullwood, " . . . tell the story of a black queer cultural history that is deep and diverse, unique and rich—and largely hidden from general public view."

The collection takes its name from the title of *In the Life: A Black Gay Anthology* by Joseph Beam, an influential writer in the black gay community. Highlights of the collection include the papers of influential writers: Alexis De Veaux, a Harlem-born writer, biographer, journalist and playwright and the author of *Spirit in the Streets* and *Warrior Poet: A Biography of Audre Lorde*; Cheryl Clarke, the poet, critic and professor who wrote the 1986 poetry book, *Living as a Lesbian*; and Thomas Glave O. Henry Award winner, whose works include *Whose Song? And Other Stories* and *The Torturer's Wife*.

In establishing In the Life Archive as an official research collection, Fullwood and his colleagues were interested in preserving the record of black LGBTQ/SGL culture and providing an institutional research base for writers, academics, filmmakers, journalists, and other professionals working on aspects of black LGBTQ/SGL culture. In addition, they were, and are, committed to using the collection to build community consciousness and provide opportunities for individuals to explore their own and others' experiences as black LGBTQ/SGL people. These goals inform an active agenda with programs that promote "discussion, debate and remembrance" across generations, ages, and cultural perspectives. The primary programming initiative is the "Ordinary People Series," which includes films, book discussions, exhibitions, and panel discussions. A selection of 2013–2014 programs reflects the variety of topics and audiences:

- A screening of Jamaican performance artist Lawrence Graham-Brown's "Rites of Passage/ Sacred Spaces 2012"
- A stage reading of playwright and dancer Djola Branner's latest work *sash and trim*
- A reading by Martin Duberman of his book, *Hold Tight Gently*, a dual biography of gay icons Michael Callen and Essex Hemphill

These and similar programs, offered continuously, help promote awareness and use of the collection, stimulate collection expansion, and ensure its dynamic quality as a living archive.

❰ **CHALLENGES.** As with so many public library archives, Schomburg faces the two fundamental challenges of funding and space. These affect all of the divisions and collections, such as the In the Life Archive, which will need support and space to grow. According to Fullwood, these challenges are "still relevant today for the leading institution dedicated to preserving and interpreting the global black experience . . . and for providing the critical counter-narrative for how blacks are portrayed in the media, history books and in public discourse."

◗ FUTURE PLANS. The ITLA will continue to acquire materials produced by and about LGBTQ/SGL people of African descent, and to highlight aspects of the collection, influential community members and timely issues through its "Ordinary People" program series.

LOCAL HISTORY CENTER
Port Washington (NY) Public Library

OVERVIEW: The Local History Center (LHC) of the Port Washington Public Library (PWPL) grew out of the library's Oral History Program, one of the most extensive such programs in a public library. Started in the early 1980s by oral history specialist Elly Shodell, the program is a central feature of the LHC, with complementary multimedia collections, interpretive activities, exhibitions, and community documentation projects. The Oral History Program, a model in and of itself, is also an example of how sustained and institutionalized oral history work in a public library setting can catalyze broader exploration of local history in the digital age.

> In the early years of the (Oral History) Program we were looking for the undiscovered voices . . . people who were hidden and undocumented, people whose contributions to life in Port Washington were not part of the formal record. Today, we are helping people find meaning in the voices and images from the Local History Collections.
>
> —Elly Shodell, Director

The PWPL is one of the major public libraries on Long Island, serving a relatively wealthy and ethnically diverse waterfront community just 17 miles from New York City. From its inception in 1892 to the present time, the PWPL has preserved and organized historic records of local organizations, individuals, and institutions. Until the 1980s these collections primarily represented the histories of residents with long-standing economic and social influence. There were few formal records of the servants who enabled life in the town's great estates, the shipbuilders, sand-miners, and baymen who sustained local economic development, or the engineers and mechanics that created one of the nation's centers of aviation production. This situation caught the interest of local resident Elly Shodell, an oral historian affiliated with the Columbia University Oral History Research Office, who recognized the possibilities for historical documentation and the need for a more inclusive history of the town. Accordingly, she conceived and implemented a new, public library-based approach to documenting the lives and work of everyday people and bringing the record of these experiences to the attention of the wider public.

In 1980, the PWPL established a program "to capture on tape the memories of those men and women who have shaped Port Washington's history, and to preserve that memory for future generations." The PWPL raised grant funds to hire Shodell to develop the program, which involved oral history documentation of maritime trades, African American families, and folk traditions. Grants from the Folk Arts program at the New York State Council on the Arts stimulated a sustained focus on folkloric traditions such as boat model building. Funding from the New York Council for the Humanities ensured strong connections with public history scholars. Shodell describes her early work as a "bridge" between academic and grassroots local history, with humanities scholars, folklorists, and oral historians all assisting in the formulation of the Oral History Program.

From the outset Shodell recognized that volunteers would be essential to carrying out an interview program. Each summer a workshop course was offered to teach community members to produce videotaped oral history documentaries. During the early projects a core group of trained volunteers was created that has continuously helped leverage the work of the program director.

As digital tools have become available the interviewing process has evolved. However, from the perspective of content, throughout its nearly three decades of development, a consistent aspect of the Oral History Program has been the emphasis on thematic projects that illuminate the history and culture of Port Washington. This approach reflects Shodell's emphasis on context and her view that oral history is part of a larger historical narrative. Another characteristic of the program has been an emphasis on sharing the content of the oral histories through a variety of interpretive programs, products, and, most recently, digital collections.

Over the years the program has carried out more than 300 interviews and resulted in more than 9,000 pages of transcripts, all of which are indexed and constitute the digital Oral History Collection. These materials have been used for historical exhibitions, radio programs, school projects, and scholarly publications. They have helped to involve the community in local history through workshops, lectures, walking tours, exhibitions, film screenings, and special events. Above all, the oral histories have led the library to develop and institutionalize archival projects on a number of key historical themes, and, subsequently, to organize a Local History Center. Today oral history is one, but not the only, component of community history documentation and programming.

The following projects suggest the variety of themes the program has explored since 1980 and the ways in which oral history was the driver for larger interpretive projects that now exist as digital archives.

PORT WASHINGTON AVIATION HISTORY. Port Washington, once known as the "Plymouth Rock of American Aviation," played an important role in the development of the nation's aviation industry for more than fifty years. The Oral History Program was the first effort to document the experiences of the many residents who worked in the industry up through the 1950s. Early interviews evolved into a larger exploration of aviation on Long Island, including development of a collection of images, documents, and artifacts to complement the oral histories, a library exhibition, a digital collection, and a book by Shodell titled *Flight of Memory: Long Island's Aeronautical Past.*

SAND AND CITY. Sandmining was an important part of Port Washington's economy for part of the twentieth century. In the early 1980s the Oral History Program documented the industry through interviews with former sandminers and their families. The oral interviews evolved into an archival project looking at the social history of sandmining and a series of exhibitions, books, and public programs. Today, transcripts of the interviews are available at the Local History Center site along with audio excerpts, photographs, video clips, and scrapbook materials in a digital collection titled Sand and City.

WORLD TRADE CENTER PROJECT. Following the events of September 11, 2001, the PWPL undertook an archival project to collect and preserve related oral histories and other relevant materials. The interviews included people who were in the towers during the attacks, emergency personnel, and relatives of people who lost their lives.

PORT WASHINGTON FIRE DEPARTMENT. To commemorate the 100th anniversary of the all-volunteer Port Washington Fire Department in 2007, the program interviewed firefighters, emergency medical personnel, and auxiliary members of the department. The interviews are now part of the Fire Department's archives as well as the LHC archives and website.

As the Oral History Program and associated archival materials expanded it became increasingly apparent that the records would benefit from a more formal and permanent structure. By institutionalizing the program the library could ensure the preservation of documentary materials, organize interpretive activities on a regular basis, and provide space for members of the public to access the collections. PWPL's Local History Center was established by the library in 2001 "to collect and preserve Port Washington's heritage, especially materials that are fragile or unique, and make it available to the public at the library and online."

Today the LHC is organized around an Oral History Office, Special Collections, Archives, and Folk Arts Projects. LHC's Special Collections house photographs, manuscript collections, oral histories, maps, ledgers, postcards, audio and video tapes, printed books, scrapbooks, and artifacts. To date, nearly 100 collections have been contributed from cultural organizations, official agencies, civic groups, families, individuals, and local businesses.

In addition to collecting, processing, and creating digital access to local history materials, LHC has carried out numerous public programs and exhibitions, from a Maritime Festival and an Aviation Kiosk at the town dock, to a Latino Festival and related exhibitions. LHC has developed lesson plans for fourth- and seventh-grade classes, using collections to enrich the local social studies curriculum. Speakers' symposia have included scholars, writers, and professors whose work illuminates the topics of LHC investigations, such as workers at gold coast mansions, and Latino history. Most recently, in 2014, LHC mounted an exhibition titled, Connections: Finding Meaning in Archival Images from the PWPL Local History Collection.

❯ **CHALLENGES.** Funding for the LHC is a continuing problem. Most grants are relatively small and do not cover digital components. With only part-time staff, LHC cannot fulfill its potential to become a comprehensive local history center in the digital age. There is also need for storage space, both physical space and extra space in the cloud.

❯ **FUTURE PLANS.** LHC plans to focus more resources on creating digital exhibitions and developing better ways to stimulate interest in local history through social media channels. In addition, staff will continue seeking donations of documents and images that complement existing collections and help fill out the history of Port Washington.

PUERTO RICAN COMMUNITY ARCHIVE
Newark (NJ) Public Library

OVERVIEW: The Puerto Rican Community Archive (PRCA) of the Newark Public Library (NPL) was officially created in 2006, following a four-year survey of records and collections across the state of New Jersey. Established through the joint efforts of the NPL and the Friends of New Jersey Hispanic Research and Information Center (Friends of HRIC), the initiative illustrates the importance of community leadership in helping public libraries take the steps necessary to organize a formal archive. Having grown in eight years from a single researcher sharing a desk and phone to an official three-person unit managing over 450 cubic feet of archival material, the story of the PRCA is relevant to other communities and libraries considering how to create a new archival unit.

Development of the Puerto Rican Community Archive here at the Newark Public Library is a poster child for community involvement in archival development. Without local leadership the research behind the Archive would not have been done, the collection would not exist and there would be no archival staff to rescue the valuable history that is out there.

—Ingrid Betancourt, Director, New Jersey Hispanic Research and Information Center

NPL is the largest municipal library in New Jersey, with a collection of more than 1.5 million books, audio and visual materials, and a Special Collections Department with unique collections of prints, photographs, and historical documents. NPL's research-level collections include the Charles F. Cummings Research Center on New Jersey, Essex County and Newark, the James Brown African American Room, and the New Jersey Hispanic Information and Resource Center. In addition, as a depository library for state documents and federal publications, NPL is an important statewide information resource.

The PRCA evolved from the long-standing commitment of NPL to provide information and services to the Latino community in Newark and across New Jersey. In fact, NPL was a pioneer in the development of such services. In the 1980s, when New Jersey's Latino communities started growing—including people from Puerto Rico, Ecuador, Mexico, Dominican Republic, Peru, and Colombia—NPL responded by recruiting Latino librarians and providing targeted services. By the 1990s Latinos had become the state's largest minority group, and in 1998 NPL established La Sala Hispanoamericana (La Sala) as a resource center for Latino residents, especially newcomers. This was a center where they could find Spanish language information and reading materials as well as classes, community connections, and cultural programs. Under the leadership of Project Director Ingrid Betancourt, La Sala became known in New Jersey and across the United States as a model for community-responsive library services.

Betancourt, her library colleagues, and members of the Latino community soon recognized the need for a research center to complement La Sala. Accordingly, in 2002, with the assistance of a Friends group, NPL created the New Jersey Hispanic Research and Information Center (NJHRIC). NJHRIC offers a research and reference collection documenting the experiences of Latinos in New Jersey, serves scholars, supports publications, and organizes exhibitions and programs that reflect the vitality and diversity of Latinos in New Jersey.

In the mid-1990s, Betancourt sought to create an exhibition on the history of the state's annual Puerto Rican parade. She found that aside from informal records held by a few individuals and organizations, there was no authentic documentation of the parade's history and meaning, nor was any institution formally documenting the history of the Puerto Rican community in New Jersey. This experience led to her interest in creating a historical archive. She subsequently met Dr. Olga Jiménez Wagenheim, professor of history at Rutgers University in Newark, who also saw the need for documenting the history of the oldest and largest Latino community in New Jersey. Together, with the support of NPL's administration, they developed a template for the NJHRIC that called for a three-tiered center: the existing Sala Hispanoamericana, an Hispanic Reference Collection, and the PRCA.

During 2002–2006, researcher Yesenia López, functioning under the aegis of the NJHRIC and supported by the Friends of HRIC and other grant funders, conducted a systematic survey of historical records of the Puerto Rican communities in New Jersey. This study was essential not only for understanding the scope, significance, and condition of potential archival collections, but also for creating a network of contacts, allies, and history contributors all over the state. López's research provided ample evidence that substantial collections of archival value existed, but that many materials were vulnerable to possible destruction or loss without improved storage, preservation, and organization.

Based on Lopez's needs assessment, NPL formally established PRCA in 2006, fulfilling the vision of community leaders and archivists and providing a framework for formal collection development and records management. Eight years later, in 2014, the Archive has grown to include over 40 archival collections including the records of organizations and personal papers of community leaders and families from Puerto Rican communities throughout New Jersey. Beyond the collections, staffing for the Archive has also grown. López, whose work had previously been funded through the Friends group and special grants, is now an official NPL employee. A grant-funded associate archivist and archival assistant are now part of the team and the library provides support in the form of space, equipment, supplies, and collegial assistance with communications and preservation.

PRCA is committed to community education, and has worked with Rutgers University, the New Jersey Institute of Technology, and other educational institutions to provide internships and work-study experiences for students. The PRCA has also created Organizing Our Community's Records: A Workforce Development Project, a summer project that assists local organizations with records management while exposing the youth participants to library and archival work.

The community support that helped launch PRAC continues today. The Friends of HRIC and NPL have worked to identify a wide variety of sources to develop and sustain PRCA. Additionally, the NJHRIC has received grants from state agencies and private foundations for archival processing and outreach.

● **CHALLENGES.** From its beginnings PRCA has faced the problem of acquiring and updating equipment and supplies, including computers and basic collection management materials. Institutionalization within NPL has alleviated this challenge somewhat. Another major issue is the danger of loss to potential collections that exist around the state—loss due to the lack of resources to conduct needed outreach and education. Betancourt states "Without greater historical consciousness, unique records are at risk of being lost to history."

● **FUTURE PLANS.** Despite severe economic restraints, NPL is committed to sustaining and expanding its work for and with Latinos in Newark and across the state. Library staff will continue working closely with the Friends of HRIC to sustain and further develop PRCA as an essential community-based resource that is preserving the unique history of New Jersey's Puerto Rican residents.

● **RELATED PROGRAM.** Development of PRCA led to a complementary initiative: the Latino Oral History Collection. During López's state records survey she encountered many Latinos who did not have documentary sources but who were able to recount their own stories or stories of significant events and issues in the Latino community. She began to record these individuals, creating the basis for a collection that is a unique resource for the history of Latinos in New Jersey. NJHRIC has organized selected oral histories into "Collections," such as the Justice Collection and the Latino Life Stories Collection, which are transcribed, digitized, and accessible online on NPL's website.

VIVIAN G. HARSH RESEARCH COLLECTION
Chicago Public Library

OVERVIEW: The Harsh Research Collection (Harsh Collection) of the Chicago Public Library (CPL), founded by Vivian G. Harsh in 1932, is a vital resource for scholarship, education, and community documentation. While it started out as the "Special Negro Collection" at CPL's Hall Branch, the Harsh Collection is now the second-largest public repository in the Midwest focused on African American history. Its diverse programs reflect the founder's vision for a center that would promote exploration of African American history and literature.

> **We have always had an open relationship with the community from the very beginning . . . we try and meet their needs. It is a two-way street that ties us—library and community—together.**
>
> —Beverly Cook, Archivist, Vivian G. Harsh Research Collection

The Harsh Collection is one of three special collections at CPL, the other two being the Special Collections and Preservation Division, located at the Harold Washington Library, and the Northside Neighborhood History Collection located at the Sulzer Regional Library. The Harsh Collection was started as a special book collection in CPL's George Cleveland Hall branch. Harsh was the first director of the Hall branch and traveled throughout the country to acquire items for the collection. She also pioneered public programming and forged relationships with authors, scholars, and civic leaders as well as diverse residents of the City of Chicago and beyond. The collection was renamed the Vivian G. Harsh Collection of Afro-American History and Literature in 1970 and was moved to the Carter G. Woodson Regional Library in 1975.

Today, the Harsh Collection includes rare books, manuscripts, periodicals, photographs, African American newspapers, microfilm, and audio collections. Primary subject areas are history, literature, journalism, religion, genealogy, medicine, law, and civil rights. Special holdings include manuscripts by Richard Wright, Langston Hughes, Arna Bontemps, Gwendolyn Brooks, and Era Bell Thompson. Scholars from around the world come to the Harsh Collection to use the papers of African American publishers, local organizations and prominent literary and civic figures. The Harsh Collection also works with the Patricia Riddell Researchers, an African American Genealogical Society, to respond to the growing interest in family history and genealogy. The group sponsors programs and maintains its (print) collections as part of the Harsh Collection.

From its beginnings under Vivian G. Harsh, the collection has functioned as more than an archive; it has always been a vital resource for scholars, students, African American history specialists, educators, and members of the general public. Drawing on founder Harsh's original vision, the programming is inclusive, with lectures, exhibitions, performances, meetings, academic symposia, author talks, and special events, many of which are organized with academic, professional, or community organization partners.

EXHIBITIONS. Small displays and larger exhibitions illuminate topics represented in the Harsh Collection.

Faith in the Struggle: Rev. Addie Wyatt's Fight for Labor, Civil Rights (2013) was an exhibition of more than one hundred items selected from the archives of Rev. Addie Wyatt and Rev. Claude Wyatt. Born in Mississippi, Addie Wyatt moved to Chicago and became famous for her lifelong struggles in the labor movement and civil rights and feminist activism.

To See Reality in a New Light: The Art and Activism of Marion Perkins (2009) was the first retrospective of Chicago Renaissance sculptor and activist Marion Perkins. The exhibition featured works loaned by museums and his family, supplemented by correspondence and other personal documents from the Harsh Collection. An accompanying catalog was produced by the community. The exhibition opening featured a panel discussion with five scholars and critics on Perkins' political life and his art. Cook notes the importance of exhibition-related programming:

> When we did the art exhibit on Marion Perkins we used the opportunity to educate the public about his history, to partner with the Art Institute and other galleries around the city that showcased black sculptors, and to talk about the development of black artists, how art and history inter-connect . . .

Other Harsh Collection exhibitions have included: Chester Commodore, an exhibition on the famed *Chicago Defender* cartoonist, featuring Commodore's political and social satirical images; and The Chicago Renaissance: A Flowering of Afro-American Culture, which revealed the Chicago Renaissance to a new generation of researchers and has resulted in a plethora of books on the subject.

PUBLIC PROGRAMS. Harsh Collection programs vary widely, from an Annual Lecture in support of the Timuel D. Black Fund, featuring a prominent historian, to the Harsh Readers Circle, an African American book club that grew out of Vivian G. Harsh's Book and Literature Forum, started in 1933.

In 2013, the Harsh Collection organized an event to celebrate publication of *The Negro in Illinois,* which was based on a multiyear research project tracing Illinois Black History and Culture over more than 150 years. The first phase of the project was carried out by a team of artists and writers, such as Richard Wright, as part of the Illinois Writers' Project in the 1940s. The original WPA interviews are part of the Harsh Collection. Brian Dolinar, editor of *The Negro in Illinois,* moderated the discussion and spoke about the importance of the Harsh Collection in enabling the research behind the book.

The Harsh Collection often collaborates with other city departments to carry out public programming that features the collection, such as On the Trail of the Great Migration: Chicago's Black Communities. During African American History Month in 2014, Cook visited four black communities and did presentations on local connections to the Great Migration, the Great Chicago Fire of 1871, and the fight for inclusion that took place in communities such as Altgeld, Pullman, and Roseland.

◉ **CHALLENGES.** The primary challenge faced by Harsh Collection staff is keeping up with the processing of the numerous archival collections donated by the African American community.

◉ **FUTURE PLANS.** Harsh Collection staff are working to make their finding aides and public domain collections available on CPL's website.

THREE

EDUCATIONAL INITIATIVES

Being in a public library is a huge distinction for me. We welcome everyone, of every age and background. We learn what they are interested in and work to respond to those interests. We also have an important teaching mission, especially with young people, that makes our work both challenging and exciting.

—Susan Goldstein, San Francisco City Archivist and Manager, San Francisco History Center/Book Arts & Special Collections

There are very few public library archives or special collections that do not carry out some form of educational programming, that is, programming designed to enrich teaching and learning in the classroom. That programming can take multiple forms: tours, outreach to classrooms, teacher institutes or history fairs, and the creation of print or digital resources for educators. Whatever forms they take, the educational initiatives under way in the nation's public library archives and special collections departments provide strong evidence that these departments play important educational roles in their communities.

How libraries implement their educational roles depends on many variables: the relationship between the public library and local educational institutions, staff capacities, budgetary limitations, the contents of the library's special collections, and the responsiveness of individual educators to the enrichment opportunities offered by the library. The variables result in a rich tapestry of educational initiatives. The 11 examples selected for this chapter, and others mentioned throughout the book, suggest the wide array of approaches to educational programming.

TOURS OF COLLECTIONS are the most typical form of educational service provided by public library archives and special collections. Many are the tried-and-true "show and tell" formats. However some institutions are shifting to a more participatory approach. Glenn Humphreys of Chicago Public Library's Special Collections and Preservation Division states:

> For years we did show and tell for school groups . . . Now the Division offers hands-on workshops and helps students work with actual primary sources, manuscripts and photos. In addition, we try to make sure that they all leave with something to help them further such as a secondary source or an e-mailed article from our newspaper archives.

Virtual tours are another form of tour developed by some libraries that benefits teachers and students unable to visit the library in person.

OUTREACH TO CLASSROOMS, at all educational levels, is another important way for local archives and special collections to fulfill their educational role. Many institutions encourage such outreach as a means of building connections between educators, their students, and the library's collections. Christina Moretta, curator of the Photography Collection of San Francisco's History Center/Book Arts & Special Collections, regularly visits classes at San Francisco State to discuss the library's photo collections and their importance for local history and for the history of photography.

As libraries do more class visitation, they are moving away from generic overviews of their collections to focus on stories and relevant items that can be discovered in local special collections. Nicholas Butler, historian at the Charleston County (SC) Library, visits middle school and high school classes in Charleston to encourage use of the Charleston Archives and to talk about topics such as Early Velocipedes in Charleston. Other librarians are moving toward a participatory approach, working directly with students, in the classroom or the archives, on local history projects. William Cook, special collections manager at the Bangor (ME) Public Library, visits middle school classes in two local schools twice a week for six to eight weeks each year to work with students on the Life on a Tidal River Community Heritage Project.

DIRECT ASSISTANCE WITH RESEARCH PROJECTS AND PREPARATION FOR HISTORY FAIRS is expanding as archivists and special collections librarians in some libraries increase their educational activities. Rather than assuming that students will visit the library and know how to use primary sources and special collections, some libraries are making concerted efforts to reach out to students and help them acquire the skills necessary for collection-based research. Denver Public Library's Western History and Genealogy Department works with the Reference Services Department to offer one-on-one research assistance to help students with classroom projects. The Hennepin County (MN) Public Library's Special Collections Department works closely with Youth Services and the Minnesota Historical Society to offer an annual one-day history fair—a History Day Hullabaloo—in support of National History Day. Through Brooklyn Public Library's Brooklyn Connections program students from participating schools can visit the Brooklyn Collection after school and receive individual assistance.

The Schomburg Center for Research on Black Culture offers a Junior Scholars Program for students 11 to 18 that involves all day sessions at the Schomburg Center every Saturday for eight months. The intensive experience, involving lectures, project development, dialogues with scholars, and field trips can have a profound impact on students. Few institutions have the resources to undertake such a program, however, Junior Scholars is a beacon project within the profession and suggests the direction that some archivist-educators would like to take.

Internships and fellowships are another form of educational programming that is also expanding in archives across the country. Special Collections departments in Cleveland, Houston, Chicago, Birmingham, Austin, and many smaller communities host undergraduate or graduate students who take on projects that benefit the institution as well as the intern. For host departments the interns can be an invaluable source of assistance, processing particular collections, contributing to departmental blogs, and otherwise helping with archival tasks that could not be accomplished by regular staff and that result in broader collections access for the public.

In some situations there are ongoing relationships between the library and the educational institution. The Portsmouth (NH) Public Library has an ongoing relationship with the Simmons College School of Library Sciences and Information. The Queens (NY) Public Library's Archives has a similar relationship with Queens College, which provides interns for the Queens Memory Project. One of the most developed such programs is the Memphis (TN) Public Library's Archival Fellowship Program with Rhodes College, which is being expanded to offer a special certificate in archival studies.

PROGRAMS FOR EDUCATORS are preferred by some archivists and special collections librarians who see the value in preparing teachers to identify and use primary materials as the most effective way to improve student awareness and use of those materials. Despite problems of teacher turnover, and the reticence of many school administrators to encourage new approaches to fulfilling standard curriculum requirements, there are library programs that stand as models for the profession. The Brooklyn Public Library's Brooklyn Connections Program is one such example. It is a departmental priority, it involves sustained relationships with specific schools, and it provides a range of practical experiences that build teachers' familiarity with special collections and the ways in which they can be used to create curriculum materials and fulfill curriculum goals.

The educational activities carried out by the Chicago Public Library reflect the high priority the library places on public education. Beverly Cook, curator of the Vivian G. Harsh collection at Chicago Public Library's Woodson Regional Library, describes a training program for teachers:

> This year's session was on the Black Arts. I gave them an orientation on what an archive is, how to utilize an archive, how to find information on our web page, the difference between primary and secondary sources, cost factor details, and any other questions they had. I brought materials out of our holdings that document the Black Arts Movement—these documents ran the gamut from correspondence, programs, journals, posters, oral history and organization records. We showed them how to read a document for more than just content, but context also. It was pretty amazing to see how excited some of these teachers became. . . .They will go back to their various classes in various locales and teach their students how to use and incorporate primary source materials into their work and studies. We are preparing the next generation of teachers, historians, librarians, and archivists. Every time I see a light bulb of knowledge go off, I get very excited because I am contributing to a better future for the profession and its users.

TEACHING RESOURCES AND LESSON PLANS constitute one of the most effective, but least visible, forms of educational support provided by special collections librarians. As they put more and more material online, and create specialized sections of websites for the use of teachers, the educational impact of their collections is increased exponentially. It is not easy to capture that impact, although some librarians report more foot traffic and increased online connections with educators as a result.

The Butler Center for Arkansas Studies' History Hub offers an instructive example of the scope and quality of online educational support that can be provided by a public library. The Hub includes lesson plans designed by educators to dovetail with specific curricular requirements, complementary resources in the form of audiovisual materials and scholarly essays, and links to the Center's online Encyclopedia of Arkansas Studies. Digital Anaheim is an unusual approach whereby the Anaheim Public Library's Anaheim Heritage Center has organized its collection of historical photographs around the topics covered in the local third grade curriculum. There are numerous other examples of lesson plans based on special collections, exhibitions, and digitization projects developed by public libraries all across the country.

Some educational projects defy easy categorization, including Cleveland Public Library's Power with Chess event, based on the library's renowned Chess Collection. Like the history fairs staged by some libraries, the event attracts young people to the library where they learn about a particular collection—young people who might not otherwise visit Special Collections.

In reviewing the following examples it is important to recognize that the designation "educational initiative" can be arbitrary and that many examples of programs in other chapters could have been included in this category. For instance, the Teen Tech Squad discussed in the chapter on Interactive Archives, an initiative organized by the Providence Public Library's Rhode Island Collection that teaches high school students to use digital tools for community history documentation, could just as well be considered an educational initiative as a community documentation project.

AFTER-SCHOOL HISTORY WORKSHOPS
Birmingham (AL) Public Library

OVERVIEW: Birmingham Public Library's (BPL) Southern History Department (Southern History) partners with the Birmingham Cultural Alliance Partnership (BCAP) to provide After-School History Workshops on civil rights and family history for middle school students. The workshops introduce students to key historical events in Birmingham during the Civil Rights era and also help them start researching their own family history. The workshops offer an example of how special collections can help young students learn about local history archives and other facets of the library.

> It was a real treat getting to know these students. They are scary smart and leading discussions and having them open up about their family traditions was a delight.
>
> —Beth Willauer, Southern History Department

B PL's special collections are divided between a Department of Archives and Special Collections and Southern History. The latter department "covers every facet of Southern life and culture," including genealogy, folklore, arts, sciences, geography, and regional history. There are also newspaper collections, a Cartography Collection, Rare Books Collection, and Caribbean Collection.

Southern History developed the After-School History Workshops in 2000 as a result of discussions with the Birmingham Civil Rights Institute, which had organized BCAP with the goal of enriching after-school time for children by introducing them to the city's cultural resources. BCAP was looking for a historical component to complement other activities such as museum trips and recreational programs. For Southern History this seemed an excellent opportunity to expose middle school students to local history materials while deepening their understanding of the local civil rights movement. The project also offered an opportunity to work with other Birmingham cultural institutions.

Southern History Department staff designed an initial workshop series of ten programs over a month long period that featured family history and genealogy materials relevant to the students and also introduced participants to Civil Rights issues and events in Birmingham. The workshops involved discussions on family traditions and the stories behind the students' names and nicknames. Students examined primary materials such as newspaper microfilm and school yearbooks. Each participant received a copy of the front page of the local newspaper published on the day they were born. Guest speakers, including members of the Birmingham African American Genealogy Study Group, presented varied aspects of family and local history. The civil rights components of the program also involved examination of archival documents and sessions with guest speakers. In the first year of the workshop series the library reached 240 students.

Over the years the program has evolved to take on broader themes, exposing students to a wide range of activities and resources at the library, including exhibitions, debate teams, and oral histories. Students have been engaged in debates on contemporary as well as historical issues and Southern History has added a session on library databases. However, the emphasis is still on local and family history and the documents that record those histories. One activity involves learning about census records in order to trace the family history of four prominent local people. Staff works with two schools in particular, providing activities four times a week after school.

The continuation of this program over 14 years illustrates how a special collection in a public library can extend beyond its usual services for scholars to introduce young people to family and community history.

◉ **CHALLENGES.** The primary challenge in carrying out the after-school program is the commitment of staff time. Curriculum design has been another challenge. According to Ben Peterson, former manager of the Southern History Department, "We do adults quite well, so it is a challenge to prepare activities that are interesting to children."

◉ **FUTURE PLANS.** Mary Beth Newbill, manager of Southern History, states that the department intends to continue offering the After-School Workshops, emphasizing local and family history. She sees the program as "part of a continuum of services provided by Southern History, encompassing people of all ages."

BLACK HISTORY 360°
The Schomburg's Summer Education Institute
and
JUNIOR SCHOLARS PROGRAM
Schomburg Center for Research in Black Culture, New York (NY) Public Library

OVERVIEW: Black History 360°: The Schomburg's Summer Education Institute (Black History 360°) is a weeklong professional development institute for educators from all levels—elementary schools to graduate programs—offered by Schomburg Education, the educational division of the Schomburg Center for Research in Black Culture (Schomburg Center). Junior Scholars is a precollege program that helps participants increase their historical literacy and deepen their knowledge of African American culture and history. Both programs are based on the Schomburg Center collections and reflect new approaches to teaching about the experiences and legacy of African Americans in the United States and globally. Both programs offer instructive examples for archival and special collections divisions in public libraries that aim to use their collections to enrich public education.

> Our programs for educators, the curricular materials, the Junior Scholars program and our tours of Schomburg exhibitions and collections are all part of a comprehensive approach to connecting students and teachers with the incredible resources that we have here at the Schomburg.
>
> —Deirdre Lynn Hollman, Director of Education,
> Schomburg Center for Research in Black Culture

The Schomburg Center, one of the New York Public Library's four research units, is one of the world's primary research collections on the African Diaspora and African American history and culture. Established by Puerto Rican librarian Alfonso Schomburg, the Schomburg preserves, interprets, and shares a wide range of documentary and creative material on the black experience. Collections are divided into five research divisions, the curators of which work closely with a Department of Exhibitions and Public Programs and the Schomburg Education Department to fulfill the educational mission of the Schomburg Center. There is an extensive agenda of exhibitions and public programs ranging from gallery talks and exhibitions to performances, symposia, and issue-oriented conversations. The Schomburg Center website offers rich resources for viewers, from in-depth digital exhibitions to essays on topics related to the collections.

As a public research library the Schomburg Center aims to share its collections with as wide an audience as possible, including educators and students. Two signature programs suggest the institution's commitment to education.

Black History 360° is a week long professional development program for educators including K–12 teachers, college and university faculty, community educators, and college students who plan to teach. In 2009, the first year of Black History 360°, there were 25 attendees; the 2014 Summer Institute attracted 125 participants from throughout the United States. There is no comparable educational opportunity for educators who seek to strengthen teaching on the history and culture of African Americans and the experiences of African people worldwide.

Black History 360° features lectures by scholars from a variety of disciplines related to the program themes. It also includes interactive workshops, community walks, and curator talks with specialists from different divisions. Participants are exposed to the Schomburg Center's rich on-site and online collections, and they are introduced to inquiry-based teaching methods that can be applied in different disciplines and with different grade levels.

Each year Black History 360° focuses on different themes that are often planned to coordinate with exhibitions at the Schomburg Center or at other historical repositories in the New York metropolitan area. The 2012 Institute themes included Black Migration/Immigration, Harlem Studies, and Teaching Africa: Past and Present. Topics featured in 2013 included Africans in India and The Art of Black America. The 2014 program included The Motown Sound: A Voice for Freedom and Abolitionist Brooklyn. Black History 360° lectures and key events are recorded and archived in the Center's Moving Image and Recorded Sound Division and some are offered on Livestream.com.

For 12 years the Schomburg Center has offered a Junior Scholars Program for young people ages 11 to 18 from the New York metropolitan area. The program involves all-day sessions at the Schomburg Center every Saturday from October to May. Like the Summer Institute, the Junior Scholars curriculum uses an inquiry-based and project-based approach to teaching about black American history and the global black experience. Participants, who are selected on a competitive basis, engage in college-style lectures, presentations, and dialogues with scholars, take part in group discussions, work on individual research, and create collaborative media and arts projects informed by the Schomburg's collections, exhibitions, and other educational resources. The program culminates each year with a Youth Summit, when participants present their projects for peers, family members, and the public.

For many participants the program has a strong impact on their educational direction and understanding of their own potential. Samuel, a three-year participant, states:

> I love reading and at the program we got books from the many people who came to speak with us and encouraged us to learn and understand our culture. I was fascinated with my video project group; I never held a camera like that before or visited a newsroom. The Junior Scholars Program not only gave me somewhere to go on Saturdays but provided me with learning skills.

Black History 360° and the Junior Scholars Program are both unique, designed and operated by educational specialists at the Schomburg Center in collaboration with the Center's curators and programming staff. They illustrate the potential for a research collection dedicated to public education to fill gaps in conventional curricula and provide enriched learning opportunities for students and educators.

⊙ **CHALLENGES.** Schomburg Education, with a rich array of educational resources for program participants and visitors to its website, has much to offer K–12 schools, especially the public school systems in the New York area. However, it has been difficult for Schomburg educators to reach school administrators and classroom teachers to make their resources and programs known and utilized in classrooms. Schools' current emphasis on assessment and the lack of time for individualized learning make it difficult for teachers to take full advantage of what Schomburg Education has to offer.

⊙ **FUTURE PLANS.** Schomburg Education will be continuing both Black History 360° and the Junior Scholars Program. In addition, the Schomburg Center has received a major grant from the National Endowment for the Humanities (NEH) to offer a special NEH Summer Institute for thirty teachers in 2015, the topic of which will be Immigration, Migration, and the Transformation of the African-American Community in Twentieth and Twenty-First Century North America.

BROOKLYN CONNECTIONS
Brooklyn (NY) Public Library

OVERVIEW: Brooklyn Public Library's (BPL) Brooklyn Collection offers a highly developed school enrichment program that is a primary service component of the special collections department. Brooklyn Connections involves teacher workshops, curriculum packets, online resources, and class visits that enable teachers and students to work with primary materials. In the 2013–2014 school year alone, Brooklyn Connections partnered with 30 schools in Brooklyn, Queens, and Manhattan to serve more than 2,000 students in 70 classes. The program is unusual for its comprehensive approach, the close working relationships between teachers and library staff, and in the combination of supports for both teachers and students. It demonstrates what is possible when a public library archive is deeply committed to improving teaching and learning.

> **The main purpose of Brooklyn Connections is to bring teachers and students into contact with the collections so that they can use them effectively for teaching and learning.**
>
> —Ivy Marvel, Manager of Special Collections, Brooklyn Collection

Brooklyn Connections draws on the wide array of historical materials in the Brooklyn Collection. These relate primarily to the history and culture of Brooklyn and New York City, with primary documents on the history of the civil rights movement in Brooklyn, architectural drawings, postcards, city directories, ephemera, family papers, and photographs. Aside from Brooklyn Connections, staff uses a variety of programs and communications to build awareness and use of the collections. These include exhibitions, a widely read blog titled *Brooklynology*, oral history projects, and a regular program of lectures and film screenings on Brooklyn topics.

Brooklyn Connections is designed to support educators and students through professional development workshops, class visits, online resources, and access to experts on the history and culture of New York City and Brooklyn. The program involves partnerships with public schools—with an emphasis on Title I, low-income neighborhood schools—to offer teachers and students access to the library's growing collection of original archival materials. Brooklyn Connections was started in 2007 as a standards-based program to help middle school students complete research projects based on original documents. Based on requests, the program expanded in 2010 to incorporate high school students. It is designed to "make the research process accessible and relevant to students as they develop critical skills such as research, primary and secondary source analysis, writing and reasoning." Brooklyn Connections complements the New York State Social Studies curriculum and the state's Common Core Learning Standards for English Language Arts and Literacy.

Brooklyn Connections involves working relationships between teachers and the staff of the Brooklyn Collection. Each participating teacher receives:

- planning assistance with Connections staff, customized project guides, lesson plans, worksheets, document reproductions, and other materials relevant to their class topics;
- tours of the Brooklyn Collection and optional professional development workshops, including tours of historic sites in Brooklyn and interactive sessions on using primary archival materials; and
- a collection of Brooklyn history books and document reproductions for the classroom.

Students from each class develop unique research projects suggested by Connections staff based on the topics and skills identified by the teachers. Each project incorporates oral, written, and visual components. All students receive:

- a hands-on tour of the collection;
- follow-up workshops in the classroom;
- optional after-school project assistance at the Brooklyn Collection;
- access to the digital resources on the Brooklyn Connections and Brooklyn Collection website;
- a copy of the Brooklyn Collection's *Young Learner's Guide*; and
- an opportunity to be recognized through the program's end-of-year activities.

Brooklyn Connections has grown considerably since it began in 2007–2008 with 10 schools and 470 students. In the 2013–2014 school year, the program involved 30 schools serving more than 2,000 students in 70 classes. Over 100 teachers, administrators, and preservice teachers attended the professional development workshops on public history and archival research. At the 2014 end-of-year celebration, the Brooklyn Collection mounted an exhibition of student work, and project manager Christine Szeluga posted the following on *Brooklynology*:

> Our annual exhibit highlights the creativity and originality conveyed in our students' final projects, which ranged from the highly academic to the wildly creative. Research topics included the abolitionist movement, neighborhood history, architecture, city planning and famous Brooklyn residents. Students produced exhibit boards, models, plays, research papers, slideshows, movies, scrapbooks and more. These projects reflect not only a significant amount of research, but also the unique personalities of our students.

❯ **CHALLENGES.** The scope and quality of the support provided to teachers and students through Brooklyn Connections depend on a dedicated but small staff. On occasion staff must work simultaneously with students and more formal researchers. However, Marvel sees this as "a mark of the special mission of the public library." Another challenge is long-term funding. Despite substantial foundation grants for Brooklyn Connections, particularly from the New York Life Foundation, the issue of sustainability is always a concern.

❯ **FUTURE PLANS.** The Brooklyn Collection would ultimately like to institutionalize Brooklyn Connections as a part of the department's routine work. Marvel states that "it is critical to carry out educational outreach on a continual basis and also to cultivate young researchers and students." Staff would also like to carry out more substantial multiyear evaluations of Brooklyn Connections to help build a full picture of its impact on participating students, educators, and the library itself.

DIGITAL ANAHEIM
Anaheim (CA) Public Library

OVERVIEW: The Anaheim Heritage Center (Heritage Center) of the Anaheim Public Library (APL) has created a digital archive—Digital Anaheim—composed of a selection of its large collection of historic photographs. Building on a partnership with the Anaheim City School District, the digital archive is organized according to the district's third-grade social studies curriculum. As the digital archive grows, future material will be integrated into the curriculum framework as well as being searchable by subject. The archive has proven useful for general researchers as well as teachers and students.

The historic photograph collection is one of the most heavily used historic resources, and the digital archive will be utilized by researchers throughout California and the world, as well as local students.

—Digital Anaheim website

D igital Anaheim is the primary online access point to the special collections of the Anaheim Public Library, known as the Anaheim Heritage Center (AHC). The collection contains nearly one million items relating to the history of Orange County, the City of Anaheim, and surrounding areas. Holdings include documents and maps pertaining to Spanish and Mexican land grants, Native Americans and German settlers, and diverse materials on winemaking, business development, family history, agricultural change, and land development in the region. AHC is located in the Carnegie Plaza building, part of the city's new MUZEO complex. Through tours, exhibitions, and special projects Heritage Center staff engage diverse audiences with the collections and with local history.

Digital Anaheim is an archive of more than 2,000 photographs covering the historical development of Anaheim and Orange County, with images reflecting the early Rancho economy and nineteenth century transportation as well as twentieth century views of Anaheim as a growing commercial center. What makes Digital Anaheim unusual is the arrangement of the collection according to the topical categories used by the Anaheim City School District for third graders. Digital Anaheim was first conceived in 1999–2000 when Heritage Center staff collaborated with faculty from the Anaheim City School District in a local history curriculum building project—the Digital Anaheim Project—that emphasized use of primary sources. Project organizers determined the potential to utilize the Heritage Center's large photograph collection as the basis for a digital collection to inform classroom teaching and other educational research. They also decided that the third-grade curriculum was appropriate as an organizational framework because it calls for including local history and writing reports on the city's history. Remote access was important insofar as the city's dispersed geography makes it difficult for elementary school children to visit the Heritage Center except for scheduled group visits. A grant from the Institute for Museum and Library Services, administered by the California State Library, helped implement the initial project.

The Digital Anaheim Project was well received, not only by third grade teachers but also by educators and students at other levels who find the topical outline helpful for research. The subjects around which the images are organized range from missions and landmark buildings to ethnic groups, labor relations, and natural disasters. The success of the initial project led to institutionalization of the archive as Digital Anaheim. To encourage educational use the Heritage Center has offered workshops on using local history sources for teachers in the city school district and teachers in other elementary schools.

❯ **CHALLENGES.** The primary challenge associated with Digital Anaheim has been the turnover of teachers assigned to particular grades in local schools. Heritage Center staff must constantly work with new teachers.

❯ **FUTURE PLANS.** The Heritage Center intends to expand its Digital Collections with several additional categories of materials, including a collection of photographs by several generations of a Japanese American family that participated in an oral history project. These and other new materials will be integrated into the current topical framework.

EDUCATIONAL PROGRAMS
Chicago Public Library

OVERVIEW: The Special Collections and Preservation Division (Special Collections) of the Chicago Public Library (CPL), located at the Harold Washington Library, and the Vivian G. Harsh Research Collection at the Woodson Regional Library (Harsh Collections) both offer educational services, programs, and hands-on learning opportunities that reflect CPL's commitment to the education of Chicago's children and students. The educational programs carried out by the two departments also demonstrate that education is an appropriate function for a library archive or special collection. CPL is an instructive model for other public libraries interested in how special collections can help strengthen teaching and learning in their communities.

We are part of a large organization and don't exist in a vacuum . . . Our role is to make history meaningful to everyone, including schoolchildren.

—Glenn Humphreys, Librarian, Special Collections and Preservation Division

C PL's educational programs for students, teachers, young people, and families are based on their exceptional collections on Chicago history and culture, including reference materials on the Chicago World's Fair, blues recordings, local theater history, and Civil War artifacts. The Harsh Collection, for instance, is the largest African American history and literature collection in the Midwest. From its inception in 1975, Special Collections has carried out services and programs for the general public and today the division is heavily committed to educational programming for all ages and academic levels. The following activities occur on a regular basis, while others, such as tours, take place on special occasions based on educators' requests.

CHICAGO METRO HISTORY FAIR. CPL is one of four other collecting institutions in Chicago that sponsor this well-known history fair, an annual competition designed to inspire participants' interest in history and improve history education in middle and high schools. Students throughout Chicago and the adjacent counties work on individual projects for several months. Projects can vary from exhibitions to research papers, performances, documentaries, or websites.

In conducting the original research for their projects, students benefit from supporting institutions. For students preparing for Metro History Fair projects, CPL offers on-site and online services. Staff in Special Collections and the History Division sponsor workshops engaging students in hands-on training with history and newspaper databases as well as with original photographs, manuscripts, and government documents. Special Collections and Children's Services offer a two-page outline of library resources, and even suggest topics of potential interest.

The Harsh Research Collection also participates in the Chicago Metro History Fair, working with both teachers and students. In 2014, for example, teachers from throughout the Midwest spent a day at the Harsh collection for a session on Black Arts. Assistant Curator Beverly Cook gave them an orientation on archives, different types of research sources, and digital collections. They examined holdings documenting the Black Arts movement, including correspondence, programs, journals, posters, audiotapes, and organization records.

EXHIBITIONS FOR CHILDREN. Special Collections recently began a partnership with the Children's Department to create fun and informative exhibitions using materials from Special Collections. One exhibition was a "pop-up" display about snowstorms following a huge storm in 2011. Historical and current photographs and graphic images prompted children to consider snow banks in relation to their own sizes, how contemporary snowstorms compare with those in prior years, what a snow drift looks like, and more. The exhibition also supported an active learning program in which children measured snowfall over the winter break from school.

BLACK METROPOLIS RESEARCH CONSORTIUM. Along with eleven other collecting institutions, CPL's Special Collections and the Harsh Collection participate in the Research Consortium's Short-Term Fellowships for doctoral candidates, scholars, writers, and artists. The selected researchers pursue their own studies or creative projects that draw from the archival collections.

EXHIBITIONS. Both Special Collections and the Harsh Collection encourage student visits to special exhibitions. The Harsh Collection's Faith in the Struggle: Rev. Addie L. Wyatt's Fight for Labor, Civil Rights and Women's Rights (March 2013–March 2014) was one of many exhibitions that have been used by local teachers and students to enrich classroom learning.

INTERNSHIPS. Many public library archives and special collections host occasional interns from undergraduate or graduate programs, especially library and information science schools. CPL's Special Collections has hosted students from Dominican University School of Information Sciences and other schools. Students spend a semester processing collections, scanning photos, compiling metadata, and helping with special project planning.

Collectively, these and other educational activities developed by Special Collections demonstrate CPL's leadership in public library special collections programming in support of education.

❯ CHALLENGES. According to Humphreys, one of the biggest challenges is developing programming that connects with middle and high school students. He states that Special Collections is trying to create participatory programs that respond to students' interests.

❯ FUTURE PLANS. Special Collections has been working with other library staff on a new library website that will offer new opportunities to showcase its assets and encourage participation in educational activities and other Special Collections programs.

LIFE ON A TIDAL RIVER
The Bangor Community Heritage Project
Bangor (ME) Public Library

OVERVIEW: Life on a Tidal River: the Bangor Community Heritage Project (Life on a Tidal River) is a multiyear initiative led by the Bangor Public Library (BPL) Archives and Special Collections (the Archives) that has resulted in digitization of Special Collections items; creation of an online community history portal; online exhibitions; the involvement of multiple classes of students and teachers; and a sustained relationship between participating schools, the local museum, and the library. The project demonstrates not only the educational value of collaboration between special collections and schools but the corollary benefits to each participating institution in terms of exposure and preservation of collections.

> **Middle and high school kids don't usually have an opportunity to create something real and lasting. The Heritage Project gives them the chance to make a visible contribution to their communities. I see a real change in the kids who get involved— they are enthusiastic and engaged.**
>
> —William Cook, Archivist/Special Collections Librarian

Life on a Tidal River is an educational outreach project of the BPL, which serves the City of Bangor and surrounding areas of eastern and northern Maine. The project draws on BPL's Archives holdings, which include photographs, genealogical and organizational records, more than 300 works by Maine artists, and a collection of rare books, some dating from the fifteenth century. For decades many of these items were kept in a vault. When Archivist/Special Collections Librarian William Cook was appointed in 2000, he began a concerted effort to process and preserve these collections and to reach out to local educational and cultural institutions to make them more visible and accessible. Life on a Tidal River was an outcome of this outreach, providing the basis for ongoing collaboration with the local history center and public schools.

Life on a Tidal River started when BPL developed a partnership with the Bangor Museum and Center for History (the Museum), the Bangor High School, and two middle schools to apply to the Maine Memory Project for support toward the joint creation of an online local history portal. With approval from the state project, the Bangor partners worked together to select the initial exhibition topics, each of which had to meet certain criteria: (1) interest to local students; (2) availability of primary research materials; and (3) collections that the library and museum were interested in digitizing.

After a brainstorming session for partners and students, and a community conversation, five topics were selected. One school, with a Maine Studies Curriculum, chose the Shep Hurd/Brady Gang as its research/exhibition topic. Students in the English/Language Arts Curriculum at another school were reading *The Diary of Anne Frank* and decided to explore what life was like for young people in Bangor during the same time period. High school students studying the Progressive Era selected the Bangor Fire of 1911 and subsequent city reconstruction. The Museum chose the Civil War based on their collection of Civil War letters and the upcoming 150th anniversary of the Civil War. BPL chose early railroad transportation in order to showcase its primary sources and pave the way for future transportation exhibitions.

Development of online exhibitions for the history portal started with classroom visits by BPL's archivist and staff from the museum to introduce participating students to their collections and help plan the student research. Students then visited the archives and the museum where they examined primary documents and analyzed photos and maps. With the assistance of teachers and project partners' technical staff they learned how to scan documents, upload images, and prepare text for the online exhibitions. The students wrote the exhibition narratives, with introductory remarks by library Archivist Bill Cook.

Since Life on a Tidal River started, additional classes have become involved each year and the roster of topics has grown. Although two schools eventually had to leave the project, the Cohen Middle School has continued the initiative. The 2014 topic, lumbering, brings into play a variety of library holdings and museum artifacts.

As a result of the project, many students have become directly involved with the local history collections, discovering resources that have helped them in subsequent courses in high school and college. Cook states: "Students who have taken part now know what we have here, and they know it is not all digitized." Cook has also noticed a "ripple effect," with increased use of the archives by local teachers and with parents coming into the library or the Archives as a result of their children's' involvement in the project.

Life on a Tidal River has generated considerable media attention, helping BPL and Special Collections promote awareness of the collections. The project has also brought about closer connection between the library and the museum and it has helped expand and enrich the library's online offerings by prompting identification of specific collections for digitization.

◉ **CHALLENGES**. Library Archivist Cook reports that the primary challenge he faces in implementing the project is fitting it into the state-mandated curriculum. Even the Maine Studies Curriculum is limited and does not easily allow the time necessary for teachers and students to engage in a hands-on, in-depth local history research. Another challenge has been the time required to work with students. During the three to four months of the school year that the project occurs, Cook devotes nearly a day a week to classroom visits or working with students in the archives.

◉ **FUTURE PLANS**. Current project partners intend to carry on the work, expanding the topics available on the Community Heritage Portal and continuing to digitize and interpret the collections that bring these topics alive.

MARION BUTTS
Lens on Dallas
Dallas Public Library

OVERVIEW: In 2005, the Texas/Dallas History and Archives Division (Texas History and Archives) of the Dallas Public Library (DPL) acquired a collection of more than 58,000 negatives by Dallas photographer Marion Butts. A newspaper editor during the postwar and civil rights eras, Butts documented all aspects of Dallas life, from segregation and sports to the State Fair of Texas. In 2010, Texas History and Archives made 1,800 of the images available through a digital collection, Marion Butts: Lens on Dallas, and created a series of online lesson plans that feature Butts' photographs for middle school students. The project demonstrates how a public library archive can use one significant collection to advance its educational purposes and showcase unique, place-based historical images.

> We knew that the Butts Collection would be in demand, but we also knew it has educational value. The photographs bring alive the events, issues and personalities of Butts' day.
>
> —Brian Collins, Archivist, Texas/Dallas History and Archives Division

Texas History and Archives is one of three DPL divisions that contain special collections materials, the others being the Fine Arts Division and the History Division. A major public library repository, Texas History and Archives covers many aspects of the history of Dallas, the surrounding area, and the state of Texas. The Manuscripts and Archives Collections alone contain materials on women's history, political history, architecture and community planning, performing arts, ethnic history, and business and organizational history in text, graphic, audio, and video formats. The division also maintains a collection of approximately 300 oral history interviews with people who witnessed or helped shape Dallas history.

Starting in the mid-1940s, Marion Butts, a commercial photographer, documented African American life in Dallas for almost sixty years. Butts was widely known for the quality of his images and for his insights into community life. Recognizing that Butts' work represents an unusually comprehensive record of Dallas in the last half of the twentieth century, Texas History and Archives acquired the large collection of his photo negatives in 2005. The images depict race relations, sporting events, churches, civil rights events, popular culture, and numerous other aspects of local life. In order to ensure their stability and future use the division obtained a grant for the Marion Butts Photography Negatives Project, which enabled staff to store the negatives in archival, acid-free sleeves and create an in-house database.

Subsequently, in order to share a portion of the collection with the general public, Texas History and Archives obtained a TexTreasures grant from the Texas State Library to digitize 1,800 of the images and make them available online. Marion Butts: Lens on Dallas, an online presentation, was launched in 2010. At the same time, Texas History and Archives created a series of online TKS//STAAR-based lesson plans targeting seventh grade students. The lesson plans, which are designed to be incorporated into state and federal curriculum standards, incorporate some additional materials from Texas History and Archives' collections. The lesson plans are divided into eight themes, including Voting Rights, Working for a Living, and Growing Up in Dallas. Each thematic plan includes an introductory statement, notes about how to use the materials in specific sections of the seventh grade curriculum, and links to relevant sections of the library's online image gallery.

❱ **CHALLENGES.** Limited staffing in recent years has slowed down efforts to increase access to Texas History and Archives, especially via digitization and online exhibitions. However, the division's staff will be substantially expanded in 2015. According to Archivist Brian Collins, "This will be both exciting and challenging as we try to get everyone up to speed and decide on projects that merit most attention."

❱ **FUTURE PLANS.** Texas History and Archives intends to publish a book of images from the Butts Collection, which will complement the educational materials and digital collection already available online.

PITTSBURGH IRON AND STEEL HERITAGE COLLECTION
Carnegie Library of Pittsburgh (PA)

OVERVIEW: In 2008, the Carnegie Library of Pittsburgh (CLP) undertook a major project to increase public awareness and use of its Pittsburgh Iron and Steel Heritage Collection (Iron and Steel Collection). With federal funding the library digitized more than 500,000 pages related to Pittsburgh's metal industries, which were critical to the growth of the city and of the nation in the late nineteenth and early twentieth centuries. The resulting digital collection provided the basis for community programming and social media outreach when it opened to the public in 2012. Preparation of the digital collection also enabled the library to create thematic lesson plans for social studies and history teachers. The project reflected the challenges of converting such a large and diverse collection into digital format. It also demonstrated the value of using technology to preserve, document, and prepare for educational use previously inaccessible collections on industrial or social history.

> **Pittsburgh's iron and steel industry was a key factor in the industrial revolution of the United States. As a public library it is our responsibility to connect customers through technology and provide access to our region's rich history.**
>
> —Dr. Barbara K. Mistick, President and Library Director

CLP maintains special noncirculating research collections in several locations. The primary source of rare materials is CLP's Oliver Room Special Collections, housed in the Main Library, which include manuscripts, rare books, photographic and nonprint materials, and the Carnegie Archives. CLP's Pennsylvania Department includes multiple resources on the city of Pittsburgh, Pennsylvania, including extensive genealogical resources, historic clippings files, the Andrew Carnegie Collection, oral histories, and the Pittsburgh Photograph Library of more than 100,000 negatives and prints.

IRON AND STEEL COLLECTION. CLP's Heritage Collection, which consists of maps, government documents, noncirculating reference books, local history, genealogy materials, and pre-1970 journals, is divided between the Main Library and CLP—East Liberty, in a closed stack area known as the Becky and John Surma Depository. Materials relating to the history of the iron and steel industries in Pittsburgh are part of the Heritage Collection, along with early trade journals that reflect the impact of iron and steel on the national economy in the twentieth century.

CLP's Iron and Steel Collection is one of the library's great research assets, with value to local students and residents as well as researchers worldwide. The City of Pittsburgh was known for decades as the "Workshop of the World" due to its giant iron and steel industries. The evolution and prominence of these industries—the owners and workers, industrial processes, labor practices, conflicts with regulators, and impacts on Pittsburgh—are documented in the Iron and Steel Collection. The size and the variety of collection formats—albums, photographs, trade catalogs, booklets, sheet music, scientific documents, and journals—made it difficult for library staff to provide easy access to the materials. In 2008, the library received an Institute of Museum and Library Sciences National Leadership Demonstration Grant to convert much of the collection to digital format, thereby enabling remote access. CLP's goals were to place the collection online and to create thematic lesson plans for educational use in Pittsburgh schools and beyond.

In order to fulfill the project goals, the library's archivist, reference and preservation librarians, and IT staff worked on the Iron and Steel Collection for three years, carrying out multiple processing tasks. Each of the 1,300 documents totaling half a million pages had to be examined, prepared, and tracked for scanning by the project manager or other staff. The items vary widely in size, type, condition and accompanying data, which made the organizing, scanning, and descriptive processes complicated. Metadata to accompany each item had to be developed. For photographs of people and places there was often little data to support identification. Because of cost considerations, the library decided to use DSpace, an open-source, online repository program to house and present data. The project team was also responsible for creating a topical framework for online searching using the structural parameters defined by DSpace.

According to Richard Kaplan, project manager and assistant manager of CLP's main branch in Oakland, "Putting together this collection has been like exploring a coal mine . . . We came out blackened by years of industrial grit."

In 2012, CLP launched the digital Pittsburgh Iron and Steel Heritage Collection, making a previously inaccessible trove of historical materials accessible for public use online. The first iteration of the digital collection includes 1,300 documents organized for searching into six broad themes. CLP staff used Facebook, blogs, and other media to generate attention to the new digital collection and placed a selection of images from the Collection on Flickr. To celebrate the opening of the digital collection CLP organized a Community Day that featured numerous activities including a screening of the documentary film "The River Ran Red" and stories about Joe Magarac, the folklore archetype of the immigrant steelworker.

LESSON PLANS. Having accomplished the first of their two goals, CLP staff focused on their second goal—namely, creation of lesson plans based on the Iron and Steel Collection. Staff of the children's and teen departments worked with Special Collections staff to develop a series of lesson plans that are aligned with the current Pennsylvania State Board of Education's Academic Standards and Content Areas for different grade levels. Staff report that the process of distilling information on the collections into topical areas that align with the various subject areas was complicated. However, the results make it possible for educators to use previously inaccessible materials to augment and enrich classroom teaching.

The lesson plans are organized for use at the elementary, middle, and high school levels. Topics include: Air Pollution (Elementary School); Immigration and Advertising (Grades 4–6); Industrial China compared to Industrial Pittsburgh, and Transportation (High School). CLP staff has conducted workshops for area teachers to advance their understanding of the Iron and Steel Collection and how it can be integrated into the regular curriculum.

● **CHALLENGES.** The Iron and Steel Collection was the largest digitization project undertaken by CLP and resulted in hundreds of gigabytes worth of computer files. Scanning such a large collection to make it usable online and for lesson plans was a daunting task. Organizing and operating the special project team for years, and managing the complex technical issues, were additional challenges.

● **FUTURE PLANS.** Project Manager Kaplan plans to add the American Marketplace Collection (see below) to CLP's digital offerings in 2015, thus expanding public access to the vast trove of historical materials associated with the Pittsburgh Iron and Steel Heritage Collection.

● **RELATED PROGRAM.** The process of converting the Iron and Steel Collection to digital format led to some unexpected benefits. The Trade Catalogues that form part of the Collection turned out to be a significant historical resource in their own right, documenting the growth of industrial and consumer products, and related marketing, that emerged as a result of Pittsburgh's massive metals industry. In a complementary project, the library was able to scan an additional 126,000 pages from 700 trade catalogs, spanning the period 1870 to the late 1940s, to form the American Marketplace Collection. This collection complements the Iron and Steel Collection and will be useful for educators at several levels.

PROGRESS WITH CHESS CHALLENGE
Cleveland Public Library

OVERVIEW: Cleveland Public Library's (CPL) Special Collections Department (Special Collections) contains the John G. White Chess Collection (White Chess Collection), the largest collection of books and periodicals on chess in existence. The library hosts an annual two-day chess event in partnership with the Cleveland Municipal Schools Chess Program called Progress with Chess Challenge. In addition, the library develops exhibitions based on its chess collections and offers online access to many collection items. Programming around the collection illustrates ways that a public library can promote young people's educational development through involvement with unusual collections, while also helping them build critical thinking skills.

Playing chess develops critical thinking skills and promotes healthy social interaction and good sportsmanship between the children—and we have lots of fun!

—Pamela J. Eyerdam, Fine Arts and Special Collections Manager

The renowned collection of books and related materials on chess is a primary feature of CPL's Special Collections. Created by John G. White, a collector of rare books, chess manuscripts, and unique editions, the White Chess Collection was established in 1899 when he donated a large number of works on folklore and Orientalia. In 1932 the library received his full chess library of more than 12,000 titles. In the 1980s the library consolidated rare holdings from other subject departments into the department now known as Special Collections, which, in addition to the White Chess Collection, includes such specialties as miniature books, medieval manuscripts, titles about the occult, tobacco, and rare architectural publications.

CPL's White Chess Collection documents the history, development, and technical aspects of the game along with records of competitions, tournaments, and players. An endowment provided by White makes possible ongoing acquisitions. The current collection numbers more than 32,000 books about chess and checkers, hundreds of unusual chess pieces, more than 6,000 periodicals, more than 50 Indian treatises, tournament records, twelfth-century Arabic manuscripts, documents from many great chess masters, and literary works that mention chess. The collection is known to chess aficionados worldwide; however, it is not well-known to the general public. Special Collections staff uses programs and exhibitions to reach beyond specialists to build connections with more diverse audiences.

For the past twelve years the library has hosted the Progress with Chess Challenge, a chess tournament for more than 500 students from the Cleveland Metropolitan School District Chess Program. Working with the local organization Progress with Chess Inc. (PWC), which is dedicated to using chess as a positive educational experience for young students, the library provides access to its auditorium and an entire floor of the main wing of the downtown library for two days during Chess Challenge. In addition, staff has donated hundreds of hours to help with planning and conducting the event.

According to PWC organizers, the Chess Challenge has "been a positive outlet for students to test their skills against one another . . . and to reap the intellectual and social benefits of chess participation." The event involves more than 500 students, grades 3–8, who compete for prizes, scholarships, and recognition. In addition to its educational benefits for student participants, Chess Challenge has exposed participants and their families to the library and, in particular, to the White Chess Collection. It has also helped widen local residents' awareness of the collection through extensive publicity associated with the event.

Aside from the Power with Chess Challenge Special Collections staff has used exhibitions to draw the attention of chess players, both young and old. The most recent chess exhibition, Women in Chess (2011), featured women chess players dating from the nineteenth century to the present day, including photographs of twentieth-century women players, records of games and tournaments, and books written by the women chess players. Another exhibition (2006), titled Chess Metaphors, Anecdotes and Proverbs, focused on references to chess—"witty, sad, and philosophical"—from fictional works and the literature of history, philosophy, and the sciences.

The department has carried out other chess-related educational programs. Special Collections staff has worked for three years with a Cleveland Institute of Art (CIA) design professor to facilitate use of the White Chess Collection by students taking her Foundation Design course. Students research various chess sets and the history of chess as the basis for designing their own chess sets as class projects. Since 2009 the library has exhibited the student-designed chess sets in the Reading Room.

❯ **CHALLENGES.** One of the ongoing challenges for Special Collections is widening awareness and use of the White Chess Collection by local chess players and researchers. Events such as the Power with Chess Challenge are helpful in that regard.

❯ **FUTURE PLANS.** Although staffing is limited, Special Collections is exploring the possibilities for extending chess outreach programs into the branch libraries.

❯ **RELATED PROGRAM.** In 2011, Special Collections, which commissions CPL's public art projects, commissioned Cleveland-based artist Donald Black Jr. to create a work celebrating the White Chess Collection for the library's Eastman Reading Garden. Black's "Power of the Pieces" featured chess tables designed with photographs of chess pieces and topped with a chessboard, 1,000 handcrafted chess pieces for public use, and a large photograph mural of two figures playing chess mounted on the library window facing the garden. The chess tables were scattered throughout the Reading Garden so that visitors could play chess at their leisure.

RHODES COLLEGE—MEMPHIS PUBLIC LIBRARY ARCHIVAL FELLOWSHIP PROGRAM

Memphis (TN) Public Library and Information Center

OVERVIEW: The Memphis and Shelby County Room (Memphis Room), a section of the History and Social Sciences Department of the Memphis Public Library and Information Center (MPLIC), partners with the History Department of Rhodes College to offer the Rhodes College—Memphis Public Library Archival Fellowship Program. Through the program the Memphis Room hosts two undergraduate history students as archival fellows during the summer months, training them in archival processes and giving them the opportunity to process specific collections. Based on their experiences some fellows have subsequently assisted with archival projects in the region or gone on to advanced studies in archival management or library science. Like other internships offered by public library archives and special collections, the Archival Fellowship Program stimulates student engagement with historical collections and helps attract young people to the archival and library professions.

> **With our Rhodes College-Memphis Public Library Archival Fellowship Program we aim to create a new generation of archivists.**
>
> —Wayne Dowdy, History Department Manager

The Memphis Room is a primary source of research materials on the history of Memphis and the broader region. Holdings include rare books, maps, business and organizational records, family and genealogy records, photographs, materials on local music, architecture and the arts, and a growing collection of films and videos. With a range of services and programs, the Memphis Room collaborates with educational and cultural organizations in the region, including Rhodes College. For more than eight years Memphis Room Manager Wayne Dowdy has lectured to classes at the college on the use of archives and special collections in historical research. Through this relationship, students from the college's history department have often done individual internships at the Memphis Room.

In 2011, the Memphis Room and the Rhodes College History Department established the Archival Fellows Program, through which two upper-level history students are selected to work for two months at MPLIC on varied archival projects. The fellows have the opportunity to work in a real-life setting while helping preserve the history of Memphis. They receive training in processing manuscript collections, basic archival preservation, and preparation of computer-generated collection guides. The students are treated as members of the staff and are expected to take on responsibility for projects that result in new finding aids or enable a collection to be placed on Dig Memphis, the library's digital archive. The fellows are paid a small stipend by Rhodes for eight weeks' work. Each Fellow is required to write a reflective essay on his or her time in the Memphis Room; some of these are posted on the Memphis Room's blog. Regan Adolph, a summer 2012 archival fellow, wrote:

> Finishing the Awsumb Architectural Collection rather quickly, we were given the opportunity to process every single Memphis blueprint we could find in the library. I couldn't have been happier—going from the basement to the storage rooms in the history department collecting numerous blueprints and using our new architectural processing knowledge . . . I know that my mix of abilities would be perfectly put to use in an archival setting like this.

In 2014, the two Archival Fellows, Katie Jakovich and Matthew Hicks, worked on the papers of Benjamin L. Hooks, the lawyer and civil rights leader for whom the Benjamin L. Hooks Central Library in Memphis was named. The Fellows' work led to inclusion of the Hooks Collection on the Dig Memphis site.

The Archival Fellowship Program has opened up professional opportunities for some fellows even before they graduate. For instance, in 2011 Rhodes College Library received the papers of acclaimed historian and novelist Shelby Foote Jr. Two former archival fellows qualified for History Department grants to help organize Foote's boxes of research notes, manuscripts, and hand-drawn maps associated with his famous three-volume work *The Civil War: A Narrative.*

In addition to the in-depth partnership between Rhodes College and its history department, Memphis Room staff also work with the University of Memphis and Christian Brothers University to host interns and conduct departmental tours for undergraduate and graduate classes. Through these efforts the library's professionals try to instill interest in the history of Memphis and in archival work in general.

◉ **CHALLENGES.** It is sometimes difficult for Memphis Room staff to devote the time necessary for training and supervising the archival fellows, especially in times of staff shortages. However, Dowdy states that: "All staff realize the importance of the Archival Fellows Program and are willing to work extra shifts on the public service desk to cover for the curator or digital projects manager while they work with the Fellows . . . the benefits to the library and the profession far outweigh the challenges."

● **FUTURE PLANS.** Dowdy and his partners at Rhodes College plan to expand the Archival Fellowship Program into a yearlong archival certificate program for Rhodes College undergraduates. The first semester will cover archival theory and practice and the second semester will consist of hands-on experience, either at the Rhodes College Library or the Memphis Room.

THERE IS NO BETTER PLACE IN THE COUNTRY FOR A CITY
The Old Dominion Land Company and the Development of the City of Newport News
Newport News (VA) Public Library System

OVERVIEW: The Special Collections Department (Special Collections) of the Newport News Public Library System (NNPLS) organized a multipart project in 2009 that centered around an exhibition—There Is No Better Place in the Country for a City: The Old Dominion Land Company and the Development of the City of Newport News (the Exhibition)—that used the Old Dominion Land Company's records to "teach the history of how the city was developed." Other project components included a traveling version of the exhibition, public programs on exhibition themes, an online exhibition, development of lesson plans, and outreach to media. The exhibition and its accompanying components demonstrate how one special collection can be presented and interpreted for both general and classroom education.

> This is an exciting exhibit, because it highlights key events in the history of Newport News and the role that the Old Dominion Land Company played in the city's development. In addition, the exhibit will help draw attention to the amazing collection of materials in the Virginiana Room at the Main Street Library, and the online exhibit will allow students and scholars to research the history of Newport News.
>
> —Dr. Julie Richter, Department of History, College of William and Mary

N NPLS's Special Collections are known as the Martha Woodroof Hiden Memorial Collection and are housed in the Virginiana Room at the Main Street Library.

Holdings include maps, manuscripts, photographs, genealogical resources, business records, yearbooks, journals, and copies of Newport News' *Daily Press* from 1896 to the present. The primary collection is made up of the papers and maps of the Old Dominion Land Company, founded in1880 by railroad magnate Collis P. Huntington. The company records comprise more than 94,000 maps, blueprints, documents, and photographs given to the city in 1979 by the son of the last company president. The records provide the basis for understanding how the area that is now Newport News evolved from a rural community in 1880 to a major maritime city by the turn of the century. Maps and records trace how, in developing the land required to extend the railway line from Richmond, Virginia, to the port of Newport News, the Old Dominion Land Company established the city's basic infrastructure, its street layout, utilities, sewage and water systems, and helped expand local shipbuilding. According to former Special Collections Branch Manager Gregg Grunow:

> The Old Dominion Land Company Records and Map Collection is extremely valuable to anyone interested in the history of the development of the City of Newport News. Therefore, it has been a goal of the Library System to both preserve and provide wider access to this treasure trove of information.

Given the importance of the Land Company records, NNPLS invested in records management and conservation. In 2009, Special Collection staff began to focus on making the records accessible to members of the general public and developing interpretive tools for educational use. With special project funding the library was able to hire a part-time researcher and an exhibition designer and to organize a local project team that included representatives of the local middle schools, the City of Newport News, and the Library of Virginia. The team developed the concept for an exhibition based on the Land Company records that could be re-created online, adapted to a panel version for travel to public locations, and that could provide the basis for educational activities designed to deepen teachers' and students' engagement with historical documents.

The main exhibition was launched with a celebration at the Main Library with dramatic readings of letters from the exhibition, keynote lectures by two historians, and period music performed by a youth orchestra. A traveling version was then circulated to City Hall, local schools, and other public locations. The online version of the exhibition offers extensive classroom resources developed by local social studies teachers, including lesson plans and special projects such as Mapping Project: Newport News Yesterday and Today.

Grunow states that the exhibition project was "a turning point for the library's Special Collections," stimulating new relationships with schools and new public awareness of the library's archives and online collections. Teacher participation extended the exhibition's classroom use and underscored the value of library-school collaboration. The city television channel filmed the exhibition and many local and regional newspapers reported on the project.

In 2009 the exhibition was cited as the Outstanding Adult Program for libraries serving a population of more than 100,000 by the Virginia Public Library Directors' Association. The online exhibition won the 2009 C. Herbert Finch Online Publication Award from the Mid-Atlantic Regional Archives Conference (MARAC).

❯ **CHALLENGES.** Special Collections staff found it challenging to accomplish a large educational project while carrying out other departmental duties. The exhibition itself took six months to complete, not including prior months of planning, hiring of part-time temporary project staff, and working with partners on the lesson plans and other attendant activities.

❯ **FUTURE PLANS.** Special Collections is working to expand NNPLS's Digital Library by digitizing collections of historical significance. Grunow explains: "By digitally preserving important and rare artifacts the library is able to provide access to the widest possible audiences, including educators and students."

FOUR

EMERGING INSTITUTIONAL MODELS

At NYPL we're engaging the twenty-first century by reimagining information networks and developing citizen archivists.

—NYPL Labs Staff

This book aims to showcase examples of public library programs that increase connections between archival and special collections and the general public. It also aims to identify ways that public libraries are changing internally as they work toward this goal. What institutions or departments are committed to expanding public access to and involvement with special collections and how does this commitment play out operationally? How are these public libraries shifting priorities and reallocating staff and other resources?

The 13 institutional and departmental models highlighted in this chapter provide some answers to these questions. Although they are operating in different community settings and circumstances—different governance and leadership structures, different institutional histories, different collections, and different fiscal and staff capacities—each one has made internal changes leading to enhanced public access. As such, they provide valuable case studies concerning organizational change in relation to special collections.

Despite the diversity of the following models there are four visible trends. One is the tendency of some larger institutions to centralize public programming activities, including exhibitions, in a single department. At New York Public Library's Schwartzman Building the Exhibition Program is responsible for all exhibitions and programs, including corridor exhibitions, pop-up displays, and major interpretive exhibitions in the Gateman Exhibition Hall. This arrangement calls for intensive collaboration between Exhibition Program staff and Special Collections staff, as well as collaboration with staff responsible for public programming, communications, and public relations. Similarly, the Kansas City Public Library has designated its Public Affairs Division as the lead developer and coordinator of nearly all exhibitions and public programs.

Another trend in some major public library special collections, such as the Austin History Center, Nashville's Special Collections, and the Houston Metropolitan Research Center, is the allocation of expanded resources for community outreach and the creation of archives that reflect particular neighborhoods or communities of interest. The Seattle Public Library, which has recently undergone a library-wide planning process, aims to reorganize even further by decentralizing certain functions in order to ensure equitable services across the system. The approach involves creating neighborhood history collections in branch libraries and greater contact between Special Collections and neighborhood patrons through programming and communications.

A third trend is visible at some urban libraries, such as San Francisco Public Library and Los Angeles Public Library, where individual subject departments that have traditionally maintained their own "special collections" have been or are being consolidated into one overarching special collections department. Consolidation is driven by needs for improved storage, better coordination of preservation, and more efficient use of staff. However, the changes are also benefiting patrons through increased programmatic capacity and more coordinated communications.

A fourth characteristic of some models is their capacity for excellence, even in the face of myriad new functions and responsibilities. These models manage to balance the old with the new, to develop special documentation projects, conduct outreach and create digital collections while also maintaining the highest standards of collections care, preservation, and research support. The Jerome Robbins Dance Division at the Performing Arts Library in New York City is an example of a special collections department that has consistently been able to integrate new activities with traditional archival functions while maintaining high levels of excellence in all its endeavors. The Pikes Peak Library District's Special Collection department has also achieved a consistent level of outreach and quality programming while also addressing collection development and management, in this case focusing on regional history.

Aside from these four trends there are no discernible connections between the other examples of institutional change cited in this chapter. However, the latter have value as distinct models within the larger picture of institutional change. The merger between the Free Library of Philadelphia and the former Rosenbach Museum and Library in Philadelphia is, to this author's knowledge, an unusual example of a contemporary public-private library merger. Similarly, the Center for Folk Life, History and Culture in Glens Falls, New York, is an unusual example of a structure that incorporates elements of a local history collection, an archive, and a folklike center. Boston Public Library's "Collections of Distinction" constitutes a special approach to promoting library treasures while also providing an effective framework for interdepartmental coordination around thematic, collection-based projects.

The most unusual model included in this chapter is the NYPL Labs Department, which was set up specifically to work with special collections to find innovative ways of applying digital tools for archival processing and citizen engagement. The projects Labs has undertaken, some of which are discussed in the chapter on Interactive Archives, have already influenced libraries in other cities, especially libraries where experimentation is a priority.

Beyond the "Emerging Institutional Models" presented in this volume, there are others that could have been included. Each of the models represents other public libraries that are reorganizing operations, communications, and programs to enhance public engagement with special collections.

AUSTIN HISTORY CENTER
Austin (TX) Public Library

OVERVIEW: The Austin History Center (AHC), a division of the Austin Public Library (APL), is a primary example of a public library archive that operates as a separate department, with its own programming, building, support group, and identity. Established as a repository for the library's manuscripts in the 1950s, the center has grown to include the archives of the City of Austin and Travis County as well as diverse records that reflect the history and culture of Austin. In recent years AHC leaders have emphasized outreach to the city's diverse neighborhoods and programming centered on exhibitions. In both respects, AHC offers instructive examples of how a historical repository can engage varied constituencies.

> **One of my strategies for running the History Center is to continually strive to make us relevant. In everything we do, from outreach to collection development to exhibitions, our primary concern is to build relevancy.**
>
> —Mike Miller, Manager, Austin History Center

O ver the past five decades AHC has established itself as the primary locus for the preservation and presentation of Austin history. Housed in the original Austin Library, a landmark building, its extensive collections include documentary material in diverse formats, from oral histories and ephemera to historic photographs, films, and business records. Specialties include music, architecture, and family history. Through outreach to formerly underrepresented communities, conducted by Community Archivists, AHC is filling gaps in its collections to ensure that they reflect the lives and traditions of contemporary residents and newcomers. To build awareness of the collections, and to stimulate their use, AHC carries out multiple public programs. The Austin History Center Association, a private, nonprofit organization, has played a substantial role in AHC's development and supports many programs.

EXHIBITIONS AND PROGRAMS. Exhibitions are AHC's primary programming vehicle. AHC Manager Mike Miller defines the goals of exhibitions as: "First, to promote awareness of who we are in Austin and what our history has been; and second, to engage the public in topics that are meaningful and of wide interest today." To fulfill these goals AHC organizes at least two exhibitions a year in its major exhibition space and two to three exhibitions in a separate gallery. The exhibitions are organized by AHC research librarians or archivists supported by design and production personnel. Recent exhibition topics include:

- Austin's Mexico: A Forgotten Downtown Neighborhood (2014)
- Deco and Moderne: Austin Architecture of the 1930s (2011)
- Building a Community: The First Century of African-American Life in Travis County (2010)

All AHC exhibitions are accompanied by public programs, some geared toward general audiences and others designed to attract special interest groups, certain ages, or residents of particular neighborhoods. They include performances, author talks, lectures, film screenings, and demonstrations. Backwards in High Heels: Women Politicians in Texas (2014) is one example of a major exhibition-program initiative. The exhibition used photos, letters, manuscripts, government records, ephemera, and audiovisual presentations to provide a historical context for an issue relevant to Austin residents today. Complementary programming included a panel discussion with women holding key positions in county and state government; a beer garden social featuring entertainment concerning women and politics, with an Ann Richards impersonation contest; a film series on women in politics; and a lecture on women in politics by a former City Council member.

AHC creates smaller exhibitions for travel to branch libraries or other community organizations. As one example, AHC created Austin Music Originals, a photographic exhibition documenting local musicians that was shown at the Terrazas Branch in 2013 and provided the backdrop for a music documentary series.

OUTREACH. Austin's Community Archivists Program, aimed at building collections and increasing community participation, is another model for public library archives. Three full-time archivists function as subject specialists and community liaisons with specific constituencies—African Americans, Mexican Americans, and Asian Americans—whose history has been underrepresented in AHC programs and collections. Their work is having an impact in terms of collection development, community relationships, and program content.

In addition to exhibitions and outreach, AHC maintains a Speaker's Bureau, offers tours of the collections, collaborates with cultural organization partners, and partners with institutions of higher education to offer internships and study opportunities to "help prepare next generation archivists."

SOCIAL MEDIA. AHC also reaches out through its online presence, with a set of online exhibitions, and through use of social media focused mainly on Facebook. AHC leaders have found it more efficient to put their energies into one primary social media channel rather than to scatter their efforts, and have had good response in terms of "likes" and feedback on Facebook. AHC also has a presence on Historypin that allows photographs from the collection to be geo-located on a map and searched by time frame.

● **CHALLENGES.** Miller cites the need for sustained funding as a major challenge. He hopes to build endowment funds over the next few years that will help to ensure the continuation of outreach staff, in particular, and enable the additional activities that will be offered when the center expands into a second building. Other challenges include the costs of digitizing AHC's growing collections while also maintaining AHC's commitment to outreach and programming.

◉ **FUTURE PLANS.** To accommodate its growing collections AHC will take over the current library building in 2016, following construction of a new central library for the system. The move will quadruple the size of AHC's physical facilities, providing increased space for preservation and documentation, as well as improved facilities for exhibition design and presentation. Miller anticipates a corollary expansion of AHC's web presence, with more collections online, a more active blog, and online exhibitions tied to AHC's exhibition program.

BUTLER CENTER FOR ARKANSAS STUDIES
Central Arkansas Library System

OVERVIEW: The Butler Center for Arkansas Studies (the Butler Center) is unusual in several ways. It is a department of the Central Arkansas Library System (CALS) and shares space in the CALS Arkansas Studies Institute (ASI) building with the University of Arkansas at Little Rock, joining the two institutions' research collections on history and culture in one facility. The Butler Center's Encyclopedia of Arkansas History & Culture is the only state encyclopedia in the country to be produced by a library system. The scope of the center's activities is also unusual, from musical festivals and genealogical conferences to an hour-long documentary on Arkansans in the Korean War. Although the center results from a special set of circumstances, it offers lessons to other institutions examining ways to diversify audiences, collections, and programs.

> **We can't just stockpile stuff and hope people will wander in. We must use our collections in as many ways as possible to help people think about Arkansas's past and future.**
>
> —David Stricklin, Manager, Butler Center for Arkansas Studies

The Butler Center was established in 1997, through an endowment from Richard C. Butler Sr., with the goal of promoting a greater understanding and appreciation of Arkansas history and culture. As CALS's special collections unit Butler

Center staff and programs are part of CALS. The majority of Butler Center funding comes from CALS's regular budget. The Center is housed in the ASI building that CALS opened in 2009, which also contains the Center for Arkansas History and Culture (CAHC) of the University of Arkansas at Little Rock (UALR). While administratively separate, the two institutions make their holdings available in one research room. The ASI building contains more than 10 million documents and photographs on Arkansas history as well as exhibition galleries and spaces for public programming.

Butler Center collections include manuscripts, oral histories, personal and family papers, documents and images that illuminate such themes as Arkansas agricultural history, the environment, genealogy, arts and entertainment, religion, industry, and women's history. The Map Collection is the largest in Arkansas, the photographic collections are extensive, and there is a growing Arkansas Sounds Music Collection. The Butler Center is also responsible for CALS's permanent art collection of almost 1,500 pieces, among them the largest public collection of art created by Japanese Americans from a single internment camp, the Rohwer Camp.

The Butler Center has many facets that, together, make it stand out on the spectrum of institutional models for public library archives and special collections. It is, simultaneously, a major repository and center for research on history and genealogy, an interpretive center, a cultural institution, *and* a creator of content and educational tools that enhance public understanding of and public dialogue about Arkansas history and culture. To carry out these various roles the center has a varied agenda.

ARKANSAS SOUNDS. The Butler Center is a locus for the study of regional music, past and present. To showcase the state's rich musical culture, the center presents Arkansas Sounds, including monthly live concerts, songwriting workshops, and outdoor music festivals.

ENCYCLOPEDIA OF ARKANSAS HISTORY & CULTURE (EOA). Launched in 2006, EOA has grown each year, with thousands of items from the collections—photographs, maps, documents, art—organized thematically and available to anyone anywhere. The project was started with a major foundation grant. CALS now supports the five staff positions necessary to continuously refine and expand the site. Between 5,500 and 7,000 people visit the EOA site daily and it is an important resource for Arkansas student and teachers, scholars, writers, and diverse audiences interested in Arkansas history and culture. As a form of digital outreach and collections access, EOA complements other activities. The most recent innovation is a mobile version of EOA, which launched in January 2013, and won the Award of Merit from the American Association for State and Local History. According to Butler Center

Manager David Stricklin, "The Encyclopedia is important not only as vehicle for expanding access to our collections but for providing the contexts and narratives that give those collections meaning."

EXHIBITIONS. With several gallery spaces available in the ASI facility, the Butler Center has a continuous schedule of collections-based and traveling exhibitions. Exhibition themes vary widely. Clinton for Arkansas (2013) drew on the Center's collection of Bill Clinton's pre-presidential papers, tracing his Arkansas political career and his impact on the state. Drawn In: New Art from WWII Camps at Rohwer and Jerome (2014) featured artwork created by people held in the Japanese-American internment camps in Arkansas during World War II. To further expand public access to the art, the Butler Center created a multimedia digital exhibition.

LESSON PLANS. The Butler Center has created dozens of free online thematic lesson plans that dovetail primary source material with the curriculum frameworks required for local history study in the state. One example is a module titled Ruled by Race, which provides a historical perspective on race relations in the state. To create these teaching modules the center hired historians and worked with the state's Department of Education to ensure compatibility with standards. The Center's K–12 educator and other staff also visit regional educational conferences to encourage teachers to use the lesson plans, and they created the Arkansas History HUB, a web-based clearinghouse for teaching materials, that is maintained in partnership with the Department of Arkansas Heritage.

SPECIAL PROJECTS. Forgotten: The Arkansas Center Korean War Project is one example of the center's capacity to carry out multipart initiatives that collect, preserve, and interpret documentary evidence of a historically significant event. The ongoing project involves gathering oral histories, building a distinct collection, organizing meetings of stakeholders, and developing curriculum-specific lesson plans. The project has resulted in a film exploring the impact of the Korean War on Arkansans.

AV/AR AUDIO VIDEO DATABASE. The AV/AR collections online offer an important means of drawing in individuals and groups who might not otherwise know about the scope of the Butler Center Collections. They include oral histories, lectures about Arkansas, and various kinds of film footage—such as a growing collection of Home Movies—with digitally searchable subject descriptions that provide a variety of sources relating to a specific topic.

BUTLER CENTER BOOKS. Though it is heavily invested in digital collections, the Butler Center carries out a robust print publication program, releasing an average of five books a year on the history and culture of Arkansas. Recent Butler Center books include *Arkansas: An Illustrated Atlas* and *Race Relations in the Natural State* by Grif Stockley.

BUTLER CENTER BLOG. The blog is defined as "a new avenue to encourage discussion between the Butler Center, other historical professionals, and our patrons out there in the blogosphere." Among its features are links to new entries in the Encyclopedia of Arkansas History & Culture.

Singly, and in combination, the activities summarized above offer instructive models for contemporary archival practice in a public library setting.

◉ **CHALLENGES.** Like many organizations with deep roots in the collection of paper resources, the Butler Center is working hard to balance the opportunities and challenges of digital formats with those of more traditional materials. Stricklin states:

> We aren't getting out of the paper business anytime soon, but we're keeping a keen eye on the costs of processing and accessibility of paper materials, as well as digital resources, along with their relative prospects for reaching people who need to know about Arkansas's history . . .

◉ **FUTURE PLANS.** Butler Center staff has several priority projects to increase public use of its research collections. One is to create more web-based resources such as mobile apps based on the EOA. Stricklin believes it is important to take advantage of the fact that schools now allow students to use mobile devices. "Having mobile apps based on solid historical materials is going to be crucial to reaching these students." Other projects include the engagement of contract oral historians to pursue collecting projects in greater depth, and exploring the use of radio or other channels to make the music and art collections more accessible.

CENTER FOR FOLKLIFE, HISTORY, AND CULTURAL PROGRAMS
Crandall Public Library (Glens Falls, NY)

OVERVIEW: Crandall Public Library's (CPL) Center for Folklife, History, and Cultural Programs (Folklife Center) is an unusual model wherein the library's archival and local history functions are combined with the documentary and programming functions of a regional folklife center. The consolidation of functions has enabled the library to strengthen its preservation and programming capacity while engaging varied audiences from throughout the Southern Adirondack Mountains and the Upper Hudson Valley.

With an infrastructure that is a cross between an archive, a gallery and a laboratory, we are redefining what a local history collection can be and we are engaging people in discovering the cultural traditions of the region.

—Todd DeGarmo, Director, Center for Folklife,
History, and Cultural Programs

S COPE AND GOAL. The Folklife Center is a part of CPL, which serves residents of Glens Falls, New York, and four surrounding counties in the Southern Adirondack region of New York State. It was formed in 1993, inspired by the American Folklife Center at Library of Congress, with seed money from the National Endowment for the Arts. Starting in 1983, the New York State Council on the Arts had provided funds for folk arts programming, with folklorist Todd DeGarmo running the programs beginning in 1986. He organized research and public programs that attracted new audiences and enabled documentation of previously overlooked aspects of the region's history, however, they were not institutionalized within the library and depended on intermittent grants.

In the early 1990s, CPL was grappling with how to care for its substantial local history collections, which had little professional oversight or educational programming. Library officials were presented with an opportunity to consolidate the overlapping functions of a special collection archives, a local history department, a gallery, and an educational resource into one center dedicated to the living cultural history and traditions of the Southern Adirondacks. DeGarmo became the founding director of the new Folklife Center; his first duties involved the renovation of a section of the library for a secure reading room, archival storage, and a gallery space. With its consolidated framework the Folklife Center has evolved a multifaceted agenda of educational programs, outreach, and participatory activities. These are usually coordinated around one of two key themes that staff selects to focus on each year. Programming is interdisciplinary, reflecting the Center's broad mission and collections and its commitment to diverse audiences. According to DeGarmo, "We have tried to create a center that offers opportunities for different kinds of interactions with regional history and culture."

EXHIBITIONS. Staff present two original exhibitions a year in the Folklife Gallery, the themes of which are the basis for related programming. The exhibitions highlight current research and collecting interests, and often serve as opportunities to build partnerships with local organizations whose work is relevant to the subject. Recent exhibitions include the following:

- Collecting Lake George: Maps, Prints, Postcards & Other Memorabilia (2014)
- Odetta: The Queen of Folk (2012)
- Foodways: Documenting the Local (2011)

MUSIC SERIES. Live! Folklife Concerts, offered in the spring and fall of each year, showcase different forms of traditional and regional music and help attract diverse audiences to the center. The concerts have also become a draw for musicians from throughout the region and the Northeast, providing opportunities for documentation.

WORKSHOPS AND PRESENTATIONS. Exhibitions are often accompanied by educational activities that involve different age groups and partnerships. At the Lake was a four-part, free lecture series supporting the Collecting Lake George exhibition. A participatory dance/narrative and craft workshops, a film series, and ethnic music performances were developed to support the 2014 exhibition, Celebrating Women's Creative Hands & Spirits. Locally sourced healthy snack workshops, cookbook authors with tastings, film series, and interactive exhibition stations were all part of the Foodways exhibition in 2011.

OUTREACH. Folklife Center staff regularly present illustrated talks to regional organizations and at professional meetings on topics ranging from "Genealogical Resources at the Folklife Center" to "Cardboard Boat Races on the Hudson."

EDUCATIONAL PARTNERSHIPS. Staff work with local educational institutions to expose young people to the Folklife Center. One program introduces students to special collections in an "Archival Treasure Hunt," moving them from document to document in a kind of timed lab test. Another is the annual Women's History Essay contest for fourth graders, cosponsored by the local chapter of the American Association of University Women. DeGarmo has also worked with BOCES Gifted and Talented Program to teach photographic and oral history skills to sixth graders.

COMMUNITY DOCUMENTATION. The Folklife Center is beginning to experiment with new media. A local foundation has provided funds for a digital documentation lab for video and sound production with editing on laptops. New projects using the new equipment are beginning, such as *Portraits,* short video documentaries about local folk artists, and *Do Tell: Learning to Perform Personal Stories,* a four-part workshop series being recorded and edited for broadcast on social media with links to the library's website.

● **CHALLENGES.** As a relatively new department within the library, and one with an atypical scope and mission, there was an initial learning curve on the part of library staff with respect to what the Folklife Center could or should be. Over time, staff have come to value the cultural facets of the center as an important part of the library's mission. Another challenge had been the need to form preservation protocols around a professionally managed archival collection, which had previously been open without safeguards regarding use. Marketing is a third challenge. With relatively limited resources for marketing in the library, the Center has had to conduct its own marketing, including digital communications.

● **FUTURE PLANS.** DeGarmo envisions greater use of digital technologies to advance the mission of the Folklife Center. Through an improved website, digitization of collections, use of social media, digital documentation tools, and more sophisticated communications the Folklife Center will expand access to its collections and bring more people into contact with the history and culture of the region.

COLLECTIONS OF DISTINCTION
Boston Public Library

OVERVIEW: Boston Public Library's 2011 Strategic Plan, the *BPL Compass*, articulated a "Principle for Excellence" that called for "the ongoing development and preservation of its distinctive special collections . . ." Based on this Principle the library has identified 18 Collections of Distinction, which provide a framework for decisions about collections management, digitization, and public programming. This strategy, which implies greater coordination across divisions, increased thematic programming, and expanded online access, gives momentum to other changes started earlier in the century, including organization of institution-wide interpretive programs and formation of a department of Digital Services and the Norman B. Leventhal Map Center. The "Collections of Distinction" approach to special collections preservation and programming offers a compelling model for the nation's public libraries.

For the first several months of my tenure, people would ask me what my priorities were with the collection. How could you choose between a letter from Phillis Wheatley or a manuscript from Louisa May Alcott or Toulouse-Lautrec drawings?

—Amy Ryan, President

Long renowned as the first publicly supported municipal library in America, BPL's Special Collections are also renowned, containing landmarks in the history of printing, arts, history, maps, literature, law, and music. From American Revolutionary War manuscripts to the Ticknor Library of Spanish and Portuguese Literature, the BPL has research resources that rank among the most important in the nation. Some collections illuminate aspects of national history, such as the Anti-Slavery Collection, while others, such as the map collections, are global in scope.

As the BPL's Special Collections grew over the last 150 years, individual divisions were responsible for managing, preserving, and providing collections access. Curators conceived, developed, and executed projects and programs without a cohesive institutional plan. Each department, no matter how creative, often operated independently, making it difficult to coordinate or prioritize preservation work, carry out cross-department thematic programming, or promote the collections as overall library assets. Several developments in the early 2000s began to change this approach, expanding public engagement with Special Collections and culminating in the articulation of a focus on Collections of Distinction.

THEMATIC PROGRAMS. In 2003, the BPL received two federal grants to preserve, catalog, and digitize the John Adams Library and to create an interpretive exhibition. The 3,500 books donated by John Adams to the people of Massachusetts are national treasures, illuminating the evolution of the early nation and revealing Adams' political and intellectual development. The multiyear project resulted in an electronic catalog accessible from BPL's main catalog, an independent John Adams Library website, transcriptions of Adams's annotations of the books, a major exhibition (2006–2007) titled John Adams Unbound, and digitization of nearly 3,200 volumes from the collection.

The John Adams Unbound exhibition, held in the McKim building in Copley Square, attracted more visitors than any previous library gallery exhibition. This exhibition marked the first time the entire Adams Library had been put on public display. It was organized around Adams's handwritten notes in the margins of his books, as well as interpretive comments from curators, historical figures, and Adams himself. Computer stations allowed visitors to access scanned images from the library. John Adams Unbound was subsequently redesigned as a traveling exhibition—funded by the National Endowment for the Humanities and organized by the American Library Association. This traveling version circulated to 20 libraries nationwide, where it provided the stimulus for varied local programs. According to exhibition curator Beth Prindle:

> Through the development of this multifaceted project, researchers and the general public are now privileged to look over Adams's shoulder at the extraordinary revolutionary times in which he lived and to explore his deeply personal reflections preserved in the margins of this remarkable library.

The John Adams Library project involved many library departments, in particular Digital Services (see below). It helped establish a model for institution-wide efforts based on core collections, characterized by coordinated work across departments to preserve, catalog, digitize, research, design, and launch a digital collection while also curating, designing, and presenting the physical exhibition and organizing attendant programs and promotional activities. The success of the John Adams Library project was a factor in the library's establishment of a department of Exhibitions and Programming in 2009, with responsibility for developing cohesive thematic exhibition and programming initiatives involving multiple departments.

Since 2010, the thematic programs model has been applied to such projects as Torn in Two: The 150th Anniversary of the Civil War (2011), a major institution-wide commemoration, and Building Boston: A Citywide Celebration of Boston's Public Spaces (2012–2013).

NORMAN B. LEVENTHAL MAP CENTER. The formation of the Norman B. Leventhal Map Center in 2004 also prompted new cross-departmental relationships and signaled BPL's leadership in digitization. Established as an externally funded entity, the Map Center is located in the central library where BPL's vast collection of more than 200,000 maps and atlases, along with a select group of rare maps collected by Leventhal, are made available to the public through exhibitions and educational programs. Maps in the collection date from the fifteenth century to the present, with a particular strength in maps and atlases of Boston, the Commonwealth of Massachusetts, and New England. To foster public engagement with these collections, the Map Center offers a Kids Map Club and K–12 programs and exhibitions on such topics as Nautical Charts and Urban Maps. The Map Center's website provides access to thousands of digitized maps. Since establishing the Map Center there have been many more map-based exhibitions and educational programs, drawing attention to maps as core special collections.

DIGITAL SERVICES. The BPL established a department of Digital Services in 2005, formalizing the increasingly important role of digitization in expanding public access to its collections. Under the leadership of Tom Blake, Digital Services plans and carries out digital projects based on library collections, with a special focus on Special Collections. Digital Services works closely with curators and with Exhibitions and Public Programs personnel, prioritizing its work-based program plans. Digital Services also provides Services to the Commonwealth through leadership and assistance in collections digitization for libraries statewide.

COLLECTIONS OF DISTINCTION. By the time that BPL undertook a planning process, starting in 2009, the new approaches to developing exhibitions and expanding digital access already had positive impacts. Special Collections benefited from greater local and national public exposure through interpretive programs that reflected coordinated planning and preparation. Public access to Special Collections increased due to digital collections as well as physical exhibitions. Many different constituents, of all ages and backgrounds, were participating in exhibition tours, workshops, lectures, performances, and other collection-based programming.

Given the cumulative impact of these activities, it is not surprising that Special Collections was singled out in the BPL's recent Strategic Plan as one of eight priorities. In fact, the plan went further, calling for an emphasis on "Collections of Distinction"; for example, bodies of material that "represent the most outstanding, expansive, and renowned of the BPL's collections." By prioritizing certain collections from the library's vast and varied holdings, staff would have a basis for making decisions regarding the care, management, digitization, and presentation of collections.

The first set of Collections of Distinction was announced in 2013. A committee made up of the library's most highly trained subject experts, together with members of the library's Special Collections Committee, established the criteria for the Collections of Distinction and identified the first 18 collections to receive this special designation. These range from Incunabula to the Sacco-Vanzetti Defense Committee Records. In announcing the designation BPL President Amy Ryan stated, "We encourage and invite the residents of Boston and the Commonwealth of Massachusetts to engage with these treasures and celebrate the cultural heritage they contain."

The Collections of Distinction now direct special collections allocations of resources with respect to acquisition, digitization, research, preservation, staff development, public access, and public programming. They also help direct the library's communications, including outreach through social media. The BPL will continue to identify additional candidates for Collections of Distinction status.

Prindle, now Manager of Exhibitions and Programming, states that the Collections of Distinction strategy has benefits beyond greater internal efficiency:

Today, our work is much, much more about outreach and public engagement . . . we can plan ahead to use all the tools we have at our disposal to feature our assets and meet people where they are rather than waiting for them to come to us.

❯ **CHALLENGES.** Library staff acknowledge the difficulty of singling out one collection over another, of codifying "distinctions" that may not be relevant to all people. The criteria for identifying Collections of Distinction were developed with great care in order to reflect varied perspectives on what is a "treasure."

❯ **FUTURE PLANS.** Exhibitions and Programming, Digital Services, Special Collections, and the Map Center are working on another major thematic program initiative for 2015 that will focus on American Revolutionary War era materials and will feature maps, prints, manuscripts, and other materials from multiple Collections of Distinction.

HOUSTON METROPOLITAN RESEARCH CENTER
Houston Public Library

OVERVIEW: The Houston Metropolitan Research Center (HMRC) and the African American Library at the Gregory School (Gregory School), both part of the Special Collections Division (Special Collections) of the Houston Public Library (HPL), are centers for scholarship on the history of Texas and the City of Houston. They are also centers for programming. HMRC has a long-standing history of educational activities and community interactions, including oral history projects, exhibitions, outreach, partnerships, and student internships. The Gregory School uses exhibitions, performances, and documentation projects to illuminate the history of African Americans in Houston. Both HMRC and the Gregory School offer lessons for other public libraries seeking to expand awareness and use of historical collections.

> We try to get out into the community as much as possible, with scanning days, appearances at local festivals and events, oral history days and presentations to educate residents about the importance of cultural preservation and to encourage contributions of personal or community history materials. We are also doing more programming to interpret exhibit themes.
>
> —Elizabeth Sargent, Assistant Director for Special Collections and Director, Houston Metropolitan Research Center

H ouston, Texas, is the nation's fourth-largest city and one of its most diverse—
qualities that are reflected in the size and variety of HPL's Special Collections.
Established in 2007–2008, Special Collections encompasses HMRC, the Gregory
School, and the Clayton Library Center for Genealogical Research, which is the
largest municipal genealogical research library in the United States.

HMRC was created in 1976 to integrate all the library's historical materials, with
the exception of genealogy, into one center for preservation and scholarship. Its
mission is "to preserve the history of Houston and to promote an understanding of
the development of its communities." HMRC holdings take many forms, including
art, artifacts, maps, manuscripts, photographs, and oral history tapes that reflect the
social and cultural diversity of the city and the state, the evolution of the economic,
political, and architectural landscape, the collecting interests of longtime Houstonians,
and the personal stories of more recent residents. Access to the collections has greatly
increased in recent years due to expanded exhibition facilities and development of the
Houston Area Digital Archive. Digitization is ongoing and is often coordinated with
the preservation, research, and curatorial work associated with an exhibition project.

In 2010, HMRC moved to a newly built Archival Wing of the Ideson Building
and in 2011 the restoration of the building's historic portion was completed. With
facilities for conservation, digitization, education, and an exhibition hall, the relocation has greatly expanded HMRC's programming capacities and visibility. The
Friends of the Texas Room is an important source of support for HMRC activities.

The historic Gregory School, the first public school for African Americans in
Houston, became part of Special Collections in 2009. Defined as "a living archive,"
the Gregory School aims to be "a resource to preserve, promote and celebrate the
rich history and culture of African Americans in Houston, the surrounding region,
and the African diaspora." It offers study collections, exhibitions, performances,
community programs, and a scholar-in-residence program.

EXHIBITIONS AND PROGRAMS. Since relocating to the Ideson Building's Archival Wing, HMRC has presented five to six exhibitions a year, most of them drawn
from library collections. The premier exhibition, Theater of Memories, Cabinet of
Curiosities, showcased some of HMRC's unique artifacts and celebrated its many
donors. Other recent exhibitions include an exhibition of glass plate negatives titled
Faces, Places and Spaces and When Camelot Came to Houston: John F. Kennedy
and the League of United Latin-American Citizens.

HMRC exhibition topics are the basis for public programs that draw in varied audiences and expand visitors' understanding of the exhibition themes. For Faces, Places
and Spaces, for example, HMRC organized a panel discussion of local photographers

about contemporary Houston photography. Exhibitions are often the focus of the library's Second Saturday Series, with presentations that highlight an exhibition theme or aspects of the HMRC collections.

To preserve the scholarship that underpins its exhibitions and to extend access to viewers who may not be able to visit the library, HMRC has designed The Houston Public Library Exhibit Snapshot, or THPLES. This innovative tool enables close viewing of exhibition texts and objects online, and interaction in the form of commentary or questions.

In addition to presenting exhibitions drawn solely from its collections, HMRC hosts exhibitions created by other institutions that illuminate aspects of Houston history. As one example, on the occasion of Rice University's Centennial Celebration in 2012, HMRC hosted an exhibition based on the University's archives. Simultaneously, HMRC mounted a complementary display on the history of the University drawn from its own collections.

Exhibitions are an important aspect of the Gregory School's programming agenda. Permanent exhibitions, including a restored 1926 classroom, introduce visitors to Houston's African American heritage, and rotating exhibitions examine specific themes such as the history of blues music in Houston. Organized Love; Ideas on Non-Violence, was an exhibition that featured contemporary artists and writers responding to the history of nonviolent struggle in Houston. Developed collaboratively with the Menil Collection and other institutions, the 2014 exhibition was accompanied by diverse public programs exploring nonviolence from historical and contemporary perspectives.

OUTREACH. The Houston Public Library has a long record of community outreach, which is carried on today through multiple activities that foster community-library interaction and help diversify collections. Recently, in an attempt to expand collections on Hispanic culture in Houston, HMRC hired a Hispanic collections archivist. She serves as a community liaison, attending local organization meetings and representing the library at local events. She also coordinates Hispanic Heritage Month, during which the library invites the Hispanic community to contribute documents, share their photos, or record their stories.

The Gregory School is equally committed to outreach. Through its Community Scanning Project, staff encourages residents to donate documents, photos, and artifacts to the archival collections.

ORAL HISTORY. Community documentation in the form of oral histories has been a consistent priority with Special Collections staff and is reflected in the many recordings created and transcribed by HMRC and the Gregory School that are available on the Houston Area Digital Archive. The African American Library at the Gregory School received the 2014 Mary Faye Barnes Award for Community Oral History.

PARTNERSHIPS AND SPECIAL EVENTS. Both HMRC and the Gregory School work with other community organizations on events that foster understanding of different facets of Houston history. HMRC takes part in the annual Houston History Book Fair, located in the Ideson Building, which advances awareness of authors whose works have been inspired by HMRC collections. In 2012, the Gregory School collaborated with the Houston Museum of African American Culture to present a panel discussion on the history of the Tuskegee Airmen, featuring local airmen.

EDUCATIONAL COLLABORATIONS. HMRC collaborates with many educational institutions to engage and support students in archival collections research. As one example, HMRC works with professors at Houston Community College and Texas Southern University to help students complete mini-archive projects. In 2013 and 2014 participating students processed small collections and others transcribed oral history interviews. In the summer of 2013, HMRC inaugurated an in-service program to introduce high school social studies teachers from the fifty-four school districts in the greater Houston area to the resources of HMRC. HMRC also launched its Student Historian Internship Program (SHIP) in the summer of 2013, enabling students sixteen years old and older to experience working in the library science and archive field.

SCHOLAR-IN-RESIDENCE PROGRAM. The Gregory School collaborates with Rice University's Center for Engaged Learning and Collaborative Learning to offer a residency that assists fellows whose research can benefit from extended access to Gregory School's archives and other HPL resources.

◉ **CHALLENGES.** Both HMRC and the Gregory School face the demands of carrying out active public programming agendas while carrying out other archival tasks and reference services. Acquisition of up-to-date equipment for recording and scanning is another challenge.

◉ **FUTURE PLANS.** HMRC and the Gregory School intend to continue their multifaceted programming. For example, HMRC is planning projects on the history of the Port of Houston and the history of the LGBT community in Houston.

THE JEROME ROBBINS DANCE DIVISION

New York (NY) Public Library for the Performing Arts

OVERVIEW: The Jerome Robbins Dance Division (Dance Division), part of New York Public Library's Library of the Performing Arts (Performing Arts Library), is the world's foremost research collection on the art and history of dance. In addition to preserving extensive written, aural, and visual collections, the division ensures the continuity and restaging of dance forms through documentation, exhibitions, community building activities, and digital projects that involve multiple audiences. The division's multifaceted agenda offers a model for other public library special collections working to sustain traditional research services while integrating new approaches to public engagement both on and off-line.

> **Public programs are the way that people know what we have. They also help people look at the collections with a particular perspective, preparing them to explore the collections in more depth.**
>
> —Jan Schmidt, Curator, Jerome Robbins Dance Division

NYPL's Dance Division documents dance forms of all types and traditions, from Elizabethan court dances and Balanchine ballets to classical Cambodian ballets and African dances. Collection formats range from manuscripts and memorabilia to stage and costume designs and audio memoirs that bring to life the personalities that have shaped the recent course of dance history. The division includes many individual collections, such as the recently acquired Mikhail Baryshnikov Archive. It also includes the Jerome Robbins Archive of the Recorded Moving Image, which preserves and makes accessible dance videotapes, films, and born-digital materials. The recordings are invaluable for those who are restaging specific works, learning a part, or passing choreography on to other dancers and students.

As stewards for such a unique collection, division staff devotes considerable effort to preservation, including digitization to ensure collections access for future generations. As facilitators of scholarship and performance, staff members support dancers, choreographers, dance educators, dance students, and professionals involved with staging dance works. At the same time, staff is committed to ensuring access for members of the public with varying levels of knowledge about dance. The division employs multiple strategies to connect these diverse audiences with the collections.

PROGRAMS AND PERFORMANCES. The Dance Division organizes a variety of programs, as exemplified by presentations during 2012 and 2013. The Dance Historian Is In was a series of film screenings with talks by dance historian David Vaughan that explored the work of particular choreographers or performers; I Was a Dancer, a presentation by Jacques d'Amboise, was one of several author talks on recently published books about dance.

EXHIBITIONS. The Dance Division regularly works with the Performing Arts Library's Exhibit Department to mount exhibitions in the Main Gallery of the Performing Arts Library. According to Curator Jan Schmidt, "Exhibitions are important tools for helping people look at the collection. They also stimulate new research and provoke discussion across the dance community." Some exhibitions are thematic; some are historical, such as Music, Dance and the French Revolution (2009); and some are biographical, such as Alwin Nikolais: Total Theater of Motion (2011).

100 years of Flamenco in New York was a major exhibition in 2013 that used art, images, artifacts, and memorabilia from Division Collections to trace the artistic evolution of Flamenco dancers in New York who helped create an "American School." As the first exhibition to document the phenomenon of Flamenco in America, the exhibition contributed to dance scholarship and helped expand awareness of Flamenco as an art form within and beyond the dance community. Like other major exhibitions put on by the Division, the exhibition was accompanied by public programs including films and three Flamenco performances in the Bruno Walter Auditorium of the Performing Arts Library.

THE ORAL HISTORY ARCHIVE AND THE DANCE ORAL HISTORY CHANNEL. The Division's Oral History Archive contains more than 4,000 audio recordings capturing the voices and ideas of dancers, choreographers, scholars, and producers working in all areas of dance. Selections from the Archive are available on the division's recently established Dance Oral History Channel. The Oral History Archive organizes interview projects that foster communications across generations and between leaders in the dance community. Speaking of Dance, for instance, is a project that involves interviews with prominent figures in the dance field who are asked to speak about the role of interpretation in dance. Distinguished dance historians and critics conduct the interviews, excerpts from which are on the Dance Oral History Channel. Some are available in full on the library's Digital Collections site.

SPECIAL PROJECTS: KHMER DANCE PROJECT (KDP). On occasion the Dance Division undertakes projects that reflect its international perspective. The Khmer Dance Project was an initiative started in 2008 when the Dance Division partnered with the Center for Khmer Studies "to interview and film three generations of artists—dancers, musicians, singers, embroiderers and dressers—who kept dance alive during and after the Khmer Rouge regime." Funded by Anne Bass, the recordings include performances and rehearsals of the Royal Ballet of Cambodia and interviews with key dancers who tried to revive Cambodian culture after the fall of the regime. In late 2013 the recordings, subtitled in English, were made available through the library's Digital Collections. The importance of the Royal Ballet of Cambodia, and of the recordings, was underscored during a public conversation between Peter Sellars and the Princess Norodom Buppha Devi, an esteemed Cambodian prima ballerina of the 1960s, presented by the Dance Division in 2013.

Memory Preserved: Glass Plate Photographs of the Royal Cambodian Dancers, a 2013 exhibition of glass plate negatives depicting performances of the Royal Ballet of Cambodia, was another component of the Khmer Dance Project. Recently rediscovered, catalogued, restored, and digitized, the 1927 images capture leading dancers performing the classical canon; they were on exhibition in the United States for the first time.

COMMUNITY BUILDING. The Dance Division works to bring together dancers, dance educators, choreographers, researchers, and others involved in the development of dance by providing opportunities and space for dialogue and connections. According to Schmidt, "Programs foster communications across the dance community, stimulating collaboration and dance creation." The On Fire with African Dance project is one example, whereby the Division's performances and informal discussions provided a forum for disparate members of one dance community to learn from one another, "helping to ensure the continuity and growth of African Dance."

USE OF SOCIAL MEDIA. The Dance Division has created a Facebook page and a blog, both of which have helped expand the division's visibility. The creation of the Dance Oral History Channel and the Digital Collections Dance Video site has also helped inform and engage patrons with the collections.

Funding for the Dance Division derives from federal and state grants, endowments, philanthropic organizations, and private donors. The Committee for the Jerome Robbins Dance Division and the Friends of the Dance Division provide important support for the Division.

❯ CHALLENGES. It is not easy for the Dance Division to sustain key projects that are over and above ongoing archival work and that add to the volume of material that must be converted into effective digital formats. While these projects are essential for capturing the voices and memories of dance performers and leaders, for linking them with future generations, and for fulfilling the Division's public education mission, they are time-intensive projects for which special support must be identified. Another urgent need is to digitize the thousands of obsolete format video materials and get the films transferred to digital files.

❯ **FUTURE PLANS.** Curator Schmidt sees the need to continue to be "ahead of the curve," using both programming and digital tools to help the Division's patrons establish meaningful connections with the collections. Through community building, special projects, and development of tools such as the Digital Collections Dance Video Site, Schmidt sees the Division moving ahead on multiple fronts to serve and engage its constituencies.

NYPL LABS
New York (NY) Public Library

OVERVIEW: NYPL Labs, a part of New York Public Library's (NYPL) Digital Library and Labs Division, partners with curators, librarians, and archivists to develop and test digital tools that enhance public engagement with special collections. With a mandate to move beyond routine digitization, and to apply the newest techniques for searching, sharing, and creating in the digital environment, Labs has undertaken collection-based projects that transform how members of the public engage with primary sources and research collections. These projects, featuring interactive websites, crowdsourcing, community annotation, and citizen cartography, offer models for other institutions seeking to use digital tools for expanding knowledge and use of special collections. Organizationally, NYPL Labs reflects the trend in some libraries to link archival and digital library functions as a means of realizing the full benefits of new digital technologies.

> **Labs developers work closely with librarians and curators to create imaginative tools, apps and experiences around library content and services, often engaging the public directly in the work of improving, organizing or remixing library information.**
>
> —NYPL Labs website

NYPL is a vast repository of human expression in all possible formats and covering all areas of human knowledge. It is the nation's largest public library system, combining 88 branch libraries with four research centers that offer "citizens of New York and the world" free access to an extraordinary array of special collections and archives. NYPL serves more than 18 million patrons a year and millions more online. With its dual role as a research library and a free public library system, NYPL is strongly committed to ensuring that members of the general public benefit from the depth and scope of its special collections.

NYPL Labs is part of the Digital Library and Labs Department, which includes Digitization, Metadata Services, and other information outreach functions. Its website states: "NYPL Labs is an experimental design and technology team working to expand the range of interaction, interpretation and reuse of research library collections and data." The concept for this experimental team grew out of the library's prior efforts to mobilize new technologies to extend access to Special Collections.

NYPL has been a leader in archival digitization, with a good proportion of Special Collections digitized and accessible in the NYPL Digital Gallery. These collections, numbering 50 million items, represent diverse cultures, languages and dialects, and cover an extraordinary array of subjects. Many, such as the vast manuscript and archival holdings, are rare or unique. Formats range from Babylonian tablets and palm leaf manuscripts to early printed books, historical newspapers, photographs, moving images and recorded performances, and, increasingly, collections that are "born digital." The research collections are not static; recent acquisitions include the papers of Katherine Hepburn and the American Jewish Committee Oral History Collection.

Although the library's large and growing Digital Collection stimulates public and student involvement with Special Collections, library leaders have recognized that digitization is not enough. Online catalogs are important steps towards remote access, but do not enable remote users to have the benefit of a new generation of digital research tools. For members of the public to have full topical, geospatial, or relational access to *all* the library's research holdings, it was clearly necessary to link digital technologists with curators and archivists in an experimental environment. In such an environment it would be possible to work with special collections materials to explore the potential for applying new methods of information diffusion and knowledge networking. Thus, in 2011, the concept for a "Lab" initiative was crystallized in the establishment of NYPL Labs.

The Labs program has a special mission to move beyond routine uses of digital technologies to explore new possibilities for improving discoverability and enriching knowledge of the collections. From its inception, Labs has emphasized interaction between special collections and members of the public, with a vision of the library as a distributed public network and a porous information environment. Open-source networks and citizen engagement are touchstones for the Labs team. David

Riordan, manager, product and R&D, explains that Labs projects "create a context for citizen involvement."

Initial Labs experiments included building participatory websites and crowdsourcing apps to involve users more closely with the collections and to leverage their skills and interest to actually improve knowledge about the collections. Early projects, such as What's on the Menu? were far more successful than library staff had expected, in both the volume and the quality of public participation. They provided proof of principle regarding the multiple benefits of increased digital interaction between archives and the general public. The successes have led to more ambitious experiments, some more technical than others, designed to improve public use of library collections. The following projects suggest the extent of experimentation taking place at NYPL and the potential impact of these types of projects for the future of public involvement with special collections.

WHAT'S ON THE MENU? NYPL's restaurant menu collection is one of the largest in the world, used by chefs, food writers, novelists, historians, and others interested in popular culture and food trends. Held by the Rare Book Division, the collection numbers approximately 45,000 items, nearly a quarter of which have been digitized and made available through the NYPL Digital Collections. Before What's on the Menu? started the searchable information on each item was minimal: the name of the restaurant, its location, and the date of the menu. The actual menu contents, the dishes, prices, organization of the meals, were only accessible through on-site examination of the original documents. To improve access to the full content of its menus, library staff aimed to transcribe each item "dish by dish." However, staff realized they had nowhere near the internal resources to accomplish such a goal. To solve this problem the Labs team worked with the curators of the culinary collections to develop a simple transcription tool that could be used by many people, and then invited members of the general public to help by assisting with the transcription process.

When What's on the Menu? launched in April 2011, the goal was to transcribe the approximately 9,000 menus available in the NYPL Digital Gallery. To the surprise of the project team, volunteers had transcribed all 9,000 menus in three months. Since then NYPL's Digital Imaging Unit has been steadily scanning additional menus for continuing public transcription. In a second phase of the project members of the public are helping to geo-tag menus for increased discoverability. The success of What's on the Menu? helped pave the way for subsequent crowdsourcing initiatives that, overall, are having a substantial impact on how the public works with, and understands, NYPL's Special Collections.

NYPL ARCHIVES AND MANUSCRIPTS. The Labs team partnered with the Manuscripts and Archives Division to produce a comprehensive discovery system for archives and manuscripts. By creating innovative approaches to digital finding aids, including a single-page interface and component-level search, Labs improved access to over 120,000 digitized pages. This is an ongoing project.

ENSEMBLE. Ensemble is a community transcription project that aims to increase access to the Billy Rose Theatre Collection's massive collection of New York City theatrical playbills. By engaging members of the public to help transcribe details on the playbills, Labs expects to produce a linked data set of historical performances, including creators and performers, that can link to theater history projects worldwide. Eventually, the Labs team hopes to work with all of the Performing Arts Library's research divisions to carry out similar projects.

MAP WARPER AND BUILDING INSPECTOR. NYPL Labs has collaborated extensively with the Map Division to develop and test varied digital tools for improving information about the Division's collections, including crowdsourcing tools. Map Warper involves citizens in rectifying historical maps to today's digital maps, while Building Inspector uses volunteers to enter and to improve computer-generated information about buildings depicted in nineteenth-century insurance atlases.

As an unusual unit in an American public library, with a mandate for experimentation, NYPL Labs foreshadows a trend towards interdepartmental initiatives or special units within larger libraries that aim to foster experimentation in the application of digital technologies to archival work. These new units and new archival-digital-curatorial initiatives are in the early experimental phases. The "experiments" undertaken by NYPL Labs are both works-in-progress and models for future adaptation and testing in other institutions and library communities.

❯ **CHALLENGES.** In the process of building, testing, and refining new digital information tools the Labs team has struggled with numerous questions. What are the appropriate standards for the metadata associated with digital objects? What is the appropriate descriptive vocabulary? How to publicly recognize individuals who participate in crowdsourcing, and how to connect these individuals with one another? As an experimental unit, Labs is able to test solutions to these problems and refine the results.

❯ **FUTURE PLANS.** NYPL Labs, which started as a program in the Office of Strategic Planning, has recently been institutionalized within the Digital Library and Labs Department, reporting to the chief library officer. This shift in status is significant, reflecting administrators' awareness of the benefits inherent in crowdsourcing along with the need to continuously experiment with new approaches to collections access.

Institutionalization of the Labs initiative has not changed Labs' original mandate to "reimagine information networks." The Labs team will continue some current projects and will work with other collections, such as the Berg Collection of English Literature, to build new digital tools for enhanced discoverability. Labs is also focusing on new technical challenges, such as building innovative educational apps with unique sources and datasets digitized from NYPL collections, and offering a "Net Artist Residency" for an artist to work in the Map Division on new approaches to geospatial data visualization.

PUBLIC AFFAIRS DIVISION AND MISSOURI VALLEY SPECIAL COLLECTIONS
Kansas City (MO) Public Library

OVERVIEW: The Kansas City (MO) Public Library (KCPL) has developed an approach for organizing, producing, and promoting public programs that situates primary responsibilities in the Division of Public Affairs (Public Affairs). In carrying out these responsibilities Public Affairs works closely with the Missouri Valley Special Collections (MVSC). The arrangement has enabled the library to build staff capacity in technical areas needed for major exhibitions, to expand online communications, and to better coordinate planning, production, and marketing of programs.

> We have discovered that there is a huge hunger for local history. People want to know more about what happened here and how it relates to what happened in the rest of the country. Through programs we are able to feed into that desire.
>
> —Henry Fortunato, Director of Public Affairs

K CPL serves a population of more than 1.7 million in the greater Kansas City metropolitan area. With a central library and nine branch locations, the library is a highly visible educational and culture resource. KCPL's Special Collections Department was established in 1960. Today, the library's Missouri Valley Special Collections consists of local history and genealogy resources, including photographs, family records, diaries, scrapbooks, organizational and business records, and ephemera.

The emphasis is on the City of Kansas City and the surrounding area, with such specialties as postcards, theater history, sheet music, and the Civil War, especially the Civil War–era conflict between Missouri and Kansas known as the "Border Wars" that began in the mid-1850s over the slavery question. Many MVSC items are digitized and form part of the library's Digital Gallery.

Prior to 2007, MVSC was responsible for history programming, which consisted of periodic exhibitions drawn from the collections, as well as regular lecture series, Missouri Valley Speakers Series. Starting in 2007, KCPL reorganized its approach to exhibitions and other forms of programming, with the goal of increasing internal coordination, building staff capacity, and expanding public awareness of the library's special collections. Public Affairs assumed responsibility for coordinating and implementing most adult programs, often working with other internal and external stakeholders, including MVSC, which continues to organize monthly Sunday history lectures. Public Affairs took the lead in developing additional history-oriented programs, including the following.

PRESIDENTIAL LECTURES. Hail to the Chiefs (2012) and Beyond the Gowns (2013) are two signature series copresented with the Truman Library Institute, the Foundation Arm of the Presidential Library and Museum in Independence, Missouri. The former focused on presidents and the latter on first ladies in American history.

CIVIL WAR PROGRAMS. Since 2011, the library has commemorated the 150th anniversary of the Civil War with an ongoing series of talks keyed chronologically to the conflict's significant moments and turning points and given by the members of the Military History Department at the US Army's Command and General Staff College at nearby Fort Leavenworth. At least five of these talks have been taped by C-SPAN's *American History TV* for later broadcast. Additionally, Public Affairs worked with MVSC to develop an exhibition about the Quantrill Raid, an 1863 atrocity resulting in the massacre of some 150 men and boys in Lawrence, Kansas, and continues working with the KCPL Digital Branch on an award-winning website that contains thousands of scanned archival documents plus new content written by scholars called *Civil War on the Western Border*.

EXHIBITIONS are also part of the programming responsibilities handled by Public Affairs, which collaborates with MVSC on curatorial aspects of history exhibitions. As one example, Cowtown: History of the Kansas City Stockyards was a major project that traced the economic and social impact of the famous stockyard. In order to mount exhibitions of this scope, Public Affairs has built a team with technical, design, and editing skills that complement the skills of the library's archivists and curators. According to Henry Fortunato, director of public affairs, "It has taken us years of experimentation and the slow but steady recruitment of the right people necessary to develop an exhibition-creation capacity."

Greetings from Kansas City: Postcard Views of a Midwestern Metropolis, 1900–1950, a 2013 exhibition, demonstrated the advantages of an in-house exhibition team. The display contained 200 early twentieth-century postcards that are held by MVSC. Focusing on the postcard as the "instant message" of its day, Greetings from Kansas City attracted a large national and international audience. Four branch libraries offered complementary programs featuring postcard images of sites and scenes from their respective neighborhoods.

WEBSITE. A special section on KCPL's website, This Week in Kansas City History, presents ongoing original history content developed by Public Affairs with MVSC and with assistance from graduate student interns at the Hall Center for the Humanities at the University of Kansas.

***MEET THE PAST* TELEVISION PROGRAM.** *Meet the Past* is a dramatized TV-style talk show developed by Public Affairs that is taped and aired by local public television station KCPT TV. The unscripted programs feature half-hour dialogues between Library Director Crosby Kemper III and actors and re-enactors portraying well-known figures from Kansas City's past such as Langston Hughes, Amelia Earhart, John Brown, Walt Disney, and Ernest Hemingway before a live audience. Program dialogues are informed by the library's history collections, such as diaries, newspaper accounts, letters, travel narratives and memoirs, which provide the interviewer and the actors impersonating the interviewees with inspiration and context. The programs are available on KCPT TV and on the library's website. Produced episodically since 2007, *Meet the Past* has been a popular program that has helped generate new attendance at live library programs as well as new media attention. It won a regional Emmy Award in 2014.

KCPL staff report that there have been clear benefits to the institution as a result of "fusing" in one department the responsibilities for creating as well as marketing programs. By centralizing rather than dispersing tasks across departments there is clearer accountability, staff skills and other resources can be allocated more efficiently, and marketing can be built into program planning from the outset. Local foundations and private funders, including the Ewing Marion Kaufman Foundation, have assisted KCPL in carrying out its expanded programming agenda with generous financial support.

Given the scope, diversity, and impact of the activities planned and executed by Public Affairs, in collaboration with MVSC and other library departments, it is not surprising that KCPL was awarded the 2014 ALA Excellence in Library Programming Award.

CHALLENGES. Along with other history archives, KCPL and MVSC face stiff competition for public attention. By aligning program development with promotion, and by having the capacity to carry out diverse programs with high-quality production values, KCPL is well-positioned to expand audiences for its local history work. According to Fortunato, "creative marketing and diverse programs are essential for success."

FUTURE PLANS. KCPL is planning two *Meet the Past* television programs for late 2014, one of which will be held at Union Station, in conjunction with the 100th anniversary of the iconic railroad terminal. It will feature a conversation with a young Ernest Hemingway, who passed through the train station frequently on his way to the Italian front in World War I and who wrote about his war experiences while a resident in Kansas City in the mid to late 1920s.

THE ROSENBACH OF THE FREE LIBRARY OF PHILADELPHIA
Free Library of Philadelphia

OVERVIEW: The City of Philadelphia has long been home to two of the nation's preeminent collections of rare books, manuscripts, Americana, and art: the Special Collections of the Free Library of Philadelphia (FLP) and the Rosenbach Museum and Library (the Rosenbach). The recent merger of the Rosenbach with FLP is now enhancing public access to both collections through coordinated exhibitions and expanded programming. The arrangement integrates two strong institutions that have a shared past and complementary collections. As the two institutions combine their operations and programs, the lessons learned will be helpful to other public libraries contemplating a merger with a local partner.

The aim of this partnership is to build and sustain collections of Americana and English literature that are among the greatest in the world while furthering Philadelphia's status as an educational and cultural leader.

—Siobhan Reardon, President

F LP, with an array of special collections, is one of the nation's major repositories for historical and literary research. The Rare Book Department alone is comprised of 100,000 books and manuscripts that span over 4,000 years. Special Collections holdings range from letters of American presidents and the world's largest collection of orchestral music, to drawings by American artists and rare editions of works by Beatrix Potter and Charles Dickens. In merging with the Rosenbach, FLP joins one exceptional set of institutional collections with another.

Founded in 1954 by A.S.W. Rosenbach and his brother Philip, dealers in manuscripts, books, and fine art, the Rosenbach is housed in an 1860s townhouse that includes paintings and sculpture, decorative arts, more than 30,000 rare books, 130,000 manuscripts, first editions, presidential letters, and a replica of poet Marianne Moore's Greenwich Village living room. Exhibitions, special events and programs are designed to enhance Rosenbach visitors' understanding of these collections. Exhibitions are the primary vehicle for public access; at any one time there are two or three exhibitions on display, most of which are accompanied by programming. An Artist-in-Residence Program engages artists who create works inspired by Rosenbach collections, ranging from poetry and dance performances to orchestral works. Through School Partnerships the Rosenbach works with several local schools to develop in-depth, multidisciplinary projects centered on an area of the Rosenbach's collections. Author events throughout the year feature books with some connection to Rosenbach collections. The Rosenbach also offers annual scholar-led Reading Groups that include examination of related items in the collections.

Several Rosenbach special events have become signature activities, attracting audiences from across the Philadelphia region and beyond. For example, the Rosenbach's 2010 Banned Books Week event, titled "Authors of Mischief," featured poets, scholars, cultural leaders, and actors reading banned and censored books from the collections.

Like so many other special collections the Rosenbach is using social media, especially blogs, to engage website visitors with specific collections. Today in the Civil War–Dispatches from the Rosenbach Collections, illustrates how the blog format lends itself to an in-depth exploration of a whole collection, in this case Civil War-era documents. Each blog is accompanied by a full or partial transcript.

MERGER. The merger of the Rosenbach with FLP has created one of the largest collections of manuscripts, rare books, and artwork in the country. It has also created new opportunities for cross-institution programming, widening public awareness of and access to both collections. Under the new partnership, the former Rosenbach Museum and Library is now the Rosenbach of the Free Library of Philadelphia.

Structurally, it is a wholly owned subsidiary of the Free Library of Philadelphia Foundation. Some Rosenbach board members have joined the Foundation's board, and the FLP president provides operational leadership. A fund established by local philanthropies supports the merger for five years, enabling the two institutions to build their collective capacity for fund development.

Although the merger was only formalized in December 2013, the two institutions are already demonstrating the public benefits of institutional consolidation through joint programming, collaborative research, development of complementary exhibitions, and expanded special events. Two examples illustrate the advantages of the merger in terms of public programming:

> Year of the Bard, the Free Library of Philadelphia's 2014 celebration of Shakespeare's 450th anniversary, included extensive collaboration with Rosenbach staff. The Rosenbach mounted an exhibition on Shakespeare's influence on James Joyce titled I'll Make a Ghost of Him: Joyce Haunted by Shakespeare, scheduled one of its Reading Groups to focus on Shakespeare and the Bible, and designed Hands-on Tours to focus on Shakespeare materials in the collections.
>
> James Joyce's manuscript for *Ulysses* is one of the highlights of the Rosenbach collections. For some years the Rosenbach's annual Bloomsday event has featured a day of programming. As a result of the merger that event is now a six-day festival with activities across the city and at the Free Library.

● **CHALLENGES.** Fundraising will be a major focus as FLP works to make the Rosenbach self-sustaining at the end of five years. It will also require a major effort to connect the FLP's more general audiences with the Rosenbach's holdings.

● **FUTURE PLANS.** FLP and the Rosenbach are already developing plans for future joint programming including a commemoration of the 150th anniversary of *Alice in Wonderland* in 2015. The Rosenbach has the world's largest collection of material by author William Dodson. FLP and the Rosenbach will spearhead a citywide celebration similar to FLP's yearlong multidisciplinary thematic programs on Charles Dickens (2013) and Shakespeare (2014).

SAN FRANCISCO HISTORY CENTER/ BOOK ARTS & SPECIAL COLLECTIONS

San Francisco Public Library

OVERVIEW: San Francisco Public Library's History Center and Department of Book Arts & Special Collections (SFHC/BASC) is made up of formerly separate units: The Marjorie G. and Carl W. Stern Book Arts & Special Collections Center and the Daniel E. Koshland San Francisco History Center. These units, and their multiple component parts, were consolidated in 2010 with the goal of achieving greater coordination and resource sharing across the units. Within this integrated framework staff carry out extensive programming, including tours, outreach, lectures, exhibitions, and demonstrations in addition to more traditional archival functions. The San Francisco experience can inform other institutions' efforts to consolidate or better coordinate their formerly separate special collections.

> Now that we are one department we are finding that there are advantages for everyone. For staff there are benefits in terms of being able to share our collective knowledge and help each other with research questions, preservation issues and curatorial projects. The public benefits from our ability to work together on exhibitions, programs and outreach.
>
> —Susan Goldstein, San Francisco City Archivist and Manager, San Francisco History Center/Book Arts & Special Collections

The consolidation of the library's various special collections in 2010 brought together a vast array of research resources that draw specialists from throughout the world. The History Center includes the archives for the city and county of San Francisco, the San Francisco Historical Photograph Collection, maps, posters, and ephemera documenting all aspects of San Francisco life and history. Book Arts & Special Collections includes collections on the History of Printing and the Development of the Book, Calligraphy and Lettering, Sherlock Holmes, the Panama Canal, Early Children's Books, and a unique collection of wit and humor. The most recent addition is the archives and manuscripts section of the James C. Hormel Gay and Lesbian Center, which includes such materials as the papers of Harvey Milk.

One result of consolidation has been expanded public programming. Prior to the reorganization individual curators of the different departments were responsible for collection development, cataloging, research, donor relations, outreach, digitization, and public programming. Within the new integrated framework, staff share reference duties, decision making about preservation and digitization, and skills in exhibition and program development. While particular staff are still identified as "curators" of specific collections, the consolidated department provides a supportive framework for their specialized work and allows for sharing of resources and knowledge across departments. It also allows for a greater focus on ways to engage different audiences with the collections.

According to Susan Goldstein, city archivist and SFHC/BASC manager, "We have an important teaching mission, especially with young people, that makes our work both challenging and exciting." To fulfill this mission, members of the department organize multiple types of programs and collaborate with local organizations in order to reach the broadest possible audiences. SFHC/BASC curator Lisa Dunseth states that "programs are a way to let people touch special collections."

EXHIBITIONS. Drawing from its rich collections SFHC/BASC mounts exhibitions throughout the year in two exhibition galleries. Some exhibitions focus on a particular collection, such as Book Selections from the Harrison Collection of Calligraphy and Lettering (2012), and some are more topical, such as San Francisco Eats, a multi-floor, cross-department exhibition that focused on the unique food cultures and the dining history of San Francisco. Two recent exhibitions illustrate the variety of exhibition approaches.

Unbuilt San Francisco (2013), a collaborative exhibition involving six institutional partners, demonstrated how public library special collections can add unique dimensions to a citywide exploration of a historical or cultural theme. Each of the participating institutions displayed treasures from its archives and hosted companion programs. SFHC/BASC presented original architectural renderings and other images representing a city very different from the reality of today. The exhibition focused on "what never was" in the public spaces of San Francisco, such as a Panhandle Parkway, and revealed multiple competing visions for the city's future.

The Portola Festival of 1909: A Party with a Purpose (2009–2010) was an exhibition of photographs, ephemera, and artifacts documenting the 100th anniversary of this landmark event, a five-day celebration to signal that the City of San Francisco had been reconstructed after the 1906 earthquake and was ready again for business and tourists. The exhibition included an accompanying video that highlighted the participation of local and international Chinese and Japanese communities. To extend access to the exhibition and the collection, library staff digitized key items, including postcards, photographs, and day-to-day accounts of the events drawn from the History Center's *San Francisco Chronicle* database.

LECTURES. SFHC/BASC offers varied talks and lectures to complement exhibitions, educate the public, or help advance knowledge-sharing across a particular special interest group or collecting community. For example, Luca Barcellona: Italian Calligrapher, was an illustrated lecture organized by Book Arts staff in 2013 and co-sponsored with the local Friends of Calligraphy. As a well-known calligrapher, graphic artist, and former graffiti artist, Barcellona attracted individuals from publishing, book arts, graphic design, street art, and calligraphy. Lectures are widely exposed through social media such as Facebook, Twitter, and the departmental blog, and are often available on YouTube.

SOCIAL MEDIA. SFHC/BASC uses social media to promote interest in collection-related programming, to focus attention on digital collections, and to engage diverse audiences with the collections. Aside from the Department's blog, *What's on the 6th Floor?* staff promotes the collections and collection-related events through Facebook, Twitter, Flickr, Instagram, and Pinterest. Staff has discovered that some channels, such as Flickr and Twitter, are especially effective in drawing people to the blog and attracting individuals who would not otherwise know about SFHC/BASC.

SPECIAL EVENTS. The variety of SFHC/BASC events reflect the diversity of collections and audiences. An Annual Valentine Broadside Printing Event is presented by SFHC/ BASC to help the public discover one of the library's "hidden treasures," a 1909 Albion handpress. Renovated in 2011, the handpress offers an opportunity for people to learn about handprinting and the artistry involved in early printed works. The event draws people of all backgrounds, many of whom have never before visited the SFHC/BASC. Local printers donate their time to work the press and to help program participants create their own valentines. The Third Annual Printing Event, held in February 2014, was cosponsored with the American Printing History Association's Northern California Chapter, and featured San Francisco's Poet Laureate Alejandro Murguia and artist Sal Garcia, who designed and signed a hand-printed valentine for attendees.

The SF Latino Heritage Fair/Digital Archiving Day, held in October 2014, was an all-day event that included workshops on community documentation and opportunities to scan family or personal photos. The program was held in the library's new DigitCenter and cosponsored with the San Francisco Latino Historical Society. Book Doctor is designed to demonstrate the process of book and manuscript preservation and to celebrate the talents of behind-the-scenes staff. During the American Library

Association's Week of Preservation, the library's special collections conservator examines books and fragile paper items brought in by members of the public. She diagnoses their problems and, for some, does a demonstration of the suggested treatment. The event helps raise public consciousness about the importance and the technical complexity of conserving items that are meaningful to an individual or to the community.

OUTREACH. SFHC/BASC staff carry out a variety of outreach activities designed to "bring Special Collections out to the community." Regular visits by the Curator of Photography to classes at San Francisco State, printing demonstrations at the city's History Fair, talks to local organizations, staff participation in meetings of local book arts groups and architectural preservation organizations—these are but a few of the activities that build relationships between SFHC/BASC and the community and ensure visibility with diverse audiences.

Shades of San Francisco is a community history and outreach project that aims to add images of ethnic and cultural diversity to the History Center Archives while broadening representation of city neighborhoods. Working with branch libraries and community organizations staff offer Shades Photo Days where residents are invited to bring in historic photographs of their families, workplaces, and neighborhoods so that the photos can be copied and added to the library's Photograph Collection. Six neighborhoods have been documented to date and others will be included as the project unfolds. Images from Shades of San Francisco are posted in an online exhibition called Picture This.

TOURS. Reflecting the department's commitment to public education, staff carry out tours of the special collections for students at all ages levels, from grammar school to graduate school. Staff also co-teach classes with teachers on topics such as the history and use of maps. Open House days for teachers and events for collectors and donors help to continually expose different groups to the richness of the collections.

❷ **CHALLENGES.** Integration of diverse collections within one department has been challenging from an administrative sense but has benefited the library and its constituents from the perspectives of access and education. Staff are better able to enhance one another's skills and knowledge on the reference desk and in other venues and to carry out both collection-specific and cross-collection activities. Current challenges are promoting awareness of *What's on the 6th Floor?* and building a new generation of donors.

Another challenge for SFHC/BASC is how to document the rapid and profound changes taking place in the City of San Francisco today. Issues of transit systems, housing access, and gentrification affect all residents; the library is seeking ways to capture dialogues on these issues and track the physical and social changes under way in different neighborhoods.

> **FUTURE PLANS.** SFHC/BASC staff have many projects in different stages of planning, while prioritizing digitization as a primary means of ensuring preservation and access. For example, the department's older audio materials are being prepared for online access as part of the statewide California Audiovisual Preservation Project (CAVPP). SFHC/BASC is working on becoming a service hub for the Digital Public Library of America, and is mounting digital materials on the DPLA. SFHC/BASC has also received grants and partnered with the Internet Archive and other groups to digitize books and maps. This work will continue, with a special focus on manuscripts and archives, as a strategy for both preservation and access.

SPECIAL COLLECTIONS

Pikes Peak Library District (Colorado Springs, CO)

OVERVIEW: The Special Collections division of the Pikes Peak Library District (PPLD) carries out exceptionally robust public programming agenda, offering a regional history center model for public libraries seeking to involve diverse audiences in historical topics and collections. Activities include an annual regional history symposium, oral history projects, exhibitions, publications on regional history, online exhibitions, partnerships with other cultural institutions, and production of historical videos and films. These projects involve considerable research, outreach, partnerships, and marketing; some have evolved over a period of years and some are recent experiments. The division's commitment to public engagement reflects that of the Library District, which has an office of public engagement and uses multiple channels to involve people of all ages with the library.

One role of archivists is to educate people and get them excited about the value of archival resources. Through different programs and products we help people see their own connections to the region's history and to the primary sources in our collections.

—Tim Blevins, Division Head, Special Collections

P PLD, which serves nearly 598,000 people in El Paso County, in southern Colorado, has one of the most programmatically active Special Collections departments in the nation. Special Collections, which is also known as the Regional History and Genealogy Department, contains maps, oral histories, historic photographs, books and manuscripts, pamphlets, government records, films, and ephemera that "illuminate the history of the Pikes Peak region." Areas of collecting focus include El Paso County, the state of Colorado, the Rocky Mountains, and family history related to the region, as well as genealogy resources for most US states. These topics provide the basis for the many public programs designed and carried out by Special Collections staff. Outreach and programming are supported, in part, by special gifts and grants.

Colorado Springs and the surrounding region are home to diverse populations, some with longtime connections to the area and many who are newcomers without prior connections to the city or the Mountain West. Recognizing this diversity, Special Collections offer programs that are varied in content and format. The goals for regional history programming are to educate and excite longtime residents *and* newcomers about the history of the region and to engage them with the special collections.

SYMPOSIUM. An annual Pikes Peak Regional History Symposium is one of the department's most visible programs. Focused on specific topics concerning "the historical people, events and trends in the Pikes Peak region," the Symposium has built a national reputation and draws more than 200 people a year. Topics range from Bigwigs and Benefactors of the Pikes Peak Region (2014) to Film and Photography on the Front Range (2011). Symposium themes often link to other programs and products.

COMMUNITY DOCUMENTATION PROJECTS. Documentation projects are undertaken to record local events or address gaps in the collection. A recent project, the Waldo Canyon Fire Collection, for example, brought together oral history interviews, documents, photographs, videos, and websites related to the devastating 2012 fire in the Pike National Forest and Colorado Springs. Special Collections Manager Tim Blevins states that "the intent was to acquire and preserve the ephemeral evidence of the destructive event before it was lost."

EXHIBITIONS are developed to provide insights into an aspect of the region's history and also to complement other library educational and programming initiatives. For instance, in 2012 a two-part exhibition on the Titanic Disaster of 1912 and the Influenza Epidemic of 1918 was organized to reinforce the All Pikes Peak Reads 2012 theme of Survival. Some exhibitions include interactive components, reflecting Special Collections' interest in experimenting with ways to more deeply engage "tech-savvy" audiences.

PUBLICATIONS. A Regional History Series of 13 books, with accompanying DVDs, chronicles "the unique and undocumented history of Colorado and the Rocky Mountain West." The book topics often piggyback on the topics of the History Symposia or departmental exhibitions.

EDUCATIONAL INITIATIVES range from tours of the archives for elementary students to organizing research experiences for teenagers that introduce them to finding aids, primary sources, and the archival profession. The library has collaborated with local schools and two other local archives on a three-year Teaching American History project in which middle and high school teachers select primary sources with which to create lesson plans. The lesson plans are then compiled into a text that is uploaded onto the Pikes Peak Library District's eBranch.

VIDEOS AND FILMS. Production and distribution of regional history videos and films are some of the defining activities of the Special Collections division. Taking advantage of the library's video production studio and cable television channel PPLD TV, the department creates products that are distributed for educational use and also sold commercially. Both the films and the videos are often related to one of the annual history symposia or regional history publications. One video that has received much attention is *Frozen to Death on Pikes Peak: A Cold Case Investigation*.

DIGITAL COLLECTIONS. The library maintains constantly growing Digital Collections, including oral histories and videos of history symposia presentations. The digital photo archives provides access to 10,000 historic photographs and lithographs that "depict people, places and events of the Pikes Peak region from 1850 to the present."

The scope of interpretive and documentary programs and materials produced and presented by Special Collections may be unmatched by any other public library special collections department outside of a major metropolitan area. The impact and reach of these presentations are considerable, making PPLD a resource for educators, researchers, students, and the general public far beyond Colorado Springs. Given the scope and quality of the programming carried out by the Pikes Peak Library District's Special Collections, it is not surprising that the department was the only public library awarded a 2014 Leadership in History Award by the American Association of State and Local History.

● **CHALLENGES.** Special Collections cites several challenges in carrying out an active history programming agenda, especially the need for marketing. Even though program attendance is excellent and content is well received, staff notes that it is "essential to be constantly communicating an active image for the department and for history in general." Another departmental challenge is the labor-intensive nature of the behind-the-scenes work to produce excellent programs and products such as transcribing oral history interviews, editing history books, digitizing photographs, or selecting presentations for the annual history symposium.

⊙ **FUTURE PLANS.** Special Collections intends to continue its multifaceted history programming agenda. Among the projects in the pipeline is development of a self-publishing program that could help authors of history publications with which the library is involved.

SPECIAL COLLECTIONS AND NEIGHBORHOOD HISTORY
Seattle Public Library

OVERVIEW: The Special Collections Department (Special Collections) of the Seattle Public Library (SPL) is undergoing a transformation that reflects a new institutional emphasis on community engagement and system-wide services. As a result of a strategic planning process, Seattle culture and history have become a primary focus for the library and for the department. Special Collections is reorganizing its approach to local history by reaching out to neighborhoods to carry out community documentation and develop a stronger infrastructure for local history collections. The department is also experimenting with digital projects to enhance public engagement with primary sources. The results of these efforts to reach people where they live and online will be instructive for other special collections seeking ways to be more connected to their local communities.

> Whether it's capturing the history of Boeing or the history of the 12th Man, the Library is committed to collecting information and providing programming about what makes Seattle unique. It is a priority of ours to make it easy for people to access, study and experience the history and cultural heritage of our city.
>
> —Public Survey, Seattle Culture and
> History Programmatic Assessment, 2014

Seattle's Special Collections contains multiple collections, such as the Aviation Collection, a collection of Northwest Art, a Genealogical Collection, the Balch Autograph Collection, and the Seattle Collection. The Seattle Collection is a primary collection, including maps and atlases, more than 30,000 historical photographs, books, yearbooks, municipal documents, clippings, oral histories, and works by Seattle artists. Special Collections are all housed at the Central Library while a separate collection of African American research materials—one of the largest on the West Coast—is housed at the Douglas Truth Branch Library. Public programming carried out by Special Collections in recent years has consisted of topical exhibitions drawn from the collections and occasional lectures or other programs.

In 2011 SPL undertook a planning initiative to engage city residents, staff, and other stakeholders in developing a common vision for the future. The resulting plan, My Library: Next Generation/Strategic Plan 2011–2015, which was adopted in 2013, articulated a vision for bringing the library "to people and places who might not otherwise come to us"—a vision with implications for Special Collections. Seattle Culture and History were identified as one of five service priorities to realize the Strategic Plan goals. Other services priorities relevant to Special Collections are Technology and Access and Community Engagement.

SCOPE AND GOALS. One result of SPL's planning is to work toward infusing the entire system with the new priority services, rather than concentrating them in a single, central location. For Special Collections this means a new focus on community documentation, working with all neighborhoods, and expanded efforts to make the special collections located at the Central Library accessible to all electronically. The goals are public access and public engagement: the strategies are community outreach and digitization. Two prongs of activity reflect Special Collection's approaches to fulfilling these goals.

NEIGHBORHOOD HISTORY PROJECT. Seattle has a long tradition of strong neighborhoods, each with its own identity and history. Local librarians and residents feel a sense of ownership in their neighborhood items. Special Collections seeks to honor that sense of ownership in the Neighborhood History Project, through which it will be a partner and a resource. The library's branches are a key part of the project. Because it is difficult for branches to maintain secure collections of original documents, Special Collections will copy all locally relevant history materials for retention in the branches and easy access for students and residents. At the same time, Special Collections intends to have branch staff more involved in collection acquisition and history programming.

Through the Neighborhood History Project, access to local materials is being enhanced by digitizing relevant collections. While there is a current website for the project, Special Collections is building a new website that will be more robust, with subject headings and GEO reference codes. Maps, real estate atlases, photos, and full-text documents will be easily searchable by neighborhood location.

The Neighborhood History Project is not only about increasing local engagement with Central Library collections, it is also about building stronger collections for and with each neighborhood. Special Collections has set up a process whereby staff from the Central Library is available to work with branch librarians and local residents to document special events, copy newly donated materials, and identify collection gaps that need to be filled. When new neighborhood history materials are added they will be integrated with other relevant local history information.

Special Collections Manager Jodee Fenton sees the Neighborhood History Project as a "gift of the digital age," whereby Seattle residents will have improved access to and use of neighborhood records and images both locally and digitally. She also expects the project to evolve over time as branch librarians work more closely with Special Collections librarians, and vice versa.

DIGITAL PROJECTS/ONLINE EXHIBITIONS. Digitization is an important part of the Neighborhood History Project, as Special Collections plans to digitize "more and more of the collections in topical areas that are meaningful to residents." It is also an important aspect of Special Collections' broader efforts to "make our unique treasures accessible to everyone digitally." Staff has implemented Digital Projects that focus on specific themes, bringing together varied materials from across the collections that illuminate those themes, creating the associated metadata, and producing high-quality digital surrogates. What makes these projects distinctive are the depth and variety of thematic material digitized for each topic. Beyond typical "digital collections," the projects allow for different levels of exploration, from single image to full-text, and for exposure to relevant content in multiple formats.

Selection of materials for the Digital Projects is based, in part, on identifying time-sensitive topics with wide appeal. For the first Digital Project, for example, staff selected items from its World's Fair Collection pertaining to the first world's fair in Seattle, the Alaska-Yukon-Pacific Exposition of 1909. With a citywide committee of curatorial, technical, and community advisors, the department spent more than two years planning how to handle the topic, what would be digitized, at what quality resolution, with what accompanying metadata, and so on. The planning group decided to include a broad spectrum of items—reports, photographs, catalogs, ephemera, and even material from a local museum—to provide an in-depth, qualitatively rich, multi-format digital collection that could be used for multiple purposes. To ensure the validity of the approach, the department then convened several dozen workshops for local historians, teachers, and students interested in the 1909 Exposition. This input helped Special Collections refine the presentation before it was launched as an online collection; it also provided an important form of community engagement.

Other Digital Projects undertaken thus far by the department include a selection of items from the collection of Northwest Art. Based on a 2010 exhibition of items from the Northwest Art Collections, the digital project aimed to ensure a "museum-quality experience" online. The Department arranged for special high-resolution photography and prepared in-depth metadata. With this approach the Northwest Art Project resulted in both a digital collection and an online exhibition.

● **CHALLENGES.** Visibility is a primary challenge for Special Collections, especially in light of the new initiatives to promote public engagement. The research that accompanied SPL's Strategic Planning revealed great affection for the library but lack of awareness about the range and depth of services being offered. This issue has risen to the top of Special Collections' list of priorities. The need for more substantial public programming and increased capacity to carry out digital projects are additional challenges.

● **FUTURE PLANS.** The new website for the Neighborhood History Project is under way, which will help fuel greater community involvement in the project and use of the newly digitized materials. In addition, Special Collections is considering new strategies to ensure that Special Collections are accessible and meaningful at the neighborhood level, including pop-up reference assistance concerning local history issues, traveling exhibitions, do-it-yourself instructions for local history exhibitions, and the provision of digital recordings of Central Library lectures delivered via the Web.

SPECIAL COLLECTIONS CENTER
Nashville (TN) Public Library

OVERVIEW: The Special Collections Division (Special Collections) of the Nashville Public Library (NPL) opened a Special Collections Center (SCC) in October 2007 with two interrelated goals: to provide an "access point" for the library's extensive historical collections of non-book materials, and to coordinate oral history projects that document the lives of Nashville residents and "their participation in history." In its structure, services, and content, the Special Collections Center offers an instructive example for other public library special collections divisions.

> **We are very deliberate in our documentary projects and public programs, looking for people who could use the collections and for ways to engage diverse communities.**
>
> —Andrea Blackman, Manager, Special Collections Division

NPL's Special Collections document the history of Nashville and Middle Tennessee, as well as the role that Nashville has played in the history of the nation. Subject areas range from geography and politics to business history and entertainment; materials include historic maps, manuscripts, photographs, scrapbooks, organizational records, architectural drawings, songbooks, oral histories, and the Christina Webb Performing Arts Collection. A Nashville Room houses Local History and Genealogy, the archives of the *Nashville Banner* are housed in a separate room, and there are also four Writer's Rooms. The Metropolitan Government Archives is a separate division that preserves the records of Metropolitan Nashville and Davidson County.

Over the past decades Special Collections has greatly expanded to include a Civil Rights Room, increased oral history and community documentation projects, educational outreach, and development of digital collections. The Department also carries out interpretive functions: exhibitions, panel discussions, and special events. With the expansion, staff perceived the need to provide a central point of public entry and project coordination. Accordingly, in 2007, NPL organized and opened SCC as a "hub" that would link people with appropriate research materials while integrating varied local documentation activities. SCC is not simply an administrative concept; it is a physical place that enhances discovery and use of Special Collections. It features computers, a research area, and a large screen displaying a digital slideshow of items that may be viewed in the center. Two kiosks offer a selection of items from NPL's Digital Collection for viewing and listening. SCC also features two interview rooms, reflecting plans to expand documentation of the lives of Nashville residents. SCC provides access to and helps coordinate multiple thematic projects including the following:

CIVIL RIGHTS ROOM AND CIVIL RIGHTS ORAL HISTORY PROJECT. During the latter half of the twentieth century, civil rights became an important collecting focus for NPL and today Special Collections houses a special Civil Rights Room and Civil Rights Collection. The latter includes primary sources that "document the leadership and contributions the city of Nashville made to the national Civil Rights Movement." The Civil Rights Oral History Project is an ongoing initiative, one of the largest such initiatives in the country. It captures the voices and memories of civil rights activists of the 1950s and 1960s, many of them national leaders in the civil rights movement. The Civil Rights Room, which carries out ongoing public programs, operates under the terms of an endowment from private donors that includes program funding.

ORAL HISTORY PROJECTS. Special Collections has long had an emphasis on oral history, based on library leaders' recognition that oral history is not only a primary vehicle for recording contemporary events that would otherwise go undocumented, but it is also an especially effective approach to engaging people with history. Andrea Blackman, manager of Special Collections, states:

> Oral history provides a venue for public discourse about the meaning of certain events or experiences. Interviewees go beyond nostalgia to reflect on the larger significance of their experiences, and the people who listen to them connect more readily than if the reports were far away and abstract.

NPL's oral history initiatives have increased in recent years in response to community events and also through association with two national programs: the American Folklife Center's Veterans History Project and StoryCorps, a national initiative to document the stories of everyday citizens. Current projects, in addition to the Civil Rights Oral History Project, include the following:

- Veterans Oral History Project
- The Nashville Business Leaders Oral History Project
- The "Everyone Has a Story" project, carried out with StoryCorps and the American Library Association in 2007–2008, that resulted in 595 interviews
- Voices of Immigrants Project, created in partnership with StoryCorps in 2013–2014, that documented the experiences of immigrants living in Nashville
- The Flood History Project, documenting the impact of a massive flood that devastated large sections of Nashville in 2010

DIGITAL PROJECTS. Special Collections has digitized many of the items in its diverse collections to create the Nashville Public Library Digital Collections. *Nashville Banner* news photos, for instance, depict people and events in Nashville during much of the twentieth century, providing unique snapshots of the city's recent economic, political, racial, and cultural history. Interviews from the Flood History Project and the StoryCorps Collections are also available online.

SOCIAL MEDIA. Special Collections uses multiple platforms to communicate with the public about events, projects and collections. They include Twitter, e-blasts, Facebook, and streaming video.

Given the scope of its activities, it is not surprising that Nashville's Special Collections has an unusual staff. There are not only archivists and reference librarians, but also oral historians, professional photographers, public history specialists, an anthropologist, and marketing staff. Technical staff within Special Collections handles digitization and development of digital archives. In addition, Special Collections has developed a process for training volunteers to carry out oral history interviews, enabling them to record far more interviews than would otherwise be possible while empowering community members as public historians.

NPL's approach to Special Collections transforms the very concept of "special collections" from a static repository of documents from a distant past to a dynamic, interactive hub for documenting, interpreting, and communicating the historical and contemporary experiences of Nashville residents. By establishing the Special Collections Center Nashville has helped to reshape the structure and identity of special collections.

● **CHALLENGES.** One challenge has been finding individuals with the varied skills and disciplinary backgrounds required to complement staff with traditional archival and reference skills. Acquisition of up-to-date equipment for history documentation and community communications is another challenge. Finally, for a collection that emphasizes oral history, there is the ongoing challenge of transcribing recorded interviews.

● **FUTURE PLANS.** Blackman sees the need for additional community documentation projects including one that focuses on the many immigrants who are settling in Nashville and one that records the experiences of members of the LGBT community. Currently, the Special Collections Center is planning a new oral history project called the Nashville Memory Project, which will enable staff to cast a broader net in their interviewing, "beyond the target populations of our existing projects." Using trained volunteers, staff will reach out to a variety of Nashville residents willing to contribute their experiences to the public record.

FIVE

EXHIBITIONS AND RELATED PROGRAMS

Exhibitions have always been a means of getting the hidden core of the library out into public view. With technologies exhibitions are changing. We can use digital tools to allow more people to access the collections on view and to engage them to interact with the collections in new ways.

—Elizabeth Sargent, Assistant Director for Special Collections and Manager, Houston Metropolitan Research Center, Houston Public Library

Today, in the context of a culture that privileges digitized images, technologically mediated experiences, and online interactions, the library or museum exhibition may seem an anachronism. Exhibitions involve direct visual contact with primary or secondary sources, offering visitors sensory and intellectual experiences that are inherently different from online viewing. Many archivists and special collections librarians believe there is no substitute for seeing the original manuscript with its crossed out words, the rare book with its famous reader's marginalia, the actual glass plate negative, the worn diary, the first edition, or the handcrafted binding. Based on the research for this publication the library professionals are correct. Paradoxically, despite a phenomenal increase in access to special collections as a result of digitization the tried-and-true exhibition is still going strong. In fact, if anything, the scope and number of exhibitions are increasing rather than decreasing. The more special collections are accessible to remote viewers, the more those viewers seem to value the immediacy of the physical object.

The projects described in this chapter demonstrate, first and foremost, that the exhibition as a form of special collections programming continues to be ubiquitous in libraries. No matter the size of the library or library system, no matter the number of exhibition cases, corridor galleries or exhibition halls, no matter, even, the number of staff—exhibitions are a consistent public service across archives and special collections. In the absence of other means of access, digital or physical, they are often the primary or the only point of connection to research collections for some members of the general public.

While exhibitions are common, they vary widely in scope, approach, and size, from small case displays presented on a rotating basis in a local history room to substantial interpretive exhibitions, with original designs and interactive elements, which are featured in major public library spaces. The 16 examples assembled for this chapter—and the many other exhibitions referenced elsewhere in the book—provide a small sampling of the varied and dynamic exhibition landscape. Within that landscape there are several trends that can be discerned.

EXHIBITIONS AS ELEMENTS OF LARGER PROJECTS

Whereas archival exhibitions have traditionally been independent curatorial initiatives, designed to showcase specific materials or celebrate an anniversary, an acquisition, or a donor, exhibitions today are increasingly planned as one component of a larger project with multiple goals. That project may start with collections processing, such as the Aerial Photos exhibition at the Portland (ME) Public Library; it often involves collections preservation; it may involve research and interpretation, such as Defining Their Identity, at the Los Angeles Public Library; it almost always generates public programming, such as New York (NY) Public Library's Three Faiths exhibition; it may be adapted for educational resource materials; and it increasingly provides the basis for expanding digital galleries and, even, creating exhibition surrogates in the form of online exhibitions. Whatever the scope of the particular project, this trend reflects a shift away from stand-alone displays to planning and coordinating exhibitions in relation to multiple departmental and institutional priorities.

DIVERSE EXHIBITION FORMATS

Many public library archives and special collections departments are constrained by limitations of space, technical skills, and staffing, and are forced to present small displays rather than larger interpretive exhibitions. Others are fortunate enough to have large exhibition halls, curators and designers, and a mandate to present and even circulate interpretive exhibitions. Due to these differences there is great variation in the sizes and types of special collections exhibitions. There are exhibitions in public corridors, in-room cases, exhibition kiosks, and special exhibition halls. There are traveling exhibitions, some of original materials, some consisting of graphic reproductions and some formatted for display in schools and smaller public spaces.

Beyond the variations in size and format there are other variations that make the term "exhibition" an umbrella for multiple viewing experiences. Today, there are "pop-up displays," highlight exhibitions, and online exhibitions. The Exhibition Program at New York Public Library is collaborating with the Communications and Marketing Department to offer small pop-up displays relating to current events or special items in the collections. According to Susan Rabbiner, assistant director for Exhibitions, "These displays underscore the Library's (and by extension, all libraries') continued relevance to contemporary audiences and serve as opportunities to further generate attention across both social media and traditional media platforms."

THEMATIC AND INTERDISCIPLINARY EXHIBITIONS

Some public library archives and special collections are emphasizing thematic exhibitions that provide a framework for diverse items and disciplinary perspectives. In this type of exhibition the inherent value of a particular object selected for display is less important than how it adds to the larger story of which it is a part. How to Cook a Possum: 19th Century Cuisine in Austin, brought together a range of items from the Austin History Center collections, such as farmers' diaries, nineteenth-century cookbooks, and images of food preparation that, in combination, offered a lens through which to examine the history of Austin food trends from social, historical, ecological, and anthropological perspectives. Kansas City Public Library's Cowtown: History of the Kansas City Stockyards exhibition used blueprints, photographs, maps, drawings, and other documents to trace the physical development of the stockyards and to examine their economic and social impact on Kansas City. Exhibitions at New York Public Library's Schomburg

Center for Research on Black History and Culture are distinguished by the extent to which they draw on different divisions and disciplines to illuminate an issue or historical phenomenon.

PUBLIC PROGRAMMING RELATED TO EXHIBITIONS

In more and more institutions, the archival or special collections exhibition is accompanied by public programs. More than a single lecture at the exhibition opening, exhibition-based programming can involve workshops, panel discussions, conversations, films, readings, teacher institutes, and digital forums—programs that complement and extend exhibition themes and help ensure that they are meaningful to diverse audiences. Cleveland Public Library's Paper Stories: Adventures in Kamishibai, Manga, Graphic Novels and Zines generated workshops on book arts and papermaking by the library's Literature Department and the Ohio Center for the Book, as well as a lecture by a prominent book artist. Newark Public Library's Edible History: How Latin American Food Evolved and Transformed the World generated performances, tastings, lectures, and films. The Free Library of Philadelphia has organized two yearlong, citywide celebrations, The Year of Dickens and The Year of the Bard, both involving other library departments and cultural institutions in thematic programming related to a major exhibition of items from the Rare Book Collection. These examples suggest the range of possibilities for exhibition-related programs that vary considerably depending on the original exhibition goals, staff capacities, access to programming partners, and overall institutional support.

EXPERIMENTAL AND INTERACTIVE EXHIBITIONS

Some of the exhibitions profiled in these pages reflect the efforts of their organizers to experiment with exhibition formats and to encourage interactivity and closer examination of individual objects by viewers. This trend to experiment can take different forms. The Providence Public Library encourages local artists to organize exhibitions and public programs based on their interpretations of items in the library's Special Collections. The Wonder Show project and the Whale Guitar as just two projects that have resulted from the artist-library collaborations—collaborations that demonstrate the possibilities for reimagining "archival" exhibitions.

Chicago Public Library's Neighborhood History Collection recently organized the Forced Migration Photovoice Project, profiled in chapter six, that used the "photovoice" process to engage a group of recent refugees in documenting and displaying their visual reactions to the city of Chicago. Chicago's Special Collections and Preservation Division invited viewers of an exhibition of street scenes by photographer Vivian Maier to take their own photos—selfies or street scenes—and submit them to the library for inclusion in the division's collection. In the first three months of the exhibition 3,000 selfies and street images were submitted.

Some institutions are experimenting with digital tools to enhance the exhibition experience. As one example, the Pikes Peak (CO) Library District's Special Collections Department mounted Framing Community/Exposing Identity: Photographs of Life at the Foot of Pikes Peak, in which the captions for selected photographs were accessible under hinged flaps that included QR codes. When scanned by a smartphone, the codes linked to brief videos of exhibition curators who explained the significance of the images. The hinged caption covers were intended to encourage museum visitors to identify each image before discovering the details. According to exhibition organizers, "Many visitors made a game of the experience—competing to see who in their group could best determine what the image actually was."

Perhaps the most experimental of all the following examples of exhibitions is the Schomburg Center for Research in Black Culture's Writing Blackness: Harlem | Paris, an exploration of the Harlem Renaissance through the Schomburg's collections that took place outside of a formal exhibition space. The exhibition, or immersion experience, was presented off-site in a two-bedroom apartment near the Schomburg, a location intended to suggest a typical literary salon of the Harlem Renaissance period.

Experiments of this sort are still few and far between. However, each example indicates the possibilities for creating new types of exhibition experiences that change the relationship between the exhibition organizer and the exhibition visitor or otherwise reshape the exhibition experience.

ONLINE EXHIBITIONS

Online exhibitions are becoming an important part of the programming agenda of many public library archives and special collections departments. The benefits to these departments are many: preservation of fragile materials that do not have to be handled or exposed to light; a stimulus for digitization; a vehicle for helping remote viewers find portals and pathways through vast online collections; and, above all, a means of expanding access to the content and the visual qualities of an original physical exhibition. For many remote users, especially those who cannot get to the library, access to an exhibition online, at leisure, is a great benefit. When archival departments add supplementary material to the original exhibition, such as links to scholarly resources or other cultural institutions with similar collections, the intellectual and artistic benefits are multiplied.

Given the many positive aspects of online exhibitions it is not surprising that more and more institutions are investing time and resources to convert on-site exhibitions into online experiences, or creating born-digital exhibitions that offer thematic explorations of varied collections or in-depth examination of particular topics within Special Collections. In fact, the number and variety of these efforts make it difficult to summarize the topic in these pages. Suffice it to say that online exhibitions are works in progress; there are as yet no "guidelines" or best practices, and there are as many approaches as there are formats for digital collections or website designs. Three examples of online exhibitions suggest the range of experimentation taking place today in public library archives and special collections departments. The Houston Public Library's The Houston Public Library Exhibit Snapshot (THPLES) is a model tool developed to bring the full experience of a library visit to remote visitors. It not only allows for development of online exhibitions but it also encourages interaction with exhibition materials. Launched with the library's 2012 exhibition Faces, Places and Spaces, the library is planning to use the tool for three upcoming exhibitions in 2015.

The Providence (RI) Public Library has created several highly original online exhibitions that prompt viewers to carry out creative activities in response to their viewing. Discussed in chapter one, these include At Play, an exhibition of whimsical items from the Providence Public Library Special Collections (2012) based on the library's Wetmore Collection of Children's Literature. The exhibition took two forms: a "real-world, physical exhibition" and a companion, online mini-exhibition that included images and instructions for creating replicas of five items, including a chess set. Special Collections Manager Jordan Goffin intended the online version of At Play to engage people in a creative process as they tried to make their own versions of the historic toys.

The Schomburg Center for Research on Black Culture offers online exhibitions on Digital Schomburg, some of which are based on physical exhibitions and others of which are purely digital presentations. In Motion: The African-American Migration Experience is an example of a major digital project based on an interpretive exhibition. With essays, maps, images, and multimedia, In Motion demonstrates the possibilities for a public library research center to provide an exceptionally rich visual and intellectual experience for online viewers.

These examples cannot begin to do justice to online exhibitions. They do, however, reflect the extent to which major institutions increasingly consider these types of exhibitions important aspects of digital services and public programming. Based on current trends, it is likely that more and more institutions will routinely develop on-site exhibitions and online exhibitions together, as a package. The synthesis of physical and digital experiences will offer members of the public more options for viewing and learning.

AERIAL PORTLAND
Portland (ME) Public Library

OVERVIEW: In 2012, the Special Collections Department (the Portland Room) of the Portland Public Library (PPL) opened Aerial Portland, the first public exhibition of photographs drawn from a massive collection of photographic negatives taken by *Portland Press Herald* photographers between 1937 and 2005. Acquired in 2009, the Portland Room is processing the collection to create a cohesive and accessible archive. The images selected for display in Aerial Portland, a "prioritized grouping," record the extent to which the physical fabric of Portland changed during the last half of the twentieth century. The exhibition introduced the *Portland Press Herald* Collection (PPH Collection) to the public and demonstrated the value of news photographs for an understanding of local history and change over time.

> The summary goal in the processing and preservation of any archival collection is to make the primary source materials available. That goal is especially relevant to the Portland Press Herald Negatives Collection, which provides an extraordinarily rich pictorial narrative of a great American city during much of the twentieth century.
>
> —Abraham Schechter, Special Collections Librarian and Archivist

PPL's Aerial Portland exhibition was a landmark event for the Portland Room, which is engaged in a multiyear process of indexing and digitizing the PPH Collection, described by Special Collections Librarian and Archivist Abraham Schechter as "an unequalled visual resource for understanding Portland's evolution during the twentieth century." The PPH Collection is a recent addition to the Portland Room, which focuses on the history of Greater Portland, including manuscripts, printed books, maps, photographs, periodicals, and directories. Collection highlights include examples of early printing in Maine, book arts, the archive of Children's Theatre of Maine, maps and atlases, and oral history recordings.

The Portland Room organizes lectures, workshops on preservation, exhibitions, and special events to promote understanding and use of its collections. The launch of the library's Digital Commons in 2013 expanded public awareness of Portland Room resources. Portland Room staff promotes Special Collections and the Digital Commons through posts on PPL's blog, *Life of the Library,* and a "Turn Back" Feature every Thursday on PPL's Facebook page.

The Portland Room first accessioned the *Portland Press Herald* negatives in 2009. Taken by news photographers over a period of seven decades, the images illuminate multiple aspects of Portland's history: architecture, business, education, religion, holiday observances, politics, ethnic traditions, professions, and urban demolition and construction projects. Schecter states that the images "enrich multiple levels in the study of Portland history . . . and, by default . . . present a history of local photojournalism and of the photographic materials themselves."

The PPH collection consists of 325 linear feet of still photography film negatives in multiple formats, offering a substantial challenge in terms of processing. It took staff three years to review, arrange, and evaluate the entire collection in preparation for creating an index. Schecter then began to prioritize the images, selecting a "first-pass 'cream of the crop'" for initial digital scanning. Each image is now being individually described. Volunteers assisted throughout the initial processing and are now working with staff to rehouse the negatives in acid-free enclosures and create a finding aid.

Images of Portland taken from the air were in the "high priority" category and they became the basis for Aerial Portland, the first exhibition to be created from the PPH Collection. The exhibition provided an introduction to the PPH Collection and showcased many of the photographs taken from the newspaper company's plane between the late '50s and early '70s. The images show, for instance, the upheaval of urban renewal, major downtown reconstruction, and highway projects between 1957 and 1974. In many cases they are the only images documenting the changes that took place in the latter part of the twentieth century—changes that shaped the look and feel of the city today.

Aside from the Aerial Portland exhibition, Portland Room staff has started to use the PPH Collection in other ways, drawing on the collection for images to round out history exhibitions and using images of PPL in promotional materials. Portland Room staff is also selectively scanning images for photo essays on the *Life of the Library* blog and has established a section on the PPH Collection in the Digital Commons.

   ❯ **CHALLENGES.** The sheer size of the PPH collection has made processing and exhibition planning a challenge. Volunteers have been essential in helping carry out the archival work that is a prerequisite to access.

❯ **FUTURE PLANS.** The next phase of the PPH Collection management project is to create a master finding aid that will make the images accessible. Thus far the database includes approximately 14,000 images; the work will continue until the entire collection has been processed and indexed. In the interim, Portland Room staff plans to organize additional thematic exhibitions similar to Aerial Portland that provide windows into the PPH Collection.

BOTH SIDES OF THE LENS
Photographs by the Shackelford Family, Fayette County, Alabama (1900–1935)
Birmingham (AL) Public Library

OVERVIEW: The Birmingham Public Library's (BPL) 2013 exhibition of photographs by the Shackelford family of photographers, Both Sides of the Lens, provided a view of Alabama in the early twentieth century from the perspective of its rural residents, many of them African American farmers. Created by the Department of Archives and Manuscripts (Archives), the exhibition was the basis for public programs and traveling exhibitions to other cultural institutions and public settings. It was one of many exhibitions organized and circulated by the Archives to broaden awareness of the cultural heritage of the region.

> We've had great success with exhibitions drawn from the collections. They remind people about the unusual and valuable items in our collections, they stimulate new research and donations, and they provide the basis for all kinds of educational programs that draw people to our downtown and into the library.
>
> —Jim Baggett, Archivist

B PL's Archives is one of the major historical repositories in Alabama, with a collection of more than 30,400,000 manuscripts, records, and images pertaining to local government, urban and economic development, industry and labor, social history, religion, sports, music, art, and literature in Birmingham and the region. In addition, Archives has one of the largest collections in existence relating to the civil rights movement in Birmingham. Under the leadership of Archivist Jim Baggett, the

Archives carries out public outreach in the form of collection-based exhibitions that travel to educational venues, bringing the exhibition content to different regions and smaller communities and promoting connections with the library and its Archives. Some exhibitions are fully digitized for remote access, while portions of others are accessible online, such as Both Sides of the Lens. Baggett notes that on-site use of the Archives and online queries are both constantly increasing, which he sees as a consequence of the combination of the original exhibitions, their exposure at off-site venues, and their online availability.

In addition to exhibitions, Archives organizes public programs that generate awareness and discussion around themes reflected in the collections. In 2013, in support of Birmingham's 50th Commemoration of the civil rights movement, Archives hosted a panel discussion titled "In Birmingham They Love the Gov'nor: George Wallace, Birmingham and Beyond." Three eminent historians discussed Governor Wallace's role in Birmingham's civil rights struggle and his continuing influence on race relations.

Both Sides of the Lens, mounted in 2013, is based on a collection of images taken by the Shackelfords, an African American couple who were photographers and farmers and who played a central role in the rural Fayette County, Alabama, community of Covin. The collection consists of more than 850 glass plate negatives that capture rural residents' lives during the Jim Crow era. Most of the images were taken outdoors, with the subjects holding a possession of their selection such as a book, tool, gun, or musical instrument, offering "authentic expressions of the lives and personalities of the subjects." Archives staff worked with a researcher from the University of Maryland at College Park to select 40 images from this collection that would "tell the story of these remarkable photographers and those who stepped in front of their camera."

According to Baggett, Both Sides of the Lens exemplified the importance of exhibitions in "helping us carry out new research on the collections and reach multiple audiences." The exhibition stimulated in-depth research on the Shackelfords in the context of American photography and Alabama social history and provided the basis for public programs including a lecture on the Shackelford brothers and a gallery talk by a member of the Shackelford family. Both Sides of the Lens is traveling to three regional museums in Alabama and a public library in Mississippi.

While Both Sides of the Lens was an important project in and of itself, it was also an expression of the Archives' ongoing efforts to identify and share images of life in Birmingham and the region. For instance, in 2003 the library mounted Common

Bonds: Birmingham Snapshots, 1900–1950. That exhibition was "one step in an ongoing initiative to seek out, collect, preserve and share Birmingham snapshots."

● **CHALLENGES.** According to Baggett, "Archives are sometimes perceived as an odd duck in the public library." While external outreach is critical, it is equally important to "reach out internally" to ensure that library colleagues appreciate archival collections. Baggett also cites the overriding need for dedicated staff that can "do justice to important collections." He envisions a future endowment for the African American collections, for instance, that would allow at least one person to concentrate on collecting, doing oral histories, curating exhibitions, and carrying out digitization projects.

● **FUTURE PLANS.** BPL has initiated a capital campaign to refurbish the central library building, curtailing exhibitions for several years. Baggett plans to use that time to organize more symposia and start documenting aspects of contemporary life that are not yet represented in the collections. As one example, Archives is partnering with the Birmingham Holocaust Education Center to do an annual series of programs and symposia on Jewish history and life in Alabama.

BREAKING THE BARRIERS
An Exhibition in Courage
Blair-Caldwell Research Library, Denver Public Library

OVERVIEW: The Blair-Caldwell African American Research Library (Blair-Caldwell Library) of the Denver Public Library (DPL) is a major regional resource on the experiences and contributions of African Americans in Colorado and throughout the Rocky Mountain West. In 2011 the library partnered with the United States Tennis Association (USTA) to present Breaking the Barriers, a traveling exhibition on the history of African Americans in tennis. The Blair-Caldwell Library used the exhibition to organize numerous complementary programs on tennis in Denver and to enrich the library's collection with oral histories, photos, and ephemera documenting past and present African American tennis players in Colorado. The project demonstrated how a research collection can localize the themes of a national exhibition through programming while exposing viewers and patrons to a neglected part of their history.

> By adding the Denver piece to the national story of African Americans in tennis we could address a subject that has not been showcased before, and stimulate new interest in the broader subject of African Americans' contributions to American sports history.
>
> —Terry Nelson, Manager, Blair-Caldwell Research Library

Blair-Caldwell Library, a branch of DPL, focuses on the "history, culture, literature, music, art, religion and politics of African Americans in Denver's historic Five Points neighborhood, in Colorado and throughout the Rocky Mountain West." Blair-Caldwell Library functions as both a circulating library and a research center. The archival collections include diverse primary sources: photographs, manuscripts, scrapbooks, letters, and audio and video interviews with a cross section of Coloradans. In addition to its services for scholars, Blair-Caldwell Library houses permanent and changing exhibitions, conducts lectures and guided tours, and offers community programming.

In 2011 Blair-Caldwell Library worked with USTA, the Colorado Black Chamber of Commerce and local groups to present a national traveling exhibition that presented the story of African American tennis players, from the 1800s to Arthur Ashe's Wimbledon win (1975). This was a topic never before showcased in Colorado, and it provided the basis for extensive programming, promotion, and collection development.

During Breaking the Barriers the Blair-Caldwell Library conducted numerous guided tours, especially for school children, and worked with teachers to integrate the story of African American tennis players into the Social Studies curriculum for grades 3 through 6. The library prepared pre- and post-exhibition educational materials and activities for teachers and families. Children were further encouraged to take part in the project through participation in local tennis clinics offered by USTA.

For adults, staff organized a four-part lecture series titled Breaking the Barriers: A Historical Perspective featuring scholars of sports and popular culture in Colorado and the United States. Blair-Caldwell also undertook an oral history project that involved collecting stories of local African American tennis players, and a panel discussion, Where Are Blacks in Tennis Today?, that featured Women's Tennis Association pros.

In addition to its extensive programming, the library worked with filmmakers and sports historians to create an original documentary short, *Crossing the Net: Denver City Park and Black Tennis Experience,* that "captured the culture, spirit and passion for tennis at Denver City Park, which embodies grassroots tennis at its best." The short was premiered by the Denver Film Society and attracted a large audience.

The programming carried out by Blair-Caldwell Library around the national exhibition Breaking the Barriers demonstrates how local library archives can use national exhibition themes to promote audience engagement with local *and* national history.

● **CHALLENGES.** Events associated with Breaking the Barriers, particularly the opening reception, were unusually large events for the library, posing some logistical challenges. Additionally, the number of guided tours was significantly higher than usual, requiring increased volunteer assistance.

● **FUTURE PLANS.** Blair-Caldwell Library is starting a project involving the collection of oral histories from community leaders and elders of the historically black communities of Colorado.

COWTOWN
History of the Kansas City Stockyards
Kansas City (MO) Public Library

OVERVIEW: Cowtown: History of the Kansas City Stockyards (Cowtown exhibition) was presented during April through December 2014 by the Kansas City Public Library's (KCPL) Missouri Valley Special Collections (MVSC) in partnership with the Division of Public Affairs (Public Affairs). The exhibition was important for several reasons. It almost did not occur because the content was nearly destroyed before the library rescued it. A major national grant from the Council on Library Resources supported the collections processing and research behind the exhibition. Above all, the exhibition subject—stockyards—has had a defining influence on the economic, social, and cultural development of Kansas City. KCPL staff worked for over a year to ensure that this important local story would be effectively brought before the public. The project reflects the role that public libraries can play in helping communities preserve and rediscover their history.

> Original exhibitions based on the Missouri Valley Special Collections allow us to interpret the history of our region, showcase our collections, and demonstrate to other organizations that their historic records and holdings will be in good hands at the Kansas City Public Library.
>
> —Henry Fortunato, Director of Public Affairs

M VSC is an important research resource on the economic, political, social, and cultural history of Kansas City and the surrounding region. Holdings include 200 specialized archival collections from individuals and organizations related to the Kansas City area, city directories, issues of the *Kansas City Star*, and regional histories. There are special collections of postcards, theater programs, advertising cards, popular sheet music, and documentary material on the Civil War, especially as it played out along the Missouri-Kansas border. Working with Public Affairs, MVSC mounts exhibitions and offers lectures that promote interest in local history and showcase library collections. Public Affairs helps in conceptualizing the exhibitions, provides design and editorial services, markets the exhibitions, and develops attendant programming. MVSC also works with Public Affairs to develop content for the Library's Digital Gallery, its digital branch, and a monthly e-newsletter titled *The Civil War on the Western Border*.

KCPL's Cowtown exhibition started in 2008 with a phone call to MVSC concerning documents that the current owner of the former Livestock Exchange Building planned to throw out. A team of librarians and archivists visited the storage room of the old Exchange and were astonished to find an enormous quantity of records strewn about—records that were slated for the garbage. They found blueprints, drawings, photographs, maps, and other documents, mainly from the office of the Exchange's Engineer. Ultimately, these documents, numbering over 5,000 items, were added to MVSC and became the basis for a three-year collections management project including research for an exhibition.

According to Eli Paul, MVSC manager, the rescued documents are of inestimable value for reconstructing the history, scope, and impact of the city's stockyards. They reveal details such as specially designed nails and screws used in the livestock pens. "Basically, you could rebuild the Stockyards based on the detailed maps, blueprints, and other documents we have."

In order to organize the records, attend to preservation issues, develop finding aids, prepare materials for digitization, and carry out the research necessary for public presentation of the collection, library staff sought special funding. In addition to the grant from the Council on Library Resources, the library received partial funding from the Ewing Marion Kaufmann Foundation.

From the initial discovery of the trove of Stockyard records, library staff recognized the possibility for developing an exhibition. An interdepartmental group of archivists, historians, designers, and public affairs specialists eventually were able to create Cowtown: History of the Kansas City Stockyards. Key exhibition themes included the construction and use of the Stockyard; the Stockyard's relocation history and how the livestock business spread into Kansas City, Missouri; and the impact of the Stockyards on the economic and social life of the city. The exhibition was widely promoted throughout the region, using public media, social media outlets, and the library's blog. Public response to the Cowtown exhibition was positive, based on comments and attendance. It was written up in *The Kansas City Star* and covered by several local television stations. In fact the exhibition was held over for an additional three months due to strong public interest. As a direct result of the exhibition, the local Folly Theater donated its archives to the library, providing a significant collection of business records, advertising materials, and hundreds of photographs offering a lens on mid-twentieth-century burlesque.

⊙ **CHALLENGES.** Preparation of high-quality exhibitions requires staff with a mix of skills. The Cowtown exhibition benefited from a strong exhibition team assembled by the library over the past several years.

⊙ **FUTURE PLANS.** KCPL expects to continue developing original exhibitions based on current holdings as well as new acquisitions. For example, the library is planning an exhibition for fall 2015 based on the newly acquired Folly Theater collection.

DEFINING THEIR IDENTITY
The Changing Role of Women in the Post-War Era as Documented by the *Valley Times* Newspaper
Los Angeles Public Library

OVERVIEW: Defining Their Identity—The Changing Role of Women in the Post-War Era as Documented by the *Valley Times* Newspaper (Defining Their Identity) was an exhibition mounted by Los Angeles Public Library (LAPL) Special Collections staff in 2014 that used newspaper photographs to dispel popular stereotypes about the roles of women in Los Angeles and the San Fernando Valley in the post-WWII era. The exhibition not only demonstrated the capacity of special collections librarians to mount significant interpretive exhibitions, it also underscored the importance of newspaper collections in helping enrich public understanding of social history.

> For a public library like ours, that is in great transition, our strengths are not just the books we house but also the programs and the special collections. The programs help people see what is special and what is relevant to their lives.
>
> —Ani Boyadjian, Manager of Research and Special Collections

L APL Special Collections include local historical materials relating to the history of Los Angeles and Southern California and other significant collections that illuminate the region's agricultural, industrial, architectural, and business history. Some components of Special Collections have national and international significance: the Map Collection, over one hundred years old, contains more than 100,000 items and represents the development of cartography worldwide; and a Rare Books Collection has over 16,000 volumes dating from the fifteenth through the nineteenth centuries. Special Collections are dispersed throughout the library in different departments; however, since 2012 LAPL has been working to consolidate rare and special collections for consistency of policies, more efficient services, and for improved preservation and access.

LAPL's visual collections are especially strong, including collections of Travel Posters, Menus, Fashion Plates, Sheet Music Covers and Bookplates. Through exhibitions and public programs Special Collections endeavors to bring these collections to the attention of the general public as well as scholars and collectors. Special Collections is also making a concerted effort to present these collections online, thereby expanding their visibility and use.

The Photo Collection is one of the most important of the library's visual collections. It includes an enormous photographic collection donated by the *Valley Times*. Published as a daily newspaper from 1946 to 1970, the *Valley Times* documented Los Angeles and the entire San Fernando Valley, a region that reflected the suburban development boom of the 1950s and 1960s. LAPL staff has gradually been making the newspaper's numerous images readily accessible online, with 7,000 images digitized to date. At the same time, staff research revealed "the not so obvious themes permeating throughout the collection such as the diverse women of the San Fernando Valley who strove to define their identities."

Defining Their Identity, on view at the Central Library from July 2014 through January 2015, results from LALP staff recognition of a paradox: the *Valley Times* images of postwar era women both did and did not conform to the stereotypes for women of the period. While some women fit the image of the consumer-homemaker and suburban mother, and others took on the role of a "Valley Girl," many others actually established their own identities in education, charity work, government, education, the arts, and a range of professions. The exhibition provided a vehicle to reexamine social stereotypes and document the diverse paths chosen by women after the war.

In concept and execution, Defining Their Identity reflects the commitment and the capacity of special collections librarians to go beyond routine preservation of their collections to research, analyze, and interpret these collections. In so doing, LAPL staff provided new perspectives on the postwar era and demonstrated the importance of newspaper collections for enriched public understanding of social history. Defining Their Identity was supported in part by Photo Friends, who also helped produce a companion exhibition catalog.

● **CHALLENGES.** Despite their size and their historical and artistic importance, LAPL's Special Collections are not widely known. Special Collections Manager Ani Boyadjian states: "Like many public library special collections we are not very good at letting people know what we have and what we do. We don't have the infrastructure to properly brand ourselves and become more visible." To address this challenge the Photo Collection is using social media, and Special Collections generally is benefiting from media outreach by the Library Foundation of Los Angeles.

● **FUTURE PLANS.** The Photo Collection, with the support of Photo Friends, is trying to accelerate the process of digitizing the entire archive of *Valley Times* images. This is a departmental priority given the historical importance of the photos.

EXHIBITIONS AND PUBLIC PROGRAMS
Schomburg Center for Research on Black Culture, New York (NY) Public Library

OVERVIEW: The Schomburg Center for Research in Black Culture (Schomburg Center), a research division of the New York Public Library (NYPL), is one of the world's primary collections on African American, African Diaspora, and African experiences. Beyond its role as a distinguished research collection, Schomburg is committed to serving its local community and all members of the general public who have an interest in black history and culture. With a Division of Public Engagement and Strategic Initiatives (PESI) and an institutional culture that promotes interdisciplinary and interdepartmental collaboration, Schomburg fulfills this commitment through extensive educational and cultural offerings that attract diverse ages and audiences. Additionally, online presentations include major exhibitions and audio recordings of programs. The scope and depth of its exhibitions and programs make Schomburg a leading example of a research library that is also a center for historical interpretation, community dialogue, and creative expression.

> The idea of an archive for most people is ambiguous: What is it, what does it do, and why it is important? We continue to educate with each exhibition and event.
>
> —Steven G. Fullwood, Assistant Curator, Manuscripts, Archives and Rare Books Division, Schomburg Center for Research on Black Culture

The Schomburg Center is one of four NYPL research units. Built from the early collection of Arthur Alfonso Schomburg, the Schomburg provides access to documentary material on black life in America and around the world, and promotes study and interpretation of the history of peoples of African descent. The Center's collections are organized into five divisions: Art & Artifacts; Jean Blackwell Hutson General Research and Reference; Manuscripts, Archives and Rare Books; Moving Image and Recorded Sound; and Photographs and Prints. The Lapidus Center for the Historical Analysis of Transatlantic Slavery is a special component of the Schomburg dedicated to research and programming on slavery. An additional department, PESI, organizes public programs and assists with acquisitions and collection management. PESI works with the research divisions to create exhibitions and programs that feature distinctive materials while fulfilling the Center's educational mission.

PUBLIC PROGRAMS. Programs offered by the Schomburg are highly varied in subject matter and format and are planned for a diverse audience of scholars, local residents, and individuals throughout the world. According to the Schomburg Center's website, educational and cultural programs "complement its research services and interpret its collections." Some programs are linked to exhibitions, providing context for the items on display, some are linked to special events or contemporary issues, and some provide opportunities for community members to explore aspects of the collections in-depth with specialists and staff. A selection of programs offered during 2012–2014 suggests the variety of topics and approaches:

- *Talks at the Schomburg*, a specially curated series of dialogues that features leading artists, historians, political analysts, and thinkers on such topics as The Intersection of Health, History and Justice (March 2012), Motown and Fashion, in conjunction with an exhibition on Motown (April 2014), and Stuck in Segregation (June 2014).
- *Readings and Performances* such as Oralizing, the Speed of Spoken Thought, an evening of poetry and music by poet Sekou Sundiata, presented in partnership with Cave Canem (September 2014).

- *Festivals*, including the Black Comic Book Festival, with pop-up exhibitions, workshops, and exhibitors (January 2013 and 2014).
- *Theater Talks* on works such as Martin Luther King Jr's "Letter from Birmingham Jail" read by Schomburg Junior Scholars (February 2014).
- *Films at the Schomburg*, usually shown in series, such as Freedom Summer, a series offered as part of a larger program, Mississippi Goddam: Commemorating the 50th anniversary of Landmark Events in the Civil Rights Movement.

EXHIBITIONS. Exhibitions are another form of programming that run parallel to and are often integrated with Schomburg Talks, performances, and panel discussions. Using documents, photographs, artwork and artifacts, and published works from its own holdings or other institutions, exhibitions examine a wide range of subjects from African American Women Writers to the African Diaspora in the Indian Ocean World. Some exhibitions look at broad global topics, such as In Motion: the African-American Migration Experience, while others are developed with a more local lens, such as Donald Andrew Agarrat, Harlem Photographer (2014). Exhibitions take varied formats: pop-up displays, major interpretive exhibitions, exhibitions developed in response to contemporary events or public issues, and online exhibitions.

- Schomburg Collects: WPA Artists 1935–1943 highlighted the work of visual, literary, and performing black artists as represented in the Schomburg's collections (September 2013).
- Africans in India: From Slaves to Generals and Rulers, presented the history of East Africans in India, many of whom attained high military and political positions. Two Online Exhibitions expanded on the exhibit's themes (February–August 2013).
- On the Road to Integration: Celebrating the 60th Anniversary of *Brown v. Board of Education*, a pop-up exhibition that explored events immediately before and after the landmark ruling, was curated by the members of the BNY Mellon Pre-Professional Development Program and was accompanied by film screenings (May–July 2014).

Online exhibitions are an important facet of the Schomburg Center's exhibition program. Numerous exhibitions are available on Digital Schomburg, some of which both record and expand on an analog exhibition of the same topic, and others of which are solely digital presentations. Titles include African-Americans and American Politics: An Exhibit from the Schomburg Center, Malcolm X: A Search for Truth, and In Motion: The African-American Migration Experience. The latter, which was based on an exhibition and funded by the federal Institute for Museum and Library Services, incorporated commissioned essays, images, maps, documents, and other media to examine the voluntary and involuntary migrations of Africans to the Americas.

Several characteristics distinguish the Schomburg Center's public programs from other public library archives and special collections' offerings. The first is the extent to which exhibitions and public programs are intertwined. Exhibitions enrich public programs, and vice versa. Another distinguishing feature is the extent to which the Schomburg Center's programs are interdisciplinary and interdepartmental. Many are thematic, requiring more than one disciplinary perspective and more than one type of collection material. Some are co-curated across divisions and disciplines. According to Steven Fullwood, assistant curator of Manuscripts, Archives and Rare Books, "the curators are constantly engaged with each other through collection development . . . as well as public programming." A third feature that distinguishes programs and exhibitions is the extent to which they are innovative in format and presentation. From pop-up exhibitions commemorating special events to off-site exhibitions such as Writing Blackness: Harlem | Paris, which took place in a nearby apartment to suggest a Harlem Renaissance era literary salon, experimentation is a hallmark of Schomburg Center public programs, offering inspiration and models for other institutions seeking new approaches to traditional programming.

❷ **CHALLENGES.** There is a need for constant development activity to support the scope of the programming carried out by the Schomburg Center.

❷ **FUTURE PLANS.** PESI and Schomburg Center curators intend to continue enriching their program offerings through interdisciplinary exhibitions, related public programs, and community partnerships. The institution will be undergoing renovations in the next three years, which will temporarily impact the number and scope of public programs.

GRIDIRON'S GOLDEN ERA
Early Days of High School Football in Grand Rapids
and
MAKING A DIFFERENCE
Outstanding Women in Grand Rapids History
Grand Rapids (MI) Public Library

OVERVIEW: Gridiron's Golden Era: Early Days of High School Football in Grand Rapids (Gridiron's Golden Era) and Making a Difference: Outstanding Women in Grand Rapids History (Making a Difference) were two exhibitions drawn from the collections of the Grand Rapids History and Special Collections Department (Special Collections) of the Grand Rapids Public Library (GRPL) that reflect the department's interest in building connections with diverse audiences. Gridiron's Golden Era proved to be one of the most popular projects carried out by Special Collections. Both exhibitions introduced new audiences to the history collections and helped attract popular and scholarly attention.

> We wanted to do an exhibit that was a little different from the past ones, a little less academic.
>
> —Ben Boss, Research Assistant for Gridiron's Golden Era,
> Local History and Special Collections Department

G RPL's Special Collections, established in 1904, is one of Michigan's largest collections of historical materials, containing periodicals, maps, family history, city directories, local newspapers, and ephemera. The Archives section contains more than a million photographs, as well as manuscripts, videos, furniture catalogs, yearbooks, and business records. The emphasis is on Grand Rapids and Kent County with additional resources on Michigan and the Old Northwest. The library's digital collections offer online access to many items. To engage Grand Rapids residents with its collections the department organizes four to five exhibitions or small history displays each year, conducts outreach, presents lectures, and collaborates with other history organizations to present an annual History Detectives symposium.

The concept for Gridiron's Golden Era originated with Tim Gleisner, manager of the Special Collections Department, who saw the possibilities to expand the audience for history exhibitions by featuring a topic with strong roots in Grand Rapids. With an array of archival materials—photographs, yearbooks, programs, news articles, and rare film clips—Special Collections staff told the story of Grand Rapids high school football beginning in 1892 and up through 1960. Different high school teams were depicted in the exhibition as well as the rivalries between these teams. Players who later went on to prominence in politics or university football were part of the story, including former President Gerald Ford and three-time Mayor Paul Goebel.

In 2009, Special Collections worked with Grand Rapids' Women's History Council to update and expand a 1997 exhibition, Making a Difference, that focused on the stories of influential women in the history of the city since 1850. Using photographs, personal records, and biographical information, the original exhibition had presented 12 women. The updated version included additional stories and explanatory panels, increasing the total number of women to 20. The exhibition, and the collections it represented, have helped attract scholars of women's history as well as donors. In fact, a major endowment has recently been set up to enable Special Collections to establish a Women's Studies Collection.

Gridiron's Golden Era and Making a Difference both illustrate the impact that different exhibitions can have on special collections. By focusing on the history of local football, Gridiron's Golden Era brought in new audiences, including more men, and attracted new publicity. Making a Difference helped attract new partners, researchers, and donors.

◉ CHALLENGES. Gleisner cites a fundamental challenge facing Special Collections, namely, the need to be balanced and comprehensive in collection development: "For Special Collections in a public library, there is an obligation to represent the entire city—its different resident groups and its many organizations. It is sometimes hard to be as balanced as we would like to be."

◉ FUTURE PLANS. Grand Rapids is undergoing major changes, in part due to expanded physical redevelopment in the downtown area and in part due to the number of recent immigrants. Recognizing the need to document these contemporary changes, Special Collections staff has started to photograph the hundreds of buildings slated for destruction or renovation. To address the need for more diverse community documentation, Gleisner plans to collect the stories of residents of different neighborhoods. He is working with nearby Grand Valley State University on a project that involves local students in documenting a primarily immigrant community. These projects will enable the library to create exhibitions on aspects of contemporary life in Grand Rapids. According to Gleisner, "Fifty years from now, anyone examining the library's Special Collections should be able to answer the question 'what was Grand Rapids like in 2013 or 2015?'"

HIDDEN FROM HISTORY
Unknown New Orleans
New Orleans (LA) Public Library

OVERVIEW: The Louisiana Division of the New Orleans Public Library (NOPL) mounted an exhibition in 2008 that featured images of people, most of whom were anonymous, drawn from the City Archives, New Orleans Parish records, and various other collections. Hidden from History: Unknown New Orleanians (Hidden from History) featured people at the margins of New Orleans society from the period circa 1882–1920—people whose lives are otherwise not represented in official records. The exhibition underscored the variety of ways that people were, or were not, officially identified, and the importance of preserving records that reflect the lives of people from all walks of life.

One of the points here is that 'Hidden History' shows the record left behind. This particular exhibit focuses on ordinary people whose lives in some way came into contact with municipal authorities . . . because the City Archives exists, because they touched the municipal record, and that municipal record is preserved, the ordinary people do not remain completely hidden, but are represented in the historical record.

—Irene Wainwright, Archivist, Louisiana Division, City Archives & Special Collections

The Louisiana Division is one of the richest sources for the study of New Orleans and Louisiana history. The collection includes rare books, official documents, newspapers, maps, manuscripts, periodicals, photographs and other image formats, motion pictures, audio recordings and videotapes, and ephemera. The Louisiana Division also houses a Louisiana Photograph Collection, a Carnival Collection, a Manuscript Collection, a Menu Collection, and extensive Genealogy collections.

To enhance access to these materials the Louisiana Division is gradually carrying out digital projects, including digitizing the City Archives Photograph Collection of more than 40,000 prints, negatives, and slides.

The Louisiana Division has traditionally informed and engaged residents and visitors by organizing exhibitions and public programs such as lectures based on its collections. Before Hurricane Katrina in 2004 the Louisiana Division mounted three to four exhibitions per year; that number is now reduced due to staff reductions. The exhibitions are usually researched and mounted by Louisiana Division staff.

Hidden from History drew from several key components of the Louisiana Division, including pre-1932 New Orleans civil and criminal court records. The exhibition was unusual for the Louisiana Division as it was organized in partnership with a guest curator and based on her research in the Louisiana Division's City Archives. Dr. Emily Epstein Landau, a historian at the University of Maryland, College Park, had carried out extensive research on Storyville, New Orleans' famous red-light district, during which she found three sets of images in the New Orleans Police Department records that documented people who had either been encountered by the police or arrested. By virtue of coming into contact with municipal authorities these New Orleanians were documented in one or more of the following ways:

- glass plate negatives showing a full-frontal portrait, with only an identifying number;
- prints showing the individual in one or more positions, with brief personal information recorded; or
- prints that included Bertillon records (a method of identifying an individual through precise measurements of anatomical features that predated fingerprints).

While some of the individuals captured in the official records were actually criminals, others were poor, homeless, or unstable. According to Wainwright, they were

> . . . ordinary people—some of them criminals perhaps, most of them simply poor. Not people whose histories you would expect to be recorded in family papers or letters or diaries that often make their way into manuscript repositories. Some, probably many, were not literate.

Other documents selected by Curator Landau, from New Orleans Parish civil and criminal court records and from other collections, revealed the various ways that these individuals came in contact with authorities—applying for a business, seeking information, seeking charity to survive—and the fact that there was little available in terms of public assistance to help them survive.

According to Louisiana Division staff, Hidden from History drew a great deal of public interest. Viewers were intrigued by the images themselves and the types of information, or lack thereof, preserved by the police department. Many viewers asked reference staff about the collections from which the images had been selected, and wondered about other individuals whose existence might have been similarly recorded. Archivist Wainwright believes the exhibition exemplifies the special role of a public library archive and, in the case of NOPL, a library legally designated as the archival repository for the city of New Orleans:

> As a public library and as the official city archive we have an obligation to document everybody, from the elites to the ordinary people, including people who are illiterate, people who do not have family papers, or people who would otherwise be hidden from history. The exhibit enabled us to draw from the city's store of "mug-shots" to reveal otherwise invisible people.

As a result of Landau's research and staff work on the exhibition they were able in some cases to identify individuals portrayed anonymously in the glass plate negative collection. And, by digitizing all of the images for the online exhibition they expect that members of the public will provide additional information on those "Unknown New Orleanians."

⦿ **CHALLENGES.** The usual challenge facing the Louisiana Division in executing an exhibition concept is the lack of staff to focus on exhibition work. Having a guest curator for Hidden from History, who carried out much of the research, was helpful in that regard.

⦿ **FUTURE PLANS.** The Louisiana Division is committed to carrying out interpretive exhibitions that can bring the stories and documents in its collections to the attention of more people, both on-site and online.

HOW TO PREPARE A POSSUM
19th Century Cuisine in Austin
Austin History Center, Austin (TX) Public Library

OVERVIEW: How to Prepare a Possum: 19th Century Cuisine in Austin (How to Prepare a Possum) was a major exhibition mounted by the Austin Public Library (APL) and Austin History Center (AHC) in 2013 that looked at early Austin food traditions—what food was local, how food was prepared, how and where people obtained food, and where and how people ate. The exhibition was intended to showcase varied items from AHC collections while also providing context for contemporary interest in local and sustainable food. The public response to the exhibition and its attendant programs was excellent and helped attract new supporters and collection users. The project demonstrates the value of organizing public history programs that are relevant to contemporary interests.

> **The current interest in sustainable eating and locally grown food was the inspiration for the exhibit because food initially—not just in Austin but all over the country and even the world—was local and sustainable. It wasn't a trend, it was just the way life was.**
>
> —Steve Schwolert, How to Prepare a Possum Exhibit Coordinator

AHC, a department of the Austin Public Library, is the largest and most comprehensive collection of documentary material on the history of the city of Austin. Holdings range from family records and architectural blueprints to films and oral recordings. Through outreach to formerly underrepresented communities, the collections are rapidly diversifying to reflect the lives and local experiences of contemporary residents and newcomers. Through exhibitions and programs AHC aims to ensure the "relevancy" of its collections to numerous constituencies.

Over the past decade Austin has become known as a "food city," with a growing number of celebrity chefs and destination restaurants, along with an emphasis on Southern food traditions and local ingredients. AHC staff saw an opportunity to tap into these trends while fulfilling their educational mission. They decided to organize an exhibition/programming initiative that would explore "the history and ideals permeating the discussion of food culture in Austin." Drawing from AHC's extensive collections of images, documents, and ephemera, the exhibition offered a historical context for current theories about Sustainable Food, Farm to Table, and Eat Local.

How to Prepare a Possum was a nine-month exhibition with continuous programming throughout. Exhibition and program topics included: what food was "local," where and how people obtained food, what it cost, how it was prepared, and where people went out to eat. Many of the items in the exhibition were the earliest food records available of their type, among them what is believed to be the first cookbook published in Austin and a diary kept by a nineteenth-century farmer detailing the activities he performed daily in the course of producing food ingredients for himself and for sale. The exhibition included records and images tracing Austin's earliest cuisine, from rancid butter to roasted possum, along with menus and mementos from Austin's first restaurants.

As with other exhibitions, AHC organized a variety of activities to deepen understanding of exhibition themes and promote appreciation of AHC collections. A four-part series of presentations on food history covered such topics as Southern Food Matters: Race, Class and Gender in Tomatoes, Biscuits and Greens and Black Enterprise: Remembering Austin's Pioneering Entrepreneurs. The final program in the series was a panel discussion featuring four Austin authors of food books.

A Beer Garden Social, billed as a 19th-Century Family Experience, was held at the historic Scholz Garden in Austin. The event included a family meal based on historic menus and recipes from AHC collections. There was a talk by a local beer blogger, a lecture on the history of beer gardens, and a concert of nineteenth-century Texas fiddle music. In addition, AHC provided a display on the history of brewing and beer gardens in Austin.

How to Prepare a Possum helped accomplish three exhibition program goals. One goal was to use preparatory research to identify relevant materials staff members did not realize they had or to find new links between collection items and an exhibition theme. In researching the history of food in Austin staff discovered items they had not previously connected with food history or had otherwise overlooked. Another goal of the exhibition program was to generate donations. How to Prepare a Possum helped raise awareness with Austin's food aficionados regarding the benefits of supporting AHC.

The third goal of the exhibition program was to widen awareness of the scope and value of AHC collections. Miller was interviewed for two live TV news segments, and the local public radio station, KUT, did a radio spot. The exhibition was also featured in the *Austin American Statesman*'s food section as well as in continued small articles about events. The coverage and the sustained programming helped to ensure a steady audience for the exhibition.

◉ **CHALLENGES.** The AHC does not have dedicated exhibition or program funding, so staff must be creative in finding ways to cover costs and to plan and organize programs—without dedicated staff to complete the many attendant tasks.

◉ **FUTURE PLANS.** The exhibition/programming project on the history of food in Austin has resulted in a project with the History Press to publish at least one book based on material from the exhibition. The book, authored by Miller (with proceeds going to the AHC), will help further AHC's mission to share the story of Austin with as broad an audience as possible.

LEAVES OF GOLD
An Exhibition of Illuminated Manuscripts
San Diego Public Library

OVERVIEW: The Special Collections of the San Diego Public Library (SDPL) include the Wangenheim Collection, one of the country's landmark collections of book arts. Between 2007 and 2010 a series of exhibitions drawn from the collection demonstrated the possibilities for presenting and interpreting special collections "treasures" for public benefit. Leaves of Gold: An Exhibition of Illuminated Manuscripts (Leaves of Gold) was among these exhibitions, offering a rare opportunity for visitors to examine premier examples of handwritten and decorated manuscripts from the sixth to the sixteenth centuries.

The exhibit of Illuminated Manuscripts allowed us to showcase the depth of our collection and to prompt visitors to consider key items carefully—who made them; when they were made; what materials they were made of; what different styles of writing were used in different places and time periods.

—Heidi Wigler, Librarian III, Special Collections

S DPL's Special Collections are housed in the Marx San Diego Heritage Center and Hervey Rare Book Room and are made up of three distinct components: the California and San Diego History Collection, which includes varied materials on Southern California and Baja California history; the Genealogy Room, which focuses on family history; and the Wangenheim Collection, which illuminates the history of books, writing, and illustration. The library has created the SDPL Digital Archive, a growing collection of digital documents, photographs, maps, and other research materials, to introduce viewers to items from the collection that heretofore have only been accessible on-site.

Leaves of Gold was one of four exhibitions drawn from the Wangenheim Collection that were intended to showcase the Collection's treasures. The Collection was donated to SDPL in 1947 by Laura Klauber, wife of local banker and civic leader Julius Wangenheim, whose avocation was the creation of a major collection on the history of the book. The Collection covers the entire history of writing, illustration, and printing, from Vellum manuscripts and Chinese silk scrolls to examples of modern private press publishing. The collection is continually expanding, with examples of early printing in San Diego and California and books created by contemporary book artists. Leaves of Gold was the largest and most visible of the exhibitions mounted by Heidi Wigler, then curator of the Wangenheim Collection.

A "rich trove" of medieval and renaissance paintings forms part of the Wangenheim Collection, including "flashes of gold on vellum leaves that have rarely been on public display." Selections from this trove were exhibited by the Wangenheim Room from August 2009 to February 2010. The exhibition, Leaves of Gold, traced the history of illuminated manuscripts including handwritten texts supplemented with elaborate decorative initials, borders, and miniature illustrations. Many of the items on display were religious texts produced by monks; later examples were created by professional artisans working across Europe. These texts were gradually supplemented by printed works in the late fifteenth century. The focal item in the exhibition was a fifteenth-century book of hours from France, beautifully decorated, with handwritten notes on the book's provenance. Other highlights included a thirteenth-century Latin bible; a Spanish missal from 1615; reproductions and facsimiles of some items and an illuminated twentieth-century manuscript of the *Rubaiyat of Omar Khayyam* illustrated by Edward Taylor Jewett.

To help visitors understand the items on display, and how they were made, exhibition organizers included interactive panels with questions about the origins, materials, and decorative styles of the items on display. The Wangenheim Room organized an accompanying lecture by Dr. Seth Lerer of the University of California at San Diego, who spoke on the evolution of illuminated manuscripts and the creation of books of hours. The exhibition was well promoted and drew new visitors to the Wangenheim Collection. A selection of items from the exhibition now forms part of the Digital Archive.

Other exhibitions were organized by Weigler to promote awareness of the Wangenheim Collection, including:

- Artist of Mist, Snow and Rain: Hiroshige and the Fifty-three Stations of the Tokaido (2009) consisted of 23 woodblock prints by the master Japanese printmaker Ando Hiroshige from one of his most famous series.
- Who Signed That? Signed and Inscribed Books from the Wangenheim Collection (2008) was a selection of rare books drawn from the collection of over 100 signed and inscribed books by various authors, book artists, illustrators, publishers, and people associated with the literary world. Authors represented in the exhibition included Mark Twain, Jack London, and Sir Arthur Conan Doyle.

- Photographs of Edward Curtis in Three Acts: Visual Representation, Empire and the Post-Colonial (2007), included the full volume of photogravures of Curtis's masterwork, *The North American Indian*. The sixth annual Wangenheim Room Lecture, by Dr. Ross H. Frank of the University of Southern California, San Diego, focused on the significance of Curtis's work.

These exhibitions offered windows into some of the treasures held by the library's Special Collections Department and helped raise public consciousness of their aesthetic and intellectual value.

> ❯ **CHALLENGES.** The position of curator of the Wangenheim Room is a part-time position that makes it difficult to plan and carry out interpretive projects. In addition, Special Collections was recently moved to a new location, which has inhibited recent development of special exhibitions.

> ❯ **FUTURE PLANS.** SDPL's Digital Archive is being constantly expanded, providing new public access to the library's extensive collections of rare books and local history, including materials from the Wangenheim Collection. On-site exhibitions from the collection are in abeyance until the move to new quarters is complete.

LUNCH HOUR NYC
and
THREE FAITHS
Judaism, Christianity, Islam
New York (NY) Public Library

OVERVIEW: Two major exhibitions presented by the Exhibitions Program at the New York Public Library (NYPL)—Lunch Hour NYC and Three Faiths: Judaism, Christianity, Islam—demonstrate the high levels of scholarship and presentation that distinguish the library's major thematic exhibitions, making them models within the library and museum professions. Each exhibition was interdisciplinary and inter-departmental; each featured an original design with interactive elements; and each catalyzed public programs that offered additional opportunities for learning and engagement. For New Yorkers and for visitors from around the world, these exhibitions and the others produced by the Exhibitions Program offer unique windows into the library's collections. The position of the Exhibitions Program as a separate entity that works collaboratively with Special Collections Departments provides one example of how larger libraries are centralizing the organization of exhibitions and related programs.

> **The New York Public Library's special collections are relatively unknown outside of the scholarly community. We develop exhibitions around themes that "open the vault" and make them meaningful to the widest audience possible.**
>
> —Susan Rabbiner, Assistant Director, Exhibitions

The Exhibitions Program was established in 1984 as a vehicle for presenting thematic exhibitions from the library's special collections that would widen public awareness of the collections and provide educational experiences for visitors. The first exhibition mounted by the Program, in the library's newly renovated Gottesman Exhibition Hall, was Censorship: Five Hundred Years of Conflict. Since then, the Program has created more than 245 exhibitions on topics ranging from the French Revolution to Garbage in New York City. Today, the Program is responsible for the development of all exhibitions in the Schwarzman Building at Fifth Avenue and 42nd Street, including Gottesman Hall for major exhibitions, and special galleries or corridor galleries for smaller exhibitions. The exhibitions draw mainly, although not exclusively, from the special collections housed in the Schwarzman Building. Extensive coordination between Exhibitions staff and curators in the different divisions helps ensure the accomplishment of the scholarship, preservation, and preparation necessary to mount a continual program of exhibitions in multiple venues. Two interpretive exhibitions mounted in Gottesman Hall during 2010–2013 reflect the Program's methods of presentation.

LUNCH HOUR NYC (June 2012–February 2013) was a major exhibition that drew on the library's special collections to explore New Yorkers' evolving approaches to noontime eating over the past century. Power lunches, school lunches, lunches at deli counters, hot dog stands, cafeterias, and Automats reflect how "New York City reinvented lunch in its own image."

Lunch Hour NYC provided a vehicle for tapping an array of materials on the social history of New York City: photographs, menus, engravings, artifacts, advertisements, magazine illustrations, musical recordings, and film clips. To contextual these materials Exhibitions staff and designers created settings that prompted the sense of being in an Automat restaurant, a home kitchen, and a school lunch table. These settings, combined with the documentary materials, communicated the differences between inexpensive Automat servings and elegant multicourse luncheons, or the fact that many places where men could lunch and conduct business or politics were out-of-bounds to women. The exhibition design also stimulated participation. Viewers could choose music about food from a jukebox, select recipe cards by opening the windows from a bank of genuine Automat machines, and do a puzzle dealing with how much and which food a tenement family could buy for 10 cents.

In order to portray contemporary lunchtime habits, the Exhibitions Program commissioned nine local photographers to go to different boroughs across the city to take photos of people eating at the same time of day for a one-week period. These photos were shown on a large wall of monitors in one area of the exhibition.

With nearly a half million visitors Lunch Hour NYC proved to be the most popular exhibition of any installed in the Gottesman Hall to date. People of all ages, backgrounds, and professions came to the library, many for the first time. They were introduced to the range and depth of the library's special collections while gaining new insights into a compelling aspect of New York history.

As with other major exhibitions presented in the Gottesman Hall, Lunch Hour NYC was augmented by complementary public programming. Educators were invited to an open house to explore the exhibition, discover the library's digital resources, and learn ways to support their classroom teaching. A series of programs at the Mid-Manhattan Library focused on writings about food and cooking, a storytelling session for very young children focused on books about "The Things That We Eat," a film series titled *Eating Out in New York* featured films that related to food and New York City, and teenagers created recipes and organized tasting events using produce from the garden at the Seward Park Library. A microsite of Lunch Hour NYC is available on the library's website.

THREE FAITHS: JUDAISM, CHRISTIANITY, ISLAM (THREE FAITHS) was another major exhibition drawn entirely from NYPL's special collections. The three Abrahamic faiths—Judaism, Christianity, and Islam—developed founding texts that have been used, interpreted, and reinterpreted for centuries. With some common and many distinctive elements, these three faiths, their scriptures, and their practice have had profound impact on ordinary people around the world over time. NYPL, with its vast and varied collections, is one of the few libraries that could mount an exhibition on the three religions. It is also one of the few libraries with the presentation capacities to make the complexities of these faiths and their connections with one another accessible and meaningful to diverse audiences.

Three Faiths was on display from October 2010 to February 2011. With items from the fifth century to the present day, the exhibition presented manuscripts, landmark printed works, scrolls and codices, prints, maps, early photographs, and liturgical or ritual objects. A large group of curators, advisors, and religious leaders contributed to the scholarship underlying the exhibition. The design of Three Faiths was distinctive, using vignettes that focused on particularly representative items, such as depictions of the Hajj, revolutionary vernacular translations of the Christian Bible, and artifacts of Jewish mysticism. The graphic designer developed a motif that referenced architectural elements found in synagogues, churches, and mosques.

To further engage visitors, a medieval manuscripts specialist worked with a design team to create a hands-on "scriptorium," or educational environment in the Wachenheim Gallery, just outside the entrance to Gottesman Hall. The scriptorium enabled visitors to compare the different materials and techniques employed by scribes and artisans of each faith. It offered interactive and educational activities, such as a light table with sheets of letters where people could trace their names in Hebrew, Greek, Arabic, and Latin alphabets, and touchable samples of the different kinds of animal skins, feathers, pigments, inks, plants, gold leaf, brushes, and tools that were used by Islamic, Hebrew, and Christian scribes to create manuscripts.

The programming associated with Three Faiths was more extensive than any exhibition-based programming before or since, including: educator programs; adult programs such as films, conversations, lectures, and performances of Hindu music and dance, Gospel choirs, and Kleszmer music; and activities for teens and children such as paper-making, calligraphy workshops, and discussions on faith. The library's Communities in Dialogue series of moderated discussions involved spiritual leaders from New York City faith organizations, and The Moth, a storytelling organization, performed Stories of the Sacred. System-wide programming enabled exploration of other faiths beyond the three featured in the exhibition. According to Susan Rabbiner, vice president for Exhibitions:

> Exhibitions can often generate themes for programs of all kinds, in the branches and here at the Stephen A. Schwarzman Building. The programs offer enormous educational opportunities and multiply the impact of the exhibitions beyond the gallery walls.

The Three Faiths website was a rich and interactive information source about the exhibition for audiences of all backgrounds. It featured blog entries relevant to the exhibition written by curators, programmers, academics, and interfaith advocates.

The website also featured "Faith on the Street," a community photography project that invited the public to submit images that captured current expressions of faith and provided an easy way for the public to engage with the exhibition on an immediate and meaningful level. Responding to this initiative, users everywhere submitted more than 531 photographs, and the submitted pictures were consequently viewed more than 26,800 times.

Three Faiths was cosponsored by the Stavros Niarchos Foundation and the Coexist Foundation. MetLife Foundation was the lead corporate sponsor of the Lunch Hour NYC exhibition and related programming. Support of the Exhibitions Program was provided by Celeste Bartos, Sue and Edgar Wachenheim III, Mahnaz Ispahani Bartos and Adam Bartos Exhibitions Fund, and Jonathan Altman.

Beyond the exhibitions detailed above there are many others that demonstrate the same thorough curatorial planning, inventive design, varied programming, and in-depth online resources. The Exhibitions Program has been, and is, a national model that has influenced other public libraries with rich archival collections as well as museums committed to interpretive programming. The American Alliance of Museums cited Three Faiths as a model for the museum profession, one indication of the exhibition's impact.

● **CHALLENGES.** According to Rabbiner, there is always a challenge in presenting exhibitions in a library setting because most people do not expect a library to have collections comparable to those of a museum. Raising funds is another persistent challenge, as is managing the execution of several exhibitions a year while planning for those in the future.

● **FUTURE PLANS.** The library is working to develop a permanent exhibition in Gottesman Hall featuring the treasures of the New York Public Library. Additional exhibition space in which to offer temporary exhibitions is also being planned. The library will continue to use exhibition themes as the basis for related programming across the system.

● **RELATED PROGRAM.** In the fall of 2013, the library's Communications & Marketing and Exhibitions departments began a joint program of pop-up displays relating to current events or relevant collection strengths. Display topics have included the 50th anniversary of John F. Kennedy's assassination, Holocaust Remembrance Day, and tributes to recently deceased luminaries Nelson Mandela and Maya Angelou. These displays underscore the library's relevance to contemporary audiences and serve as opportunities to further generate attention across both social media and traditional media platforms.

THE NATURE OF NATURE
Depictions of the Natural World from the John Wilson Special Collections
Multnomah County (OR) Public Library

OVERVIEW: The Nature of Nature: Depictions of the Natural World from the John Wilson Special Collections (The Nature of Nature) was an exhibition mounted by Multnomah County Public Library's John Wilson Special Collections (JWSC) in 2013. Using nature images as a cross-cutting theme, staff showcased an array of items, from illuminated manuscripts and illustrated nineteenth-century scientific works to 2012 artists' books. The high quality of the curatorial work makes this presentation an outstanding example of a topical exhibition that reflects the scope and depth of a public library special collection.

> Special collections are truly important in a public library. They represent the interests of the local community, historically and today. They will be even more significant in the future especially as library collections become more virtual and electronic.
>
> —Jim Carmin, John Wilson Special Collections Librarian

Multnomah County's JWSC consists of more than 12,000 volumes, including the founding collection of rare books donated by John Wilson in 1900. One of the core subject areas is the History of the Book, including thirteenth-century manuscripts, numerous incurables, a rare Klemscott Chaucer, and examples of fine press printing. Other strengths include Pacific Northwest history, Native American literature, children's literature, and literary works, especially by D. H. Lawrence and Charles Dickens. Exhibitions have traditionally been used by the JWSC to introduce members of the public to the library's treasures and to stimulate their interest in further exploration of the collections.

Natural History is one of the key topics represented in the JWSC, with well-known items such as a three-volume first edition of Pierre Joseph Redoutee's *Les Roses* (1817–1824). Other important but less well-known sources include an almost complete set of an early French magazine, *Journal des Roses* (1877–1917) and early books on fly-fishing and ornithology. Recognizing the growing public interest in the natural world and the need for conservation, Special Collections Librarian Jim Carmin decided to undertake an exhibition that would focus on nature. His introduction to the exhibition stated:

> Capturing the natural world—animals, plants, and landscape—has long been a human preoccupation, dating back to the earliest of cave paintings and continuing on to today's painters, printmakers, and photographers . . . Some of these early books used images as scientific endeavors, a first recording or observation of a particular species; others presented images as spectacular aesthetic objects; and some did both. This exhibition includes some of the finest of these materials, combined with other spectacular prints, photographs and original artwork drawn from the deep and diverse holdings of the John Wilson Special Collection.

Two characteristics make The Nature of Nature stand out. The first is the topic itself, which enabled staff to draw on so many different items in the JWSC. Some items dated before the advent of printed books, others were landmarks of early printing, such as the *Nuremberg Chronicle* (published in 1493), and some were contemporary artists' books, including one that featured a special rock found near the Pacific Ocean. In format the items ranged just as widely, from lithographs and paintings to woodblock prints and a long accordion fold-out book with hand-colored illustrations of traditional Japanese flower arrangements.

The second distinctive characteristic of The Nature of Nature is its traditional approach to presentation. Unlike many exhibitions today, there were no interactive stations, video screens, or apps. The focus was solely on the primary sources—the colored engraving, illustrated poems, early photographs, prints, and paintings. With a selection of items and accompanying captions that reflected deep knowledge of the JWSC and of the exhibition subject, The Nature of Nature was a model of curatorial excellence.

The emphasis on primary sources proved effective. The Nature of Nature was popular with general audiences and scholars alike, and elicited positive commentary in print media and social media. The exhibition was accompanied by a series of special viewings of a rare set of four-volume double-elephant folios of copperplate engravings from John James Audubon's *Birds of America* (1827–1838). These viewings enabled members of the public, in small groups, to experience the vibrant colored engravings at close hand.

❯ **CHALLENGES.** As with so many other special collections units in public libraries, the demands of collection management, digitization, research services, and acquisitions compete with exhibition development. Nevertheless, Carmin and his staff try to mount between two and four exhibitions a year to build knowledge of the JWSC.

● **FUTURE PLANS.** JWSC staff aims to increase digitization of collections, and, in the process, hopes to develop digital exhibitions based on the in-library exhibitions.

● **RELATED PROGRAMS.** JWSC is a growing collection, with several recent donations that have prompted exhibitions. David Lee: A Poet's Papers, was a 2014 exhibition mounted in the library's Collins Gallery that celebrated Lee, an award-winning poet, former Poet Laureate of Utah, and part-time resident of Oregon. Drawn from a large gift to the library from the poet, the exhibition included photographs, manuscripts, ephemera, and correspondence. The opening reception featured younger poets reading Lee's works.

PAPER STORIES
Adventures in Kamishibai, Manga, Graphic Novels and Zines
Cleveland Public Library

OVERVIEW: In 2013 Cleveland Public Library's (CPL) Special Collections Department (Special Collections) mounted Paper Stories: Adventures in Kamishibai, Manga, Graphic Novels and Zines (Paper Stories), which examined traditional and contemporary approaches to storytelling on paper. To complement the exhibition, the Ohio Center for the Book, housed in CPL's Literature Department, offered papermaking demonstrations and "Street Stories" workshops. The exhibition and its attendant programs were part of Cleveland's citywide Octavofest, a celebration of reading and book arts. The Paper Stories exhibition and the participatory programs demonstrated the depth of the library's book arts resources, provided opportunities for viewing, learning, and creating, and augmented the related programming taking place across Cleveland.

> **Through exhibitions, programs in the branches, and collaboration with local institutions we are letting people know that we have rare and relevant things.**
>
> —Pamela Eyerdam, Manager, Special Collections

C PL's Special Collections Department, which contains rare books on chess, Islamic manuscripts, miniature books, World War II posters, and rare architectural publications, also has a growing collection of graphic novels, zines, and contemporary artists books along with traditional forms of stories on paper. In recent years, under the leadership of Pamela Eyerdam, Special Collections has increasingly taken a leadership role in the cultural community of Cleveland, including working with partners to present collaborative programs, offering educational opportunities for students of different ages, and mounting exhibitions and public programs on artistic and cultural themes.

Each year Cleveland offers Octavofest, a month of coordinated programming on books and bookmaking that takes place throughout the city and the region. Special Collections was a founding member of Octavofest and began participating in the event in its first year, 2010. Amy Dawson, then Special Collections librarian, coordinated a variety of programs: a lecture entitled Curator, Educator, Artist: The Book Arts Revealed; a panel discussion on Book Arts by noted scholars and curators; "Show and Tell" presentations by local book artists on topics such as papermaking, book designing, and altered books; and creation of a book by these artists that was added to Special Collections.

In 2011, Special Collections partnered with the Ohio Center for the Book to mount two exhibitions curated by Literature Department Manager Dawson: Bound by Art: Bindings and Illustrations from the Lockwood Thompson Collection, including examples of modern twentieth- and twenty-first-century art and unique and unusual bindings; and Baron's Mail Art Collection: Display of Works on Paper. These exhibitions provided fresh opportunities to expose and interpret items from Special Collections while enriching Octavofest.

For the 2013 Octavofest, Special Collections mounted Paper Stories, an exhibition that drew from the library's collection of zines, comic books, and other forms of contemporary bookmaking. Paper Stories was intended to "celebrate storytelling that uses visual elements enhanced by text and color." Through unusual and colorful examples from the collections, the exhibition explored Japanese storytelling traditions on paper, such as Kamishibai, or paper-theater, which originated in Japanese Buddhist temples, and Hokusai Manga, which includes landscapes, flora and fauna, everyday life, and the supernatural. The exhibition also celebrated less formal and emerging forms of books and paper arts. By including new storytelling forms such as zines the exhibition responded to the interests of young people and added a special dimension to Octavofest.

To complement the Paper Stories exhibition and to draw family and youth audiences, the Literature Department's Ohio Center for the Book offered eight papermaking workshops that related to the exhibition. These "Street Stories" programs encouraged participants to create a book arts box based on the "Building Stories" graphic novel by author Chris Ware. In turn, Chris Ware was a featured presenter at the library's October 2013 Writers and Readers Series.

❯ **CHALLENGES.** Special Collection's capacity to engage broader audiences in the collections is limited primarily by insufficient staff and time. With more staff and time the department could increase outreach to partner organizations and develop more programs for students, artists, and members of the public.

❯ **FUTURE PLANS.** Special Collections Manager Eyerdam plans to expand collaborations with local organizations to bring new audiences to the library, and to continue participating in the highly successful Octavofest.

STREET LEVEL
A Stroll through Hartford's Past, 1900–1930
Hartford History Center, Hartford (CT) Public Library

OVERVIEW: Street Level, a 2013 exhibition of glass-plate negatives from the city's planning department that traced the construction and destruction of Hartford streets during the twentieth century, proved to be one of the most popular exhibitions put on by Hartford Public Library's (HPL) Hartford History Center (History Center). Audiences of all ages were interested in how the streets and buildings in their neighborhoods had changed. The exhibition demonstrated the importance of preserving records from municipal departments and how they can be used to engage people with community history. It also illustrated the trend toward coordinating digitization and presentation for greater internal efficiency and wider public access.

> We are lucky to have an enormous collection of images—glass plate negatives—taken over the course of the twentieth century by unknown photographers. These images are accessible . . . they intrigue people and draw them into the larger story of how Hartford has changed over time.
>
> —Brenda Miller, Chief Cultural Affairs and Public Programs Officer

The History Center contains a large multimedia collection that reflects the evolution of the city of Hartford over 300 years. With city directories, photographs, artwork, and books published or authored in Hartford (some dating from the eighteenth century), postcards, scrapbooks, trade publications, and photographs, there are rich research resources. Within the overall Hartford Collection, there are specific collections that contain thousands of images offering rich possibilities for exhibitions and community history projects. These include photographs from several city departments: Engineering, Health, Parks, and the Hartford Housing Authority. The photo morgues of *The Hartford Courant* and *The Hartford Times* are other primary photographic resources.

Starting in 2013, the History Center began a major project to digitize and make available online more than 1,000 historical images of Hartford that were made on glass-plate negatives. Taken mainly by unidentified photographers and city employees, the images depict Hartford in the early and mid-twentieth century—Model T automobiles, trolleys, streets under construction, businesses, and buildings. This major initiative will greatly enlarge the History Center's Digital Repository.

The Street Level exhibition, presented in 2013 in the library's Cultural Corridor exhibition gallery, offered a sampling of the glass-plate negative images that reveal how the city's streets have changed over time. Taken primarily during the early decades of the twentieth century, they depict changes in the layout of the city and changes in the look, size, and uses of the actual buildings, some of which are still part of the cityscape.

Street Level attracted and engaged audiences of different ages and backgrounds, demonstrating the extent to which people are interested in learning about the evolution of their neighborhoods and landmarks. The exhibition introduced many people to the History Center and also drew them to the online collections. According to Chief Public Affairs and Public Programming Officer Brenda Miller, ". . . this exhibition is one of the hooks that helps people become engaged with community history." The History Center will be publishing a corresponding book in 2015, *Hartford Through Time*, containing more than 90 of these twentieth-century images coupled with how the places appear in photographs today, taken from the same angle.

The organization of the Street Level exhibition as part of a larger digitization and publication project exemplifies a national trend to coordinate preservation, digitization, and presentation. Digitization of the glass-plate negatives on exhibition was made possible, in part, through a Heritage Advancement Award from the Greater Hartford Arts Council and with funding from the Society of the Descendants of the Founders of Hartford.

❯ **CHALLENGES.** Developing and sustaining a digital collection are one of the major challenges for the History Center. Everything requires staff and materials: standardizing the metadata, georeferencing, creating the appropriate image formats, and preparing digital material for a digital archive.

❯ **FUTURE PLANS.** History Center staff see an "exciting future for digital collections and how they can be shared." They will continue to seek funding for thematic projects that expand citizen connections with collections.

WIT & HUMOR COLLECTION EXHIBITIONS

San Francisco Public Library

OVERVIEW: The Schmulowitz Collection of Wit & Humor (Wit & Humor Collection) of the San Francisco Public Library (SFPL) is regarded as the world's largest such collection, with works spanning 450 years and including more than 35 languages. Each year San Francisco History Center/Book Arts & Special Collections (SFHC/BASC) mounts an annual Wit & Humor exhibition drawn from the collection, with accompanying public programs designed to draw in diverse audiences. The 2013 exhibition, which focused on jobs and drudgery, was titled On the Clock: A Playful Guide to Working Life. Deliberately planned to appeal to nonspecialists, the exhibitions and programs help introduce visitors to an unusual collection.

> **These kinds of programs are very important to fulfilling our mission. They help us reach different audiences and connect people with unique items that do not exist elsewhere.**
>
> —Andrea Grimes, Curator, Schmulowitz Collection of Wit & Humor, San Francisco History Center/Book Arts & Special Collections

The Wit & Humor Collection is one of many special collections within the SFHC/BASC. It is named for Nat Schmulowitz, a lawyer and book collector, who donated 93 jest books to the library on April Fools' Day, 1947. He continued to add to the collection over the course of his lifetime and funds associated with the collection enable acquisitions to the present day. The collection consists of more than 22,000 books and 250 periodical titles, electronic media, and ephemera, as well as the donor's personal archives. Titles range from the mid-eighteenth-century English *Anecdotes of the Learned Pig* to essays by Woody Allen and copies of *Mad Magazine*.

Starting in 1954 staff overseeing the Wit & Humor Collection have created annual topical exhibitions that reflect the comic nature of the items in the collection. These typically open on April Fools' Day and are accompanied by public programs and/or films. The 2013 exhibition, On the Clock: A Playful Guide to Working Life, focused on jobs, employment, and the drudgery of the working life. According to the library's announcement, the exhibition "will guide you through a deliberately foolish field of job opportunities." Titles on display included *50 Jobs Worse Than Yours* and *How to Cook Husbands*.

In conjunction with On the Clock, two well-known local comics performed at the library: Will Durst in "Elect to Laugh" and Josh Kornbluth in "Haiku Tunnel." A three-part film series also augmented the exhibition and performances. The library's General Collections and Humanities Department mounted a complementary display of book covers titled Works for Me: Diligence and Drudgery.

The 2012 Wit & Humor exhibition, titled Innocents Abroad: Travels with the Schmulowitz Collection of Wit & Humor, featured travel journals, scrapbooks, letters, postcards, and ephemera, in multiple languages and dialects. Well-known film comedies based on travel were shown in conjunction with the exhibition. In 2010 the annual exhibition theme was A Dog's Life (With a Special Appearance by Cats): Selections from the Schmulowitz Collection of Wit & Humor. The exhibition featured the work of classic magazine illustrators, beloved characters from newspapers and comic books, and dog-related anecdotes and images from around the world.

> **CHALLENGES.** Andrea Grimes, curator of the Schmulowitz Collection, cites the need to "appeal to all ends of the audience spectrum, from serious researchers and collectors, to elementary school children on school trips . . . It is always challenging to create exhibitions and present collections in ways that will appeal across the board, without oversimplifying the content."

> **FUTURE PLANS.** SFHC/BASC staff expects to continue building the Schmulowitz Collection and using exhibitions and programs to educate and entertain members of the public.

WONDERFUL WIZARDRY OF BAUM
Buffalo and Erie County (NY) Public Library

OVERVIEW: In 2014 the Special Collections Division (Special Collections) of the Buffalo & Erie County Public Library (B&ECPL) mounted Wonderful Wizardy of Baum, an exhibition of 14 first-edition works by L. Frank Baum, author of The Wonderful Wizard of Oz. Inventive in design, elements of the exhibition were distributed throughout the library, including a "Yellow Brick Road" leading to the Rare Book Room. The exhibition was popular with the public, drawing many visitors to the library and to Special Collections. It demonstrated how a public library can use thematic exhibitions and related programs to build new public audiences.

We feel strongly the need to open up the vault to share the fabulous works in our Special Collections with the public. After all, these collections belong to the public; they are not ours to hold on to.

—Mary Jean Jakubowski, Library Director

B&ECPL, a federated library system with eight branches in the City of Buffalo and 22 member libraries in adjacent Erie County, is known for the depth and breadth of its Special Collections. Holdings consist of nearly 500,000 items—manuscripts, maps, organizational archives, scrapbooks, phonograph discs, and musical scores—that focus primarily on the history of Buffalo and the Niagara Frontier, genealogy, and music history. The Rare Book Collection includes more than 5,000 items of local, national, and international significance, from Shakespeare's First Folio to Mark Twain's original manuscript for *Adventures of Huckleberry Finn*. Exhibitions showcasing aspects of the Special Collections have traditionally been mounted in the Central Library's Grosvenor Room, Mark Twain Room, or corridor locations.

Wonderful Wizardry, an exhibition that opened in January 2014, was an unusual exhibition for Special Collections. Not only did it focus on a children's book, but graphic elements were positioned throughout the Central Library and Oz-themed programming occurred at other libraries in the system. Internally, Special Collections staff worked with the library's Development & Communications, Graphics, and Public Services departments to plan and coordinate the project as a system-wide initiative. The popularity of the topic, the exhibition's creative design, and system-wide programming helped the exhibition to gain a large public following.

The basis for Wonderful Wizardry was the library's collection of first editions of Oz books. Thirteen of fourteen books were displayed, along with *Wizard of Oz* collectibles, illustrations, and related publications. The exhibition explored Baum's early life, the writing and the marketing of the 14 Oz stories, how they were subsequently adapted for stage and screen, and how they influenced American culture over time. Displays in the central library's Ring of Knowledge—a sculpted circle in the main lobby of the central library where events, displays, and other programs take place— in the Grosvenor Room and on the library's main floor featured Oz-inspired graphics and Oz-related items from the music collection.

To complement Wonderful Wizardry, Special Collections also mounted Early Music of L. Frank Baum. This display drew on the collection of vintage sheet music to look at Baum's early music, starting in 1900, as well as to trace his impact on American music and American culture.

Oz-themed programs took place at the central library and in branches throughout the course of the exhibition, including lectures on the making of the Oz movie and displays of costumes inspired by Oz. B&ECPL incorporated Oz into its three-month winter reading initiative with "The Wonderful World of Reading" theme. Additionally, the annual Take Your Child to the Library Day offered daylong showings of Oz-related films. The distributed programs expanded access to the Oz theme even for those who could not visit the exhibition at the central library.

B&ECPL took advantage of the popular Oz theme to promote the exhibition through print media and social media, including Facebook, Pinterest, Flickr, and Twitter. Media releases were e-mailed to local, regional, and national publications as well as to library cardholders, lawmakers, and schools. All 37 library locations in the system were provided with exhibition posters and program ideas.

❯ **CHALLENGES.** B&ECPL has experienced extreme budget cuts in recent years, resulting in staff and service reductions. Public programming that has occurred, including exhibitions, has been due to library leaders' and librarians' commitment to making the rich collections accessible to the entire community.

❯ **FUTURE PLANS.** B&ECPL is planning to ramp up its exhibition activities starting in May 2015 with the opening of a landmark exhibition based on its renowned "Milestones of Science" collection of first editions of the world's most significant scientific discoveries. A larger display space and major thematic programming will signal the importance of the 197 items in the collection, many of them key works in the history of science.

SIX

INTERACTIVE ARCHIVES

Des Plaines Memory is a work in progress . . . we are operating in a dynamic environment and trying to apply archival principals to the ever-expanding possibilities that come from today's technologies.

—Steven F. Giese, Digital Projects Librarian

Public libraries have consistently played an important role in helping patrons keep up with innovations in digital tools—tools to help find and retrieve information, tools for communications, and tools to promote creative expression. Just as they did with public access computers over the past two decades, libraries today are helping patrons stay ahead of the digital curve by lending Kindles, offering online book clubs, teaching advanced computer skills, and creating Maker Labs. This same role is playing out in how these libraries' archives and special collections departments are applying digital tools to enhance collections access and build new community connections. More and more professionals in these departments are experimenting with new approaches to interactive archives in the public library setting. According to Renee DesRoberts, archivist at the McArthur

Library in Biddeford, Maine, "I have a foot in both worlds—one in local history and one in technology—which gives me a chance to experiment with new technologies to put information in the hands of folks."

As with other categories of programming in this book, there is no single approach to interactive archives and digital programming. Variation and experimentation hold sway. In fact, in no other aspect of archival work is there so much innovation. From the use of QR codes in history tour apps to crowdsourcing projects that enhance knowledge of key collections, special collections librarians are experimenting with a multiplicity of paths to increased interactivity in the archival environment. These experiments can be roughly grouped around five purposes:

1. Enhance traditional programs.
2. Attract younger audiences.
3. Foster public participation—direct or indirect, on-site or online.
4. Leverage citizen knowledge to improve documentation of collections.
5. Enhance and expand online communications.

Several examples profiled below illustrate how digital tools can enhance traditional exhibitions. The Houston Public Library Exhibit Snapshot (THPLES) developed by the Houston Metropolitan Research Center demonstrates how a digital tool can bring the full experience of a library exhibition to remote visitors. In fact, with the capacity to present details on individual exhibition items and respond to viewers' questions or comments, some might find the online THPLES exhibition experience preferable to the physical experience.

A number of libraries are experimenting with the development of tools that engage young people with special collections. The Hartford History Center has worked with the Connecticut Center for Advanced Technology to design the Keney Park App, a game app that introduces users to geolocation technology while building their interest in history and history collections. The Sacramento Public Library's Sacramento Room, which is emphasizing outreach to young people, has created a highly successful app with QR codes for a self-guided tour of a popular historical district and is planning to create similar apps for other parts of the city.

The largest number of examples profiled involve tools that foster participation, both online and on-site. Within those, the majority of examples are one form or another of a virtual community archive. Denver's Creating Your Community Project, a social archive, was one of the first projects to demonstrate the value of building community collections online. It sparked other efforts to build online community collections such as digital scrapbooks and virtual archives. The Allen County (IN) Public Library has led creation of a regional digital album and has attracted substantial donations of records, images, and stories; and the Columbus (OH) Memory Project has brought together digitized local history resources for classroom and community use. The Des Plaines (IL) Memory Project and Richland County (SC) Library's Midlands Memory Project are but two of the many similar projects in existence or in the initial phase of development. Santa Monica Public Library's Share Santa Monica, launched in 2013, is too new for a full description in this book. However, it has already gained a following and begun to build an online archive of historical and contemporary images.

Community mapping projects are another form of participation facilitated by new digital tools. DC by the Book and Neighborhood Stories, a pilot project of the Queens Memory Project, illustrate two different approaches. The former uses digital mapping techniques to create a crowdsourced map of literary references to the District of Columbia, while the latter uses Historypin technology to engage residents of different Queens neighborhoods in building multilayered history maps. Smaller libraries are also working with Historypin software and others, such as the Tigard (OR) Public Library, are using ESRI Story Maps to develop community history maps and tours.

NYPL Labs stands out as the leader in designing and testing tools that can leverage citizen knowledge to enhance collections documentation. Labs has worked on a number of innovative projects such as Map Warper that demonstrate the possibilities for leveraging citizens' contributions for the benefit of the library and its users. San Francisco Public Library, as well, has gained substantial new information about its historical photographs and local maps as a result of crowdsourcing initiatives such as OldSF and History Mysteries. It is likely that such projects will increase as the tools become easier to manage and librarians get more accustomed to the concept of citizen cartographers or citizen historians.

Beyond the use of digital tools for community history albums, virtual exhibitions, literary mapping, crowdsourcing, and history gaming, there is another whole array of digital applications being used by special collections staff in public libraries to (1) extend their communications with patrons and remote visitors, and (2) promote their programs and collections. These include blogs, Flickr pages, Facebook, Twitter, Tumblr, and other social media platforms.

There are widely varying approaches to the uses of social media and these approaches are not static. They are in constant flux. Some archival departments are investing considerable time and effort in maintaining Facebook pages and populating Flickr with images from historical photo collections. Others find these efforts too time consuming given their traditional archival responsibilities. Yet other departments have created departmental blogs, and invested considerable effort in preparing substantial posts, only to find that briefer communications using social media platforms can be just as effective in building a constituency for their collections and audiences for their programs.

The approach taken by the Special Collections Division of the Enoch Pratt Free Library in Baltimore, Maryland, reflects the way in which institutions are constantly shifting their uses of social media and adjusting their investments of time and energy as they learn what outlets are most effective for communications. At Enoch Pratt Special Collections staff prepares blog posts on the library's *Pratt Chat* blog, offering stories of items in the collection or information on acquisitions and upcoming events. Similarly, Special Collections provides information for the library's Facebook page and Twitter account. According to Michael Johnson, manager of Special Collections, "We are experimenting with uses of social media and are finding that fast, short Twitter messages and Facebook announcements are as effective as longer blog posts in building new audiences."

As special collections departments increase their use of digital tools and social media, there will inevitably be more community archives and increased community participation. At the same time, these departments continue to carry out traditional functions including collections management, research services, and, increasingly, public programming. The challenge today, which was voiced by many professionals interviewed for this publication, is finding the right balance between routine archival tasks, programming, and online communications. The examples that follow suggest how some institutions, despite limitations of staffing and other supports, have managed to carry out experiments that offer instructive examples for the profession and that may help to shape the next wave of professional-citizen interaction around public library special collections.

ALLEN COUNTY COMMUNITY ALBUM
Allen County (IN) Public Library

OVERVIEW: The Allen County Community Album (Community Album), developed and maintained by the Allen County Public Library's (ACPL) Genealogy Center, provides a virtual framework for organizational and institutional records, historical documents from local families and individuals, and images reflecting the experiences of residents of all ages in Fort Wayne and the surrounding counties of Indiana. The

Community Album is an excellent example of the national trend to establish community archives in public library special collections.

> In helping to create a virtual community album people feel connected to one another and part of a larger whole. They realize that local history is not just one person's history, it is everyone's perspective, from everyday Jill and Jack to the Fire Chief and the Mayor.
>
> —Curt Witcher, Director, Allen County Public Library Genealogy Center

ACPL's Genealogy Center, which serves Fort Wayne and the surrounding communities of northeastern Indiana, developed the Community Album as an outgrowth of its commitment to family and local history. The Genealogy Center, with one of the largest existing collections of family history, is a major resource not only for the region but for students of family history from across the country and the world. Despite its considerable resources for family history research, the Genealogy Center did not have an equivalent community archive. In 2008, to address this need, the Genealogy Center started the Community Album. The Genealogy Center provides an ideal infrastructure for a digital community archiving project, with excellent equipment and a pool of dedicated, talented, and trained volunteers who can help with scanning. The goal is to preserve and make accessible local records, stories, and images from institutions, organizations, families, businesses, and individuals.

The Community Album includes historical collections previously acquired by the Genealogy Center and growing numbers of historic resources, especially images, donated by groups and individuals. The Album also includes special groupings of items such as the images submitted during four annual Teen Photography Contests organized by ACPL Youth Services Department, and images donated by participants in ACPL's annual Day in the Life of Allen County program. The following sample collections suggest the diverse themes represented in the Album to date.

THE FIREFIGHTERS PHOTOGRAPH COLLECTIONS was started by a local collector of images and artifacts and is now being expanded with donations from fire companies and individual firefighters across the region. This collection is important not only for its record of firefighting but also for its documentation of places, buildings, and people in twentieth-century Fort Wayne.

FORT WAYNE AND ALLEN COUNTY HISTORY COLLECTION encompasses the majority of the items donated to the Album by local residents. Focusing on people, places, and organizations, it is continually expanding through outright donations or scanned images and documents provided by citizens. According to project organizers, "this collection will become an increasingly important complement to other collections and will provide an ongoing vehicle for capturing the memories of this community."

HARTER POSTCARD COLLECTION, donated by the author of *Postcard History: Fort Wayne*, with the majority of the images coming from the "Golden Age" of postcards, a period from about 1905 to 1917.

Collectively, these bodies of historical material constitute a unique virtual scrapbook, or album, that is proving to be a galvanizing tool to engage community members with local history and the Genealogy Center. The Community Album is continually being enhanced depending on the pace of community donations and the Genealogy Center's capacity to digitize and create metadata for the collections.

The Community Album provides the library and its community of users with an important tool for education, preservation, and community involvement. It is a model for other libraries interested in creating community archives.

● **CHALLENGES.** The Community Album has proven so successful that bandwidth capacity is now a major challenge. Another issue is staff capacity to digitize and create metadata for new collections. The design of the Album also requires attention, to ensure that it is more "fun, intuitive and interactive." To this end, staff plans to open a dialogue with the community to learn what features are most desirable and effective.

● **FUTURE PLANS.** The Genealogy Center intends to create an Oral History Program that will complement the Community Album while building new content. It will focus on oral history as storytelling and will engage individuals of all ages and backgrounds. Staff envisions a taping program similar to that used by the national program StoryCorps. Another area that Genealogy Center leaders are targeting for expansion is work with artists and the promotion of community driven art as a form of local history and local interpretation.

CATABLOG

McArthur Public Library, Biddeford (ME)

OVERVIEW: The Archives and Special Collections (ASC) unit of the McArthur Public Library (MPL) in Biddeford, Maine, has created a Catablog for Local History, Genealogy, Archives, and Special Collections (Catablog) that combines elements of a digital archive, a local history blog, and a community forum. Using WordPress for its basic structure and as a content management system, the Catablog demonstrates how a library with relatively limited technical resources can develop and manage a site that not only enhances access to historical collections but also generates new information on those collections.

A library does not need a big IT department or lots of dollars to put together an online framework for increasing public access to special collections.

—Renee DesRoberts, Archivist

MPL, which serves Biddeford, a small coastal city in southern Maine, has a varied local history collection that has been known to local historians as a key information resource. However, members of the general public have been less aware of the depth and value of the historical materials. When Renee DesRoberts was hired in January of 2007, her training as an archivist provided an opportunity for the library to focus attention on ASC. Several activities resulted, the first being development of *Backblog*, a blog that highlights collection items and local history events. Another result of the new attention to ASC was an emphasis on digitization and the creation of online access points. In addition, through its participation in the Maine Memory Network, ASC has been able to expand the amount of material on the Network's Biddeford section. The results of these activities were quite obvious. DesRoberts states that, "We saw that the quantity of patrons attempting to access our collections was increasing along with the quantity of material available online."

In 2009–2010, MPL participated in, and helped develop, the Biddeford History and Heritage Project, a collaboration between the library, the local high school, the Maine Memory Network, and the Maine Historical Society. DesRoberts played an important role by helping high school students research and digitize items for this project and by building the digital infrastructure for content. The project led to establishment of a local history website.

In 2010, in order to further enhance public access to its historical collections, MPL created the Catablog, a combination digital local history archive, virtual catalog, and community forum. Organized as a WordPress blog site the Catablog brings together materials from all of the library's varied special collections, along with digital surrogates, online access tools, and commentary by library staff and public users. As the library scans and uploads materials it creates "posts" that include an abstract of the collection, a description of scope and content, and tags that provide further clues as to the collection contents.

The Catablog is unusual in several respects. It is more than a routine digitization project in which entire collections are made available electronically with little categorization or guideposts to finding specific themes or items. MPL's Catablog presents like kinds of materials together, cutting across the boundaries of formal collection titles or archival categories (genealogy, etc.). The menu enables people to search through seven primary categories: Electronic Texts, Finding Aids, History Index, Images, Veterans, Biographical Resource, and Scrapbooks. Some materials are presented via Indexes; the section on Finding Aids offers tools to help in searching the site.

The Catablog does not impose a thematic structure on the digital objects, other than the seven categories through which they are made accessible. Through both the post titles and the menu categories, it is structured to facilitate searching for individual items or groups of items so that users can create their own projects and online exhibitions. According to Archivist DesRoberts, it is "an access tool that enables the library to reach out to people and help them see and learn."

While DesRoberts has designed and developed the Catablog, she has had assistance in scanning and other tasks from library colleagues and volunteers. One of the advantages of the design is that it has been relatively easy to put in place and should be relatively easy to replicate.

There have been numerous positive outcomes for the library and for patrons as a result of the Catablog. For instance, library staff has noticed a "huge" increase in online use of historical materials versus in-library transactions. In FY2013, staff recorded 106 transactions in which 405 individual items were accessed. In contrast, the Catablog was accessed 4,370 times. These numbers suggest the impact of digital access on the visibility and use of special collections.

Use of social media related to the Catablog has also benefited the library. Queries on the library's Facebook page and comments on the Catablog forum have elicited new information on many items in the collection, particularly the photographs, and attracted new library patrons.

Library Director Jeff Cabral states:

> We are excited to make these items more widely available and accessible with digital scanning so that they can be searched and seen by students, historians, researchers, genealogists and interested members of the community . . . All in all, that makes for a richer collection and a more interested and participatory community, helping build involvement and interest, and ensuring Biddeford's stories will always be told and seen.

◉ **CHALLENGES.** DesRoberts cites several challenges in developing the Catablog, one being the difficulty of "being a lone arranger," that is, an archivist who works alone. She has been able to accomplish a great deal as the sole archivist, however, she sees the potential, with more staff, to expand the Catablog's content and use.

⊙ **FUTURE PLANS.** The library intends to continue uploading images and information from its historical collections, especially the newspaper collection. Staff also plans to continue adding images to the Maine Memory Network. They see value in having as many access points to their collection as possible.

CINCINNATI PANORAMA OF 1848
Public Library of Cincinnati (OH) and Hamilton County

OVERVIEW: The Public Library of Cincinnati and Hamilton County's (PLCHC) Fontayne and Porter Daguerreotype, popularly known as the Cincinnati Panorama (the Panorama), is a rare panoramic view of the Cincinnati waterfront taken in 1848 that was recently brought to life using specialized tools that both preserved the object and revealed its features in microscopic detail. An interactive electronic display presenting the Panorama, and its details, has stimulated dialogue with individuals worldwide who have contributed new information about many of the Panorama's features. Their knowledge, in turn, has enriched understanding of related items in the library's collections and important aspects of Cincinnati history, from business history to genealogy. The Panorama demonstrates how the application of new scientific and digital tools to the examination of one special object can stimulate rediscovery of community history.

> **What has happened has been dramatic. Through one object people around the world have joined a conversation about the history of Cincinnati and provided us with content that we never would have otherwise known about.**
>
> —Patricia Van Skaik, Manager, Genealogy and Local History Department

The Panorama is one of the treasures of PLCHC's Genealogy and Local History Department (Local History), which houses major collections of maps, photographs, rare books, broadsides, and prints. Specialties include the history of the City of Cincinnati and the Ohio and Mississippi River Valleys, books on exploration of the Americas, African American History, Bibles, and authors such as Lafcadio Hearn and Ernest Hemingway. Local History is also known as one of the nation's oldest and largest genealogical research centers.

Charles Fontayne and William S. Porter created the Panorama in September 1848, when photography was in its infancy. It is considered the earliest surviving photograph of an American city and one of the finest examples of Daguerreian photography. The daguerreotype technique, the earliest practical method of photography, was normally used for portraits rather than landscapes. Fontayne and Porter's riverfront view of Cincinnati demonstrated an innovative use of the new medium, making the seven-foot-long framed Panorama a landmark in the history of photography.

To capture the breadth of the Cincinnati waterfront, Fontayne and Porter panned their camera, capturing a series of segments of the growing city's skyline. The resulting images, eight whole-plate daguerreotypes, were dubbed by the photographers the "Daguerreotype View of Cincinnati." The original photograph hung on the walls of the library for the first half of the twentieth century, before its removal to secured storage as a preservation measure. It remained out of public view for 60 years.

In 2006, the library contracted with the George Eastman House International Museum of Photography and Film in Rochester, New York, an internationally known center of photographic preservation, to use the latest technology to preserve the Panorama and to explore the possibility of returning it to public view. Before determining a final treatment plan, the George Eastman House examined the condition of the underlying structure of the image. Using an exceptionally high-resolution microscope the conservators took more than 11,000 separate images of the Panorama, section by section, at up to 32 times magnification. In documenting each section at this level of detail content that had not been easily visible before was now revealed: buildings, signage, topography, boats, people, and even the names of products on the city's waterfront.

The optical science that enabled documentation and restoration of the Panorama also enabled rediscovery of Cincinnati, especially its waterfront, at a crucial moment in its evolution as a key commercial port. This unusual fusion of science and social history also generated new questions about the history of Cincinnati and use of new digital tools to stimulate citizen participant in answering these questions. Restoration of the Panorama was funded through a combination of private grants and support from the federal Institute for Museum and Library Sciences.

Upon completion of the Panorama preservation the Genealogy and Local History Department created the content for an interactive electronic display allowing viewers to examine the newly revealed Panorama in detail, and to zoom in and connect to a historical narrative, original documents, and other related mid-19th century images. The display, available on large screens in the main library and online, gives people the ability to explore the Panorama in ways that would previously have been impossible. The library has also incorporated contributions from viewers concerning family names, stores, shipping, and landmarks. This new knowledge about the social, economic, and architectural life of Cincinnati has not only helped identify previously undocumented images in the Panorama but also added to information about other related items in the collections such as the history of local businesses, religions, families, and so forth. Patricia Van Skaik, Local History Manager, states:

> It is amazing what this one project has done in terms of community engagement. By using new technologies to preserve, reexamine and present the Cincinnati Panorama we have not only brought it back into public view but also opened up avenues for recovering the history of Cincinnati . . . the Panorama is a Time Machine that continues to grow.

The Cincinnati Panorama has been an important catalyst for connecting different audiences of all ages with the collections. Department staff visit fifth grade classrooms to talk about the Panorama, work with high school students on Panorama-related history projects, give tours of the Panorama and related collections, and make presentations to historians, conservators, educators, and photographers.

◉ **CHALLENGES.** The process of documenting the condition and researching the content in the Panorama was time consuming and labor intensive, however, the outcomes were exceptional. Another challenge for Local History staff was carving out the time to do the research and writing that made the interactive platform so successful. According to Skaik, "new forms of archival work need to be integrated into the regular tasks of archival and special collections librarians."

◉ **FUTURE PLANS.** Local History will continue to build its knowledge of nineteenth-century Cincinnati through exploration of the Panorama, including communications with visitors to the Panorama interactive display. Beyond the Panorama project, the department is planning projects that extend access to local history programming through use of digital tools. Working with the local organization Art Works, for example, the library is developing historical content from its collection that will electronically link to an artist-created map/mural depicting life in one of the city's historic German neighborhoods.

◉ **RELATED PROGRAMS.** Local History carries out numerous public programs: exhibitions, including online exhibitions; a Veterans Oral History Project; and collaborations with educational and professional organizations around historical themes and projects. Some programs are videotaped and available via podcast. The department worked with WGBH and PBS to create the local content for a national app on Abolition and also worked with FOX 19, a local television station, to help develop a Cincinnati Timeline that appears on the station's Facebook page.

COLUMBUS MEMORY
Columbus (OH) Metropolitan Library

OVERVIEW: Columbus Memory: Visualizing Columbus's Past (Columbus Memory) is a digital repository of Columbus history developed jointly by the Local History and Genealogy Division of the Columbus Metropolitan Library (CML) and the Columbus History Society. Columbus Memory brings together historical materials from existing archival collections and other institutions and individuals. This collaborative initiative encourages public and institutional contributions and provides access to thousands of primary documents, images, maps, and artifacts pertaining to the city of Columbus and the surrounding area. Columbus Memory is also designed for classroom use, particularly for Ohio's third-grade students.

> This project is something that the Columbus Library can offer for residents that no one other institution can do. It provides a means of preserving and sharing historical collections, it enables classroom use of primary materials, and it broadens Columbus residents' understanding of their local and regional history.
>
> —Angela O'Neal, Local History and Genealogy Division Manager

CML's Local History and Genealogy Division provides researchers and members of the general public with a wide array of resources: maps, city directories, census records, family history information, city histories, newspapers, and genealogical databases. Key collections include African American History, Huguenot History, Insurance Maps, Historic Images of Columbus and Northern Ohio, postcards, and historic Columbus buildings. Many items are digitized and form part of the library's Digital Collections.

Starting in 2008, CML staff and staff from the Columbus Historical Society (CHS) discussed a joint project to digitize and share local history collections with the public through an online repository. Several factors prompted their planning. Other digital archives projects had been started in Ohio, demonstrating the possibilities for bringing institutional collections together to create online local history collections. Both institutions anticipated increased interest in the city's history during the 2012 Bicentennial, and wanted to have an online archive of the city available. In addition, library staff was seeking ways to support the library's commitment to helping city schools achieve their reading and writing goals for Columbus third graders.

In 2009, the library received a one-year grant to establish a digital archive of Columbus. The project was launched in August 2010 with three initial goals: (1) to establish an online archive of Columbus history; (2) to create a tool for classroom use by Columbus City Schools' third-grade teachers; and (3) to provide the means for local institutions such as historical societies to digitize their material. In the first phase of Columbus Memory library staff worked with CHS to scan and upload close to 3,000 items. In that first year, they benefited from significant donations, including a large postcard collection and a collection of sheet music. Over time they have added collections of Columbus-related material from many organizations including the German Village Historical Society and the Ohio Historical Society.

Beyond institutional donations, an important aspect of Columbus Memory is the inclusion of items owned by residents who agree to have them included in the online collection. The library scans these items, records the information provided by the donor, and uploads them to the site. In this way the overall picture of Columbus Memory is enriched by noninstitutional collections, and residents are able to have a direct role in shaping the historical record of their community. To encourage donations, CML operates a community collection process whereby customers can "drop off" historical materials at the library's branch locations. After going through a short intake process, library staff transport the item(s) to the main library for digitization and metadata. The items are then returned to the branch and the customer notified that they are ready for pickup. CML staff also organize scanning events at branches, attend community events, and sometimes digitize items on-the-spot.

To fulfill their educational goal project staff created tools for teachers that would help them use the site as part of the third-grade social studies curriculum. State academic standards require students to learn about historic events and place them on a timeline, and to learn about primary documents, images, and maps. To meet these requirements, CML staff created a teacher resource page that includes an interactive timeline of the city, essays on topics of local interest, and lesson plans written by Columbus Historical Society staff. The partners have also worked with local teachers to familiarize them with the site and how its content can enrich third-grade social studies.

Library staff organizes varied public programs related to Columbus Memory to generate interest in site content and deepen understanding of particular topics. For instance, during 2014 African American History month the library worked with a charter school to offer a story contest for young people. Students were encouraged to write stories based on an image, document, or map they found on Columbus Memory. The program was designed to engage residents and to stimulate participants to use both creative and writing skills to interpret a historical topic.

Columbus Memory is marketed in several ways. The library has a special feature on Facebook and Twitter pages titled "Historic Photo Friday" that takes viewers to the Columbus Memory site. The site has a bimonthly newsletter and is visible on multiple social media channels. CML also operates a Historic Columbus images board on Pinterest. In 2013, library staff were able to improve their site use tracking through a software upgrade that included being able to tell what particular items attract the most interest. For example, full-text materials such as genealogy books, yearbooks, and newspapers are proving to be more heavily used than photographs. Staff are considering the impact on digitization priorities and may shift to digitizing more text-based materials in the short term.

CML has taken the lead in organizing partners, maintaining the site, and reaching out to attract new donations. The project initially involved close collaboration between the library and CHS. The partnership has now expanded to include other contributing institutions such as the Columbus Jewish Historical Society, the Columbus Development Department, and the Urban League. In addition to these collaborative relationships, educational use of Columbus Memory has been one of the most positive outcomes. The Columbus 2012 Bicentennial Commission included the site as part of a toolkit designed for use in the schools, which helped to ensure use by teachers, a primary target audience. Students from local schools also can do social studies projects where they use the digital collection before coming in to the library, allowing the time in the library to be much more focused.

Angela O'Neal, Local History and Genealogy program manager, states that the project has multiple benefits:

> For the library, Columbus Memory opens up special collections to individuals and institutions worldwide, thereby extending the library's reach beyond Central Ohio. It enables preservation of collections, it ties into the library's goals for enhancing the literacy skills of third graders, and it helps staff get feedback and expand collections in ways that would otherwise not be possible.

CML was awarded a grant from the federal Institute for Museum and Library Services (IMLS), administered through the State Library of Ohio, to create Columbus Memory. In 2010, the State Library of Ohio cited Columbus Memory as an Exemplary Program in its LSTA Report to IMLS:

> Columbus Memory is an example of how digitization partnership projects should be planned, implemented and evaluated and as a model for library and historical society/museum cooperation and collaboration.

◉ **CHALLENGES.** The process of collecting historical materials from organizations and institutions can be challenging, requiring that protocols be in place to ensure that legal releases are completed, materials are documented properly, and that customers understand the selection criteria for the project. Another challenge is the need for appropriate equipment to maintain the site and keep it operating in a sophisticated online environment.

◉ **FUTURE PLANS.** Columbus Memory continues to grow and add new partners throughout central Ohio. As its scope expands CML is working to develop a new name and brand for Columbus Memory. There is also an emphasis on promoting the collection through digital media to expand use both locally and worldwide. Library staff recently uploaded metadata from the digital collection to WorldCat. In addition, in 2013, CML received a grant from the IMLS/LSTA to create a Digital Hub in central Ohio. Part of a larger, statewide project that resulted in four Digital Hubs, the Central Ohio Hub project will offer specialized equipment, storage, and consulting services to libraries and other organizations in the region.

CREATING YOUR COMMUNITY
Colorado's Social Archive
Denver Public Library

OVERVIEW: Creating Your Community: Colorado's Social Archive (CYC) is a three-part "social archives" project that includes an interactive website, preservation education in the community, and digitization of collections donated by the community for inclusion on the website. Building on an earlier project to digitize collections donated by residents of Denver's historic neighborhoods, CYC enables users to add content to the collection of community-generated materials and to interact with one another. The project is a collaboration between Denver Public

Library's (DPL) Western History/Genealogy Department (Western History) and a variety of partner institutions. As a forerunner of other community memory projects and interactive websites, CYC offers an example of how to use a combination of outreach and digital technologies to increase community participation in local history collecting.

> **While archives generally work behind the scenes organizing and preserving historical documents, records and photographs for future generations, the hippest archives are seeking to embrace participatory culture to create social archives which include anyone with an interest in helping to collect and preserve local history.**
>
> —Creating Your Community/Website Introduction

CYC was developed by Western History, one of the largest public library special collections in Colorado, which includes many distinct collections such as: Western Art, maps, railroad history, Western and Colorado settlement, genealogy, medical history, the city of Denver, and conservation. The Blair-Caldwell African-American Research Library is also a part of the department. Western History is used by researchers throughout the country and the world interested in the Trans-Mississippi West. However, until relatively recently, the department did not have substantial materials on Denver's neighborhoods or smaller communities in the metropolitan area. To address this need Western History created a social archive, or community history forum, known as Creating Your Community (CYC).

CYC started initially as Creating Communities: Digitizing Denver's Historic Neighborhoods. The Project was prompted by staff visits to Denver neighborhoods for which they had no documentary materials. In seeking out primary sources, they realized that such sources exist—in people's houses, scrapbooks, shoeboxes, and attics—but that their owners, proud to bring them out and talk about them, would not part with the originals. Jamie Seemiller, who became project administrator for Creating Communities, states:

> A light bulb came on. . . . the idea of not taking the originals for the collection but, rather, copying them and leaving them with their owners . . . in this way we could create a local history Facebook.

In 2007, Seemiller and her colleagues applied for and received a three-year federal Institute for Museum and Library Services (IMLS) grant for Creating Communities.

The funding enabled Western History staff to develop a cadre of partners such as municipal and county offices, educational institutions, and historical societies, and to gather information on Denver neighborhoods from these partners and official records. These materials were digitized and brought together in a centralized digital repository. This first project phase demonstrated how diverse groups could collaborate to create a rich historical information database easily accessible by local residents.

In 2010, the department received a second multiyear IMLS grant to expand the project into a participatory archive. Creating Your Community: Empowering Individuals and Safeguarding Communal Heritage through Digital Community Archiving (CYC) built on the original project concept by conducting more outreach to a wider group of citizens in the region and expanding the partner base to the greater Denver metropolitan area. The second grant made it possible to hire technical and other specialists to help conduct outreach, develop software, establish appropriate policies regarding rights, and create born-digital neighborhood collections. The project also included education to help participants learn how to preserve family and local records. Project staff conducted 60 to 90 scanning events per year and reached out to the public at fairs, markets, high school reunions, and other "big memory events." Denver residents responded, with more than 1,000 submissions of personal content in the two-year project period, ranging from Twitter messages to photo albums.

According to department staff, the CYC model is based on the concept of "participatory archives," which enable users to share and connect with their history. "By diminishing the top-down approach to history collecting and history making, the project focuses on residents as 'content experts' rather than library archivists or partner organizations."

Since 2013, department personnel have been working on ways to sustain the most useful and popular components of the project as part of the department's Digital Collections and regular programming. Within Western History's Digital Collections website visitors have the option to visit CYC, and to do many of the functions that were developed during the prior project phases. In that way the library continues to offer a highly participatory and personalized approach that enables users to continue to contribute local, personal, and family items to share with the wider community. Users can "curate" their own collections with images from DPL and the original partner sources, while doing so within the context of the library's Digital Collections.

Western History uses a variety of approaches to engage residents and visitors with its resources. A newly designed website, launched in September 2014, invites viewers to "explore" Western History's collections and offers user-friendly portals for entering different subject areas such as CYC. Staff uses social media channels to strengthen the department's visibility and encourage viewers to use the collections and take part in CYC and on-site programs. Western History also uses Historypin to interact with members of the public who want to take part in Departmental projects and/or contribute their own historical records.

> **CHALLENGES.** Western History staff report that the primary challenge is to sustain the project as a fully participatory endeavor, given the high level of internal technical expertise required and the growing storage costs. Without special funding there is only one staff member to work on the project, limiting outreach and the capacity to be technically up-to-date. Staff had anticipated the issue of sustainability, and developed plans for integrating CYC with its Digital Collections and the Western History website, thereby maintaining key portions of the project as part of a stable institutional platform.

> **FUTURE PLANS.** Staff plan to continue working on CYC, to the extent possible, with an emphasis on integrating and sustaining it within the library's evolving digital communications infrastructure.

CROWDSOURCING PROJECTS
San Francisco Public Library

OVERVIEW: San Francisco Public Library's (SFPL) History Center/Book Arts & Special Collections (SFHC/BASC) has used crowdsourcing and other social media tools to engage specialist volunteers and members of the public in helping to contextualize digitized images and maps with detailed descriptive information. Through a series of crowdsourcing projects, including OldSF and History Mysteries, and through hackathons and organizational partnerships, the library and its users have benefited from new knowledge about digital assets that depict the evolution of the City of San Francisco.

The impact of social media on what we are doing is huge. We are getting enormous and helpful feedback from community members who can identify the content and locations of photographs in the collection.

—Christina Moretta, Curator, Photographic Collections,
San Francisco History Center/Book Arts & Special Collections

The Daniel E. Koshland San Francisco History Center, a major component of SFHC/BASC, contains a rich research collection that documents all aspects of San Francisco life and history. Holdings include books, periodicals and newspapers, historic photographs, maps, posters, manuscript collections, and ephemera. In order to raise the profile of these collections, increase public engagement with history, and fill in knowledge that heretofore did not exist, the library has developed a series of projects that involve community partnerships, crowdsourcing, and the use of social media tools. The involvement of knowledgeable volunteers and enthusiastic members of the public have made possible digitization of key portions of the collections while also adding to collective knowledge about the city and its neighborhoods.

OLDSF. OldSF is based on the Historical Photograph Collection that contains photographs of San Francisco and California, and works on paper, ranging from 1850 to the present. The collection includes street scenes, views of buildings, neighborhoods, residents, and famous personalities along with the extensive photo morgue of the daily *San Francisco News-Call Bulletin* with images dating from the 1920s to 1965. The collection also contains slides, stereoviews, albums, postcards, cabinet cards, and lantern slides of local subjects.

Starting over a decade ago library staff began to digitize its historical photographs, with more than 40,000 now available for public access online. However, while digitization made materials more accessible, especially to researchers, they were not necessarily better known to the public at large. In addition, while the digital images could be searched by neighborhood, street, date, building, person's name, and keywords from a library database, essential information on content was still missing for a large number of the images, limiting the searchability and usefulness of the collection. OldSF was started in order to involve geocoding experts and enthusiasts in helping situate the library's historical photographs geographically. Using a large map of the city and tools developed by two volunteers, participants have geocoded approximately 14,000 images from the collection. OldSF has drawn over 300,000 visitors since its launch in mid-2011.

HISTORY MYSTERIES. In 2014, the Historical Photograph Collection partnered with Historypin, as part of the latter's "Year of the Bay Project." The first batch of 500 images, 1964 photographs taken by local photographer Alan Canterbury, kicked off the experimental project History Mysteries. Based on the mapping work accomplished through OldSF, the photographs all had location codes. The "mystery" to solve was to overlap the older photographs on current street views and to see how the locations look today in comparison. Users with Historypin accounts can make comments and suggestions about locations, dates, and street views. The Historypin comments are complemented by tweets and Facebook comments added in by staff. As the project has taken off, the focus has started to be more and more neighborhood specific, with people examining photos, for instance, of Divisadero Street or particular locations in the Western Division neighborhood. This is a continuing project.

1905 SANBORN MAPS PROJECT (1905). is based on the SFHC/BASC Map Collection, which includes a full set of Sanborn Insurance Maps—the only set to survive the 1906 San Francisco earthquake—and large format maps from different periods in the city's history. Through a partnership with local map guru David Rumsey the library was able to digitize the Sanborn Maps. The online maps generated new interest in the overall collection and a local design and technology studio created a geolocating alignment tool, enabling hundreds of 1905 Sanborn Insurance maps to be matched to current maps of San Francisco. The 1905 project was followed by the digitization of 164 San Francisco Aerial Views from 1938 offering large-scale black and white photographs for public use online.

As a means of stimulating public participation in History Mysteries and prior crowdsourcing projects, the library has held several "hackathons" in different neighborhood locations. Using rarely seen photographs from the library's collections—or those of its hackathon partners—library staff help people use a variety of technological tools to help build better historical information. Hackathon partners include the California Historical Society and the San Francisco Maritime National Historic Park. The hackathons and online dialogues are expanding the constituency for the library's historic maps and photographs.

As SFHC/BASC has experimented with these and other crowdsourcing initiatives, staff has made sure to build visibility for the projects through other social media channels: Twitter, Facebook, Tumblr, and so on. In this way they are able to use different social media for different purposes, with each reinforcing the other. Flickr has proven to be an especially useful tool for expanding access to the Historical Photographs Collection. After staff uploaded an initial set of 20 photographs, the set received 2,250 hits per month. These levels of use have continued as additional photos have been uploaded.

❯ CHALLENGES. One initial challenge in carrying out the crowdsourcing projects was the need to integrate the Historical Photograph Collection outreach with the library's overall website. However, as the online photographic collection has developed its own identity, that issue has become less important. SFHC/BASC also faces the challenge of staff shortages which slow down the process of digitizing photographs and creating related metadata.

❯ FUTURE PLANS. According to Photographic Collections Curator Christina Moretta, the Historical Photographs Collection is an "amazing" collection, with much that has not yet been digitized. She plans to focus on creating the metadata necessary for digitizing images and continuing to put images online. She also intends to continue the crowdsourcing projects, which have had such positive results.

DC BY THE BOOK

District of Columbia Public Library

OVERVIEW: DC by the Book is an interactive web-based map that locates fictional references to District of Columbia locales. Developed by the District of Columbia Public Library's Special Collections Department (Special Collections), and benefiting from contributions from individuals and groups, the site includes a wide range of citations. By featuring and crowdsourcing information on the literary landscape of the District of Columbia, organizers are involving diverse audiences in contributing to and learning about local history and literature.

> Projects like DC by the Book are invaluable. They give us the confidence to experiment and to reach new audiences in new ways.
>
> —Kim Zablud, Manager, Special Collections

DC by the Book is a special project of Special Collections, which was formed in 2008 to join multiple components: the Black Studies Center; the Peabody Room Collection, which is focused on the history of Georgetown; a major collection of illustrated children's books; and the library's long-standing collection of Washingtoniana, encompassing documents, maps, organizational archives, photographs, news clippings, and the DC Community Archives. Department staff developed DC by the Book as a way of testing the use of digital tools to engage new audiences with the library and with community culture and history. The project reflects the vision of Special Collection Manager Kim Zablud, who asks: "Special Collections work in an urban public library is about exciting different segments of the community. What can we accomplish for each neighborhood and for the public at large?"

DC by the Book is an interactive web-based map that locates fictional references to District of Columbia locales. Started by two senior staff, one in Special Collections and the other in administration, it involves collaboration between librarians, experts in local fiction, local history organizations, and visitors to the site. Unlike most other literary maps, DC by the Book does not focus on authors but, rather, shines a light on the streets and life of Washington. It expresses the nonfederal character of the nation's capital, and engages readers of fiction to contribute their favorite place-based references.

Contributors to DC by the Book highlight and crowdsource passages from the (largely undiscovered) body of literature set in DC that illuminates its social and geographic history. Special events and "mapathons" at branch libraries stimulate public involvement. Organizers curate the recommended passages to ensure a level of consistency and presentation. Users plug in a location, with a specific address or a neighborhood, to browse through multiple relevant entries nearby. DC by the Book received a start-up grant from the federal Institute of Museum and Library Services and has received additional support from local partners and the Humanities Council of Washington, D.C.

Started in 2012 the project has grown rapidly, stimulating interest and contributions from readers of all ages and parts of the country and from many organizations. It offers opportunities for integrating works associated with historical events, such as a Civil War Fiction Book List, and with contemporary special events, such as a set of passages associated with the city's annual Local Pride Festival. Citations range from the Greek-owned diner in George Pelicano's *The Turnaround* to the 1945 description of Foggy Bottom as an industrial wasteland in Aly Monroe's novel *Washington Shadow*. In its focus on fiction the site explores "the nonfederal civic life of Washington and its character as a city."

The curators of DC by the Book are gratified by the project's success. It has not only stimulated new public involvement with library collections but it has also prompted staff to create spin-off applications including Tours and Apps. Using the content embedded in the site, library staff has organized walking tours, including a highly popular tour of sites associated with "Harlem Renaissance in DC." Organizers have also created apps for self-guided tours using iPhone or Android devices. Each tour features a route of sites that have been depicted in fiction and is accompanied by a map for easy navigation. Some stops on the tours include photographs, audio, and historical information to enhance users' experiences. Tours of Foggy Bottom and U Street/Howard are complete and others are in the works.

DC by the Book is both experimental and visible, and has launched Special Collections on a path of using technology to create content in surprising new ways. There has been no prior effort to identify and aggregate the many fictional references to District of Columbia, much less an effort to do so using a combination of archival expertise and the knowledge of readers to build an interactive digital reference map. The map, expressing the character of the city through literature, provides a wholly new perspective on how the nation's capital has been described, perceived, and exploited for imaginative purposes. The accumulation of contributions from members of the public, who represent the widest possible spectrum of backgrounds, provides another perspective—that of the reader.

 ● **CHALLENGES**. With the strong response to DC by the Book, Special Collections faces the need to "define the boundaries of the project." With so many potential avenues and citations to explore, and so many different interest groups and neighborhood organizations to involve, the project has taken on a life of its own. One part-time staff member is now dedicated to the project, and others become involved with outreach events. Special Collections is dedicating resources to select aspects, and building capacity with librarians throughout the system in order to define and sustain the project.

 ● **FUTURE PLANS**. DC by the Book curators are looking ahead to other ways that they can institutionalize DC by the Book and engage even more varied audiences. Having asked people to help build something, and presented the data in ways that are rich and interesting, library staff now plan to involve such audiences as local business owners, teachers, writers, photographers, and more. They may work with teens on a summer series to curate a new tour. The programming will help attract attention and participation. Special Collections also plans to expand its involvement in digital humanities and map-based storytelling through collaboration with the local nonprofit MapStory.

 ● **RELATED PROGRAMS**. DC by the Book is one of several strategies for engaging the public with special collections. Oral history is another strategy. Special Collections organized interviews on the occasion of the fiftieth anniversary of the historic March on Washington, and has started an oral history project titled U Street: Memories from Duke Ellington to capture the stories and experiences associated with the U Street area, which has historically been a cultural crossroads in the city. Special Collections staff is also working closely with managers at the branch libraries to connect residents of different neighborhoods to their own histories through "Know Your Neighborhood" history workshops. These programs consist of a program series built around community interests, featuring dynamic speakers and opportunities for community interaction around topics of local interest. The events, which have drawn substantial attendance, have also helped to identify documents and stories to add to the library's collections.

DES PLAINES MEMORY
Des Plaines (IL) Public Library

OVERVIEW: Des Plaines Memory is an online archive of historical materials that reflects the historical and social development of Des Plaines. It is a collaborative effort of the Des Plaines Public Library (DPPL), the Des Plaines History Center (History Center), and Des Plaines residents who contribute content by uploading directly to the website. Started in November 2011, the project is continuously evolving in response to community interests and technology capacities. Des Plaines Memory is an excellent example of the trend in public libraries to take the lead in their communities in experimenting with digital tools that stimulate involvement with community history.

> **Des Plaines Memory is a community- driven project . . . Our role is not so much to build collections, but to facilitate the user-generated content.**
>
> —Steven F. Giese, Digital Projects Librarian

Des Plaines Memory emerged from discussions between DPPL and the History Center regarding the potential to join forces to engage more people with local history. DDPL's history collections are limited, consisting of books, telephone directories, local newspapers on microfilm, and vertical clippings files. The History Center archives contain larger collections of documents, artifacts, and photographs, but public access is limited to in-person visits. In 2011, staff from both institutions took part in ILEAD USA (Innovative Libraries Explore, Apply and Discover), an initiative developed by the Illinois State Library to prepare library and archives staff to carry out digital projects. Through this initiative the History Center received funding to start digitizing its archival collections—the basis for Des Plaines Memory.

DDPL leads the history archive project, with a Digital Projects Librarian who manages content and handles technical issues. The partner organizations invite community residents and local groups to submit images, records, and stories pertaining to personal, family, and local history. The project has received many contributions that have expanded the collective knowledge of the city of Des Plaines from the early 1800s to the present day. Materials range from photographs, postcards, documents, and artwork to firsthand information about individual items from the history center archives not previously known to the sponsors. The project is evolving as the sponsors and the project manager respond to local needs and interests. Steven F. Giese, manager of the site, states:

> Des Plaines Memory is a special digital collection, but it's intended to be used as a platform for storytelling—collective community storytelling—that complements formal research. In many ways we are doing what libraries have done all along, that is helping people access stories and useful information.

Outreach has been one useful strategy for building Des Plaines Memory. According to Giese, the community of users has been built person by person, by establishing relationships with library and History Center stakeholders. He works with organizations and individuals who request help in managing and scanning their records. He does not mediate or filter what people want to include on the site; he sees his role and the partners' roles as facilitating use of the site by the public.

Use of social media has been important in building a constituency for Des Plaines Memory. Facebook, Twitter, Tumblr, Flickr, and Pinterest pages drive visitors to Des Plaines Memory. Unexpectedly, the Des Plaines Memory social media accounts have generated smaller, satellite communities of followers that may or may not contribute to the digital archives. Giese believes that engaging in social networks adds value to the brand, and he frequently posts "bonus content" to the new followers.

◉ **CHALLENGES.** Giese states that "the big challenge is how to be responsive, flexible, and experimental as the project evolves. Like a shark, it has to keep moving forward or die." Successful partnering with community groups is another issue. "Sometimes organizations want to share what they have with the world but become uneasy about putting their materials online." In addition, as the site expands, there will be issues of sustainability in terms of staffing and server storage costs.

◉ **FUTURE PLANS.** No immediate changes are foreseen for Des Plaines Memory. The next significant phase will likely involve integrating the digital collections with programming at the library and History Center.

EXPERIMENTS IN CITIZEN CARTOGRAPHY
New York (NY) Public Library

OVERVIEW: New York Public Library's (NYPL) vast collection of sheet maps, books, and atlases provides the basis for two experiments in "citizen cartography" being carried out by the Lionel Pincus and Princess Firyal Map Division (Map Division) in partnership with NYPL Labs (Labs) and open-source software developers (Topomancy LLC). The first project invites citizens to help georeference the library's antiquarian map collection using the NYPL Map Warper, a tool created by Topomancy and supported by Labs. The second project involves "engineers, tinkerers, designers and map aficionados" to use another new tool, built by Labs—Building Inspector—that involves tracing the geography of New York's past. Both projects demonstrate how a research collection can involve members of the public by using their knowledge to improve information about and access to the collections.

> We are mobilizing citizens of New York to fill in their own history. Everyone involved is learning and contributing. There is serious quid pro quo. We are benefiting from the skills and perspectives of participants while they are developing closer connections to the collections.
>
> —Matt Knutzen, Geospatial Librarian, The Lionel Pincus and Princess Firyal Map Division

NYPL's Map Division is one of the most important map collections in the world. Its holdings include more than 433,000 sheet maps and 20,000 books and atlases published between the fifteenth and the twenty-first centuries. The collections represent the entire globe; many items are unique or rare; some have broad international significance and others reflect the evolution of New York and its environs. With a diverse constituency that includes planners, architects, geographers, historians, ecologists, novelists, and archaeologists, the Division has long been a center for research and discovery concerning "place" and "space."

In 2008–2009 Map Division staff started to work closely with a newly formed unit, NYPL Labs, that had a mandate to design and test digital tools for enhancing knowledge and use of the library's research collections. Having accomplished a significant amount of digitization, Map Division leaders were interested in exploring how to create indexes and pathways into the digital collections and, also, how to leverage New Yorkers' knowledge of the city to enhance the metadata associated with local collections. Geospatial Librarian Matt Knutzen recalls early discussions about crowdsourcing:

Once we had scanned and digitized a critical mass of material from our holdings we started to ask ourselves "what are we going to do with it? Is this just a digital service copy or is it something else?" We realized that more detailed descriptive information would be needed and that we might leverage the experience and knowledge of interested members of the general public to improve the usability of the collections.

Working together, Labs technologists, map librarians, and curators explored the possibilities for creating new tools that would transform digitized maps from routine digital photos to contextualized, searchable digital objects. Two significant projects, both of which are ongoing, were the result of their collaboration. Both projects benefit from support to NYPL Labs from the National Endowment for the Humanities; Map Warper was also supported by the federal Institute for Museum and Library Services.

MAP WARPER. Map Warper was one of the early projects undertaken by Labs, working in partnership with contracted software developers and the Map Division. The project focused on a collection of nearly 9,000 historical maps of New York City that had been digitized but were not contextualized or connected to other items in the collections. The Map Division decided to experiment with georectification—a process used by cartographers to rectify maps in relation to the earth—to create a tool for enriching the information associated with each map so that it could be linked to other maps. The resulting Map Warper tool is actually a suite of tools, used by Map Division staff but also available to members of the public, that aligns or rectifies historical maps to today's digital maps. By rectifying early maps and old atlas sheets with later maps and contemporary maps, users and researchers can explore the evolution of the New York cityscape over time.

Development of the Map Warper tool was the start of a public engagement process that has involved recruitment and training of "citizen cartographers" who are helping build a virtual, historically layered, atlas of New York City. The Map Division has built a series of courses to help volunteers interested in participating in the map warping project. Recruitment has taken place via blog posts, social media channels, and professional associations. Some professors at LIS schools have assigned the project while in other classes students have participated as a public service elective. Individuals from a variety of disciplines are involved, ranging from landscape architects and urban planners to architectural historians. Volunteers are registered in an account management system. As of August 2014 there were 12,000 registered Map Warper participants, and a constant flow of maps being rectified.

BUILDING INSPECTOR. A second collaboration between the Map Division and Labs addresses the need to extract information from nineteenth-century insurance atlases. The insurance maps offer rich detail such as building footprints, addresses, and construction materials. For students of New York's history, these details, in combination with other related historical documents, can help flesh out the story of a building, a block, a family, or a historical era. Despite their significance, before Building Inspector the only way to capture the details embedded in the maps was to do so manually on the computer.

To harvest the valuable content in the library's New York insurance maps, Labs staff first created a computer vision algorithm; that is, a process whereby computers can recognize and transcribe building shapes and other data on digitized insurance atlases. The computer output is good, but not perfect. The Building Inspector tool is a mobile-friendly web app that enables users to check the computer transcriptions and identify other valuable information building by building. They can add street numbers, classify buildings with colors, and fix incorrect building outlines. To ensure a consistent level of quality no data input by members of the public is permanently entered or published until many other "inspectors" have checked it and at least 75 percent of them have agreed with the entry.

Knutzen describes the Building Inspector process as "massively distributed historical geodata barn-raising." Many of the same volunteers who work on Map Warper have also helped with Building Inspector. Focused originally on Manhattan, a second phase of Building Inspector involves transcriptions from atlases depicting Brooklyn. By using a distributed network of citizens to both enter information and review data entered by other helpers the project provides an infrastructure for accomplishing exponentially more data capture than would ever be possible with library staff alone.

❯ **CHALLENGES.** Both Map Warper and Building Inspector provide "proof of principle" that citizens can help enrich archival information and, in so doing, gain deeper understanding of special collections. Despite success, project developers face the problem of sustaining these efforts. In the rapidly changing information technology environment, it is difficult to keep the attention of supporters and funders. However, project managers are committed to institutionalizing the projects and continuing citizen involvement.

❯ **FUTURE PLANS.** The Map Division will continue to collaborate with NYPL Labs on experiments that "transform digitized collections into discoverable data through public engagement." One concept for the future involves using data from maps to track changes in Native American populations over time. Another has to do with linking information gleaned from maps with digital objects in other parts of the library's vast collections. The scale of such projects will require citizen archivists of the sort that have been involved in Map Warper and Building Inspector.

THE HOUSTON PUBLIC LIBRARY EXHIBIT SNAPSHOT

Houston Metropolitan Research Center, Houston Public Library

OVERVIEW: The Houston Public Library's (HPL) Houston Metropolitan Research Center (HMRC) has developed an innovative software tool, The Houston Public Library's Exhibit Snapshot (THPLES), that enables remote viewers to experience in-library exhibitions through a virtual tour, close-up views of exhibition panels and captions, access to details on individual images and objects, and opportunities to ask questions about or comment on the objects and exhibition themes. By delivering collections-based exhibitions for visitors who cannot attend physically, the library is maximizing access to its collections and expertise while using its physical and digital spaces for the benefit of an unlimited public. This model for participatory virtual exhibitions was demonstrated with HMRC's 2012 exhibition Faces, Places and Spaces. It reflects efforts by archivists and curators to use new strategies for engaging on-site and online visitors with collections and exhibitions.

> **The Houston Public Library's Exhibit Snapshot is a tool that helps us fulfill the library's mission to "Link People to the World." Exhibit Snapshots for our in-library exhibitions complement these exhibitions, preserve them in digital format, and enable anyone, anywhere to access them and interact with them. The Snapshot tool also makes our internal work more efficient by linking preservation and research with digitization, education and outreach.**
>
> —Elizabeth Sargent, Assistant Director for Special Collections and Director, Houston Metropolitan Research Center

In 2011 HPL completed a major project to restore its landmark Julia Ideson Building, including a new Archival Wing for an elegant exhibition hall and expanded spaces for public services, public programming, digital functions, and collections care and processing. HMRC is now able to present and interpret more of its collections, thereby attracting more people to the library and to the archives.

Prior to moving into the Archival Wing of the Ideson Building, HMRC carried out a regular schedule of exhibitions in the galleries at the Central Library. Drawing on its rich collections HMRC offered major exhibitions and smaller displays. Within its expanded public spaces HMRC presents a regular schedule of exhibitions, most of which are based on the library's own collections, along with a few that involve collaborations with community partners to showcase aspects of Houston history.

With the move to expanded quarters, HMRC has devoted more resources to exhibitions while also dovetailing exhibition work with other departmental priorities such as digital access. In the process of planning for expanded exhibition work HMRC staff identified three considerations to inform their work: (1) to highlight materials from the collections that might not otherwise be known to the public; (2) to use library exhibitions to create virtual exhibitions that can "remain alive to inspire and inform online visitors over time"; and (3) to encourage on-site viewers to interact with the materials on display.

To accomplish the second objective HPL digital staff worked with HMRC staff to design a special software tool titled THPLES. THPLES offers online visitors a virtual and interactive exhibition experience. Visitors can take a self-guided 360 degree tour of the exhibition, they can zoom in to read exhibition panels and captions, examine close-up views of individual objects and images, search an image database, and enter commentary or ask questions about these items.

The design of THPLES allows HMRC to achieve a number of complementary goals: greater internal efficiency by linking archival processing, research, digitization, exhibition design and production, and online communications; stronger links between the physical archives and the Houston Area Digital Archives, especially for remote visitors; and increased community engagement with the collections.

In 2011, HMRC and HPL digital staff used Faces, Places and Spaces, the second major exhibition in the renovated Ideson Exhibit Hall, to demonstrate THPLES. The exhibition was based on a major collection of glass plate negatives depicting Houston and its citizens from the late 1800s, many of which had already been scanned. HMRC staff selected representative images and organized them into individuals and groups (Faces), street scenes and buildings (Places), and interior and exterior spaces for social gatherings (Spaces). These categories allowed visitors to situate the individual images in a historical context and to make personal and local connections.

As with all major exhibitions, HMRC offered public programs related to the exhibition themes. For their regular Second Saturday series of presentations on aspects of the collections, they organized a dialogue between the HMRC photo archivist and an expert on the history of photography. They collaborated with the Childrens' Services Department to organize programs, including a family program that involved creation of fictional stories about the faces on view in the exhibition. Lectures and movies rounded out the programming, which helped engage visitors beyond the display itself.

HMRC supported development of THPLES through its annual budget and with the assistance of the Digital Projects Manager. The Houston Public Library Foundation, which regularly supports HMRC exhibitions, assisted with Faces, Places and Spaces, as did the Houston Arts Alliance.

THPLES has proven to be highly successful, enabling remote viewers to experience the original exhibition in full while also having access to other relevant sources.

❯ **CHALLENGES.** The design of THPLES was in and of itself a challenge, requiring special technical skills for software development. Involvement of the library's Digital Projects Manager and other technology staff was essential to its completion. It has also been a challenge to obtain the copyright clearances necessary for use of THPLES in future exhibitions.

❯ **FUTURE PLANS.** HMRC staff intends to integrate THPLES with other major exhibitions, using it to broaden access and interaction with the library's special collections. HMRC staff is also planning to expand THPLES to include curriculum kits and lesson plans for classroom use.

JOHN CAGE UNBOUND
A Living Archive
Music Division, New York (NY) Public Library for the Performing Arts

OVERVIEW: John Cage Unbound: A Living Archive (John Cage Unbound) is an experimental archive developed by the Music Division of the New York Public Library for the Performing Arts (Performing Arts Library) to "allow the world to experience" its John Cage Music Manuscript Collection. In content and design the site reflects the philosophy of avant-garde composer John Cage, featuring crowdsourced videos of performances narrated by musicians, students, and others working to interpret Cage's music. It also includes select copies of Cage's manuscripts, photographs, and ephemera. As a source for research, a performance forum, and a stimulus for new compositions, it is an instructive example of a new type of archive, a "living archive."

We want to inspire and engage with John Cage's unique vision of music and its role in the world. In doing so, we hope to advance our knowledge of Cage and his work by sparking a global conversation among musicians, artists, and creative thinkers.

—Jonathan Hiam, Curator of American Music and The Rodgers and Hammerstein Archives of Recorded Sound

The John Cage Music Manuscript Collection is a relatively recent addition to the Music Division of the Performing Arts Library, one of the most comprehensive music collections in the world. The Division documents "the art of music in all its diversity," from jazz and popular music to opera and chamber music. With great strengths in historical materials the Division also collects works of contemporary composers. The American Music Collection, a major component of the Division, documents American classical and popular music and the Iconographic Collection contains images in diverse formats, including 100,000 photographs, relating to musicians, composers, performers, and performances. Other collections feature sheet music, autograph manuscripts, clippings and programs, printed books, scores, and periodicals.

The Division is a center for musical scholarship and a catalyst for performances and musical creations, with a broad professional constituency of performers, conductors, composers, and students of music. According to Jon Hiam, curator of American Music: "We feel that fueling creation is part of our mission."

The John Cage Collection includes manuscripts of nearly all of Cage's musical works as well as sketches and other pre-compositional materials. These materials were acquired in tandem with the archive of Merce Cunningham. The John Cage Trust collaborates with the Music Division in the organization and presentation of the items. With an initial goal of cataloging the John Cage material for use by scholars and musicians, Music Division staff has also sought ways to present the collection that would reflect Cage's unconventional approach to music making, expand the audience for his works, and generate new musical responses. Hiam states:

> The Division's usual digital projects have been functional and austere, offering basic levels of discoverability for hardcore scholars and specialists. The John Cage project was something we wanted to experiment with in order to engage a wider public and professional audience, offering a door into a research collection and a forum for new interpretations of Cage.

Music Division staff decided to carry out an experiment in patron interaction, designing a website that would engage "musicians, artists and creative thinkers" in an online exchange about Cage's work while also stimulating new performances. The resulting site, John Cage Unbound—A Living Archive, is a video archive that presents the work of one of the 20th century's most significant composers while also offering a forum on Cage's work with examples of new performances.

Three goals governed development of John Cage Unbound: (1) encourage user-generated content; (2) reach as many students as possible; and (3) get as many different voices involved as possible. The resulting website reflects these goals. It features crowdsourced videos of performances that were created especially for the site, narrated by musicians, composers, and others who discuss how they prepare for and perform Cage's works. Some of the videos were developed by the library as models for user contributions and others were submitted by remote users. The site also contains digital copies of a select number of manuscripts in the Cage collection plus images and ephemera from other parts of the Music Division that help provide context for the Cage scores. The site is distinguished by its design elements, in which Cage's hand-drawn lines guide users as they scroll through the site.

John Cage Unbound was a pilot project undertaken cooperatively by the Music Division and the library's Communications Division, without special funding. It was a grassroots endeavor that reflected staff creativity and musicians' willingness to assist. There have been numerous responses to the website. Students as well as more seasoned performers have submitted examples of their own interpretations of Cage's works and, even, their own compositions in the spirit of Cage. One submission was a "Water Walk" that featured the sounds of different objects on and in water.

Launch of the project coincided with the centennial of Cage's birth, in September 2012. The Performing Arts Library and the Music Division commemorated the centennial with a live event that featured a performance by Margaret Leng Ten, one of the artists showcased in the online performance videos, an announcement of the publication of *John Cage's Prepared Piano*—a new edition of the library's periodical series—and the official launch of the John Cage Unbound website.

Site developers have learned a great deal from the experimental archive, such as whether and how to use social media channels to build audiences, and the need for audio tools to enrich users' experience of the music. Developed as an experiment, the site has achieved its goals of "inspiring and engaging," and providing a central access point for anyone interested in Cage.

The combination of user-submitted content, performance videos created especially for the site, links to videos posted on other platforms such as YouTube or Vimeo, selections from the Cage Collection, and other related research materials makes a robust and dynamic site that contrasts with more conventional online catalogs of manuscript collections.

❯ **CHALLENGES.** Developers of John Cage Unbound have confronted challenges that reflect the nontraditional content and original configuration of the site. One is the question of whether or not to integrate a finer research component into the site by including every Cage piece with links to the online catalog and the Cage publisher's catalog. Another challenge is how to distinguish clearly between the performance videos produced by the library as examples and those submitted by site users. These and other challenges will be dealt with if and when the site becomes more than an experiment and is institutionalized.

● **FUTURE PLANS.** Since 2012, when John Cage Unbound was launched, NYPL has undergone internal changes that affect the Communications Division and digital projects in general. There is now a more centralized Digital Portal that could provide a stable digital home for the site and help address issues of maintenance and technical upgrading. Music Division staff are exploring the options for institutionalizing the site, either through the Digital Portal or as an ongoing feature of the Music Division site and a point of interrogation for the John Cage Music Manuscript Collection.

KENEY PARK APP

Hartford (CT) Public Library

OVERVIEW: The Keney Park App, recently developed by Hartford Public Library's (HPL) Hartford History Center (History Center) in collaboration with the Connecticut Center for Advanced Technology, is a game that leverages young people's familiarity with smartphones to introduce them to geolocation technology and to the history of one of Hartford's primary public parks. As a "mystery," that has to be solved, the app game also prompts participants to become involved with the library's History Center collections. The process of developing the app prototype has enabled History Center staff to experiment with interactive game design and with ways to use digital tools to engage urban youth with community history.

> In a city like Hartford, where people have such social, economic, and language needs, it is a challenge to figure out how to make a difference with our special collections. If we can get the right hook, we can affect how people, including young people, perceive their community and their place in that community.
>
> —Brenda Miller, Chief Cultural Affairs and Public Programming Officer

HPL's History Center is a multimedia research collection that reflects the more than 300-year history of the city of Hartford. The collection includes Hartford imprints, city directories, scrapbooks, trade publications, art, ephemera, postcards, photographs, nearly complete runs of the city's historic newspapers, and a collection of books by Hartford authors. Through programming the History Center involves adults with the collections; staff is also concerned about reaching more young people. They recognize that many students are unaware of the history collections and the ways in which they might access and use material relevant to their interests, school projects, and their community.

The Keney Park App serves as an "electronic field guide" and a game based on the rich history of one of Hartford's public parks. Designed as a quest, the app prompts participants to explore the History Center collections in order to solve challenges embedded in the game. The app was developed as an experiment, catalyzed by staff perception that many teenagers, while used to digital media, especially smartphones, were using it primarily to consume popular culture. They were not being exposed to new educational tools and games or applications such as geolocation technology.

Working with the Connecticut Center for Advanced Technology and a group of volunteer educators, History Center staff first explored several concepts for using technology to engage teens in history. "We concluded that gamification would allow for broad participation and enable us to present a platform for research and exploration as part of a mystery and a quest." The goal was to use game techniques to create an app that would: (1) be used where the kids are, i.e. "on their phones"; and (2) stimulate them to take part in a quest to explore the history of one of Hartford's most historic parks.

The History Center crafted a narrative scavenger hunt as a vehicle to get students playing and "competing." The quest involved not only learning GPS and geo-tagging, it also introduced them to primary sources in the library's collection and basic research skills.

As a prototype the app has been tested with groups of students. Among the findings is the need to be sure that young people can read maps, and the importance of using software that can work on multiple types of smartphones and digital devices. The game design and the supporting software have subsequently been tweaked and the app is now awaiting a new round of testing with both educators and young people. The federal Institute for Museum and Library Services funded development of the Keney Park App through a Sparks Grant, which assists in the development of innovative projects.

❯ **CHALLENGES.** According to Brenda Miller, Chief Cultural Affairs and Public Programs Officer, "The greatest challenge was how to make it fun. It required a backstory that would fit the history of Hartford, the park, the eras we were focusing on, historical figures and fictional elements like a villainous society—this all took a tremendous amount of time."

⦿ **FUTURE PLANS.** Following the next round of testing, the app prototype will be further refined. History Center staff is committed to improving the game to the point that it will be easily accessible by all youth and provide a compelling gateway to the History Center collections.

PARTICIPATORY EXHIBITIONS
Chicago Public Library

OVERVIEW: Two recent exhibitions presented by Chicago Public Library's Special Collections—the Special Collections and Preservation Division located at the Harold Washington Library (Special Collections) and the Northside Neighborhood History Collection at the Sulzer Regional Library—involved experimentation with interactive tools to promote public participation. Both engaged contributors and viewers in new ways, and both provoked positive public responses. The exhibitions reflect the trend toward interactive presentations and provide instructive models for other institutions.

> Our patrons have enthusiastically embraced the interactive components of our exhibitions, from children measuring snowfall to adults contributing photographs to our Flickr account. We are actively exploring new interactive technology options for future exhibitions.
>
> —Glen Humphreys, Special Collections Manager

FORCED MIGRATION PHOTOVOICE PROJECT (PHOTOVOICE PROJECT). The Neighborhood History Collection is a long-standing community archive that is expanding as new waves of Chicagoans contribute their memories and documents. Librarian Julie Lynch has been working to increase documentation of contemporary residents, especially newcomers:

Future generations will wonder what it was like to live in the North side at the beginning of the twenty-first century. People are not keeping scrapbooks or diaries or even photographs anymore . . . we have to find other ways to document communities.

In one experiment to address this challenge Lynch used a process known as "photovoice" that allows participants to learn about photography and document their lives through images and stories. To apply this process she sought out a group of people who had been resettled to Chicago from other countries and invited them to tell stories about their impressions of Chicago. Staff from Heartland Alliance's Marjorie Kovler Center for Survivors of Torture and its Refugee and Immigrant Community Services identified nine individuals who had been forced to immigrate and who now live on the Northside. The library loaned digital cameras to the group and asked them to capture images that reflect their new life in Chicago. The group met weekly to share their photos and stories. A local foundation assisted with direct expenses for the project.

Each Photovoice Project participant donated a sample of their work to the library. From these donated photos, they selected one picture to be included in a library exhibition and wrote a description to accompany it. One result of the Photovoice Project was the formation of a new collection of photos and stories from people affected by forced migration. Another was a community-curated exhibition, in the sense that the content was selected and created by project participants. In combination, the collection and the exhibition enabled other community residents to share the newcomers' experiences. In addition, the project gave voice to the participants, many of whom had come to the United States as refugees or asylees. One contributor to the project, Duvin, a former resident of Central America, provided the following picture caption:

> I like this picture a lot because somehow it makes me see how life can change from one moment to the next . . . It also makes me think that everyone has the power to make the necessary changes for a better life.

VIVIAN MAIER: OUT OF THE SHADOWS. Chicago's Special Collections is a major resource on the City of Chicago, with holdings ranging from Illinois in the Civil War to Chicago parks, theater, music, and political history. Through exhibitions, a blog, digital collections, and public programs, Special Collections works to involve members of the public with local history and culture.

In 2014, Special Collections mounted an exhibition of photographs at the Harold Washington Library Center that were taken by Chicago-area resident Vivian Maier. Maier was not a known photographer; she was a housekeeper and nanny throughout her life. Based on a book by Richard Cahan and Michael Williams, the exhibition featured street photographs and self-portraits, mainly everyday people and scenes, taken from the 1950s to the 1970s.

The Vivian Maier exhibition revealed an important but overlooked photographic talent—it also provided an opportunity to engage exhibition visitors who are used to using digital tools to record their lives. Exhibition organizers invited viewers to take their own portraits or street views and to contribute them to the library's Special Collections. As of August 2014, the invitation had resulted in over 3,000 submissions of selfies and street photographs to the library's Flickr account or website address. Many will be added to the collections. Staff is also considering exhibiting a selection of the images elsewhere in the library.

The Forced Migration Photovoice Project and the Vivian Maier: Out of the Shadows exhibiton both reflect the trend in public library special collections to incorporate digital tools into traditional programs as a means of engaging new and younger audiences. They are applicable in other institutions and community settings.

● CHALLENGES. Staff carrying out the Forced Migration Photovoice Project faced two hurdles. The first one, recruiting participants, was solved through working with a partner organization. The second one, finding a time when all participants could meet together, was solved through special scheduling. For the Vivian Maier project, Special Collections staff faced the challenge of managing the unexpectedly large public response to their call for patron-submitted photographs. They had to order extra film and batteries for the cameras in the exhibition hall, and they had far more online submissions than they had expected. These problems, however, were also indications of success in terms of eliciting participation.

● FUTURE PLANS. The Northside Neighborhood History Collection has finished another photovoice session with newcomers to Chicago and will repeat the program in 2015. With respect to future exhibitions that include interactive components, Special Collections Manager Glen Humphreys states that CPL is strongly committed to experimenting with new tools for visitor participation.

SEVEN

LECTURES, CONFERENCES, AND BROADCAST PROGRAMS

Public Library archives are different from academic archives. As part of "The People's University," they have a broader customer base and a mission to make everything as accessible as possible to everyone. That is why public library archives are so special ... where else can you get a history lecture from an expert for free?

—Wayne Dowdy, Manager, Memphis and Shelby County Room

As archivists and special collections librarians seek to expose their collections, attract new patrons, and engage these patrons with ideas and information, they are looking at traditional program formats as well as less common approaches. The formats referenced in this chapter—lectures, conferences, and broadcast programs—are not new, and, yet, they still draw audiences and have value in the public library archival setting. They reflect the variations in programming that can be found within a department or an institution as well as across the library landscape. Most importantly, they reflect a trend toward experimentation with tried-and-true program formats.

Lectures, which are so ubiquitous in the library archive setting, are a format still preferred by many archivists and special collections librarians. They use these events to expose patrons to new scholarship and new ideas relevant to the collections, to stimulate participants to engage in dialogue with one another and with experts, and to deepen participants' understanding of issues embedded in the collections. In the context of national research that indicates more and more older adults, especially baby boomers, are seeking formal and informal learning opportunities, collection-based lectures, symposia, and panel discussions offer natural opportunities to increase adult learners' recognition of special collections as lifelong learning destinations.

The following examples of lectures and lecture series vary widely, from the Sacramento Public Library's Capital Decades, a multi-event annual series that features lectures on the history and culture of specific twentieth-century decades, to the annual Hackley After Dark Lecture Series on the history of music at the Detroit Public Library. Each of these attracts regular participants and newcomers, each showcases new scholarship relevant to the library's collections, and each has garnered media exposure for the library and the special collection. Some library lectures are made available as podcasts, on Vimeo or on YouTube. These lecture approaches indicate that the lecture is not a program type of the past, but is being continually renewed for the benefit of the sponsor collection and the audiences who enjoy this form of learning.

The conference or symposium is another program type that is not new for special collections librarians but has been relatively uncommon. These programs are more typically carried out in academic or special libraries with ready access to scholars and other specialists and regular opportunities for extended discourse based on collections. What does seem to be a trend in public libraries is an increase in regional history symposia or conferences related to an important aspect of a library's special collections.

The Pikes Peak Regional History Symposium is unusual for its scope and size, and for the extent to which the library coordinates Symposium topics with other activities going on in Special Collections, from publications to broadcast programs. The Symposium is also unusual in that it features citizen scholars as well as academics. Similar to the Grand Rapids Public Library's History Detectives symposium, the criteria for selection of presenters emphasizes the local significance of the topic and the quality of the research to be presented. Conferences on specific topics are less common to public library special collections, although there are exceptions, such as the Butler Center for Arkansas Studies' conference on Korean War Veterans. The one-day event helped stimulate wider awareness of the Butler Center's effort to document the impact of the Korean War on Arkansans, brought together diverse stakeholders whose participation has been crucial for collection development and documentation, and helped solidify organizational partnerships that have been important in implementing the Korean War project.

Broadcast programs are a third form of public programming represented in this chapter. They are few and far between, and they usually require substantial resources for implementation, and, yet, it is telling that some special collections librarians are committed to continuing and revitalizing this program format in the form of television and radio programs, videos, and documentary films. The Memphis Room, produced by the Memphis and Shelby County Public Library's cable access television station, features Wayne Dowdy, manager of the Memphis Room Collections, interviewing local individuals who have made important contributions to the community or gained national recognition for their professional, cultural, or educational achievements. The historical documentaries produced by the Pikes Peak Public Library for broadcast on its library television channel demonstrate use of the library's production facilities for local history education and communications.

Finally, Discoveries from the Fleisher Collection, discussed in chapter 1, is a long-running monthly radio series based on the Free Library of Philadelphia's Fleisher Collections that is distinguished by the quality of its scholarship and the extent to which it draws listeners' attention to unusual and rare items in its collection.

While broadcast programs are limited in number, they suggest the benefits of using broadcast outlets to build audiences for special collections.

CAPITAL DECADES
Sacramento (CA) Public Library

OVERVIEW: Capital Decades is a month long program of lectures, displays, films, and special events "that explore what everyday life was like in Sacramento during the featured decade." Created and produced by the Sacramento Public Library's (SPL) Special Collections staff, Capital Decades has engaged diverse audiences in exploring the social and cultural landscape of successive decades in the twentieth century. Capital Decades has also galvanized community partners who offer complementary programs that are helping rebrand local history and the Sacramento Room.

> **To capture people's attention and get them into the library we have to go in the direction of more creative programming. We try to offer something other than the usual history lecture, to show rather than tell.**
>
> —Amanda Graham, Library Services Specialist/Archivist

T he Sacramento Room at SPL's Central Library houses SPL's Special Collections, which features the history of Sacramento and Northern California, printing and the book arts, musicians and songwriters, local history, and local authors. While Sacramento Room resources have been known to researchers they have been less well-known to general library users and Sacramento residents. In 2010, when a full-time archivist joined the staff, SPL started to offer programs designed to engage general citizens with local history and to increase the visibility of the Sacramento Room as a source for learning and entertainment. History tours have proven especially popular, along with an annual Haunted Stacks event in the Sacramento Room; an Archives Crawl, in conjunction with other local archives; and SacQR, an app for mobile devices that enables a self-guided tour of Sacramento's K street. According to Amanda Graham, the new archivist:

> Events have to be fun and instructive. They have to surprise people and tease them with interesting activities, images, objects and ideas that connect with their interests and lives.

The most ambitious of the new programs is Capital Decades, an annual series of lectures on the history and culture of a specific decade, highlighting arts, music, fashion, film, and literature. The lectures are complemented by fashion shows, dance instruction, movie clips, and visual displays drawn from the collections that help people connect with the issues and trends of the decade. Library staff carry out the outreach necessary to involve program partners.

The Capital Decades Program on the 1920s, held in 2011, reflects the variety of partners, topics, and formats that characterizes each annual series:

> City Life, a panel discussion with local historians and researchers on 1920s Sacramento through the lens of architecture, transportation, popular culture, Prohibition, and local speakeasies. Fashion and Styles, a partnership with the Sacramento Art Deco Society, featured a vintage fashion show. Motion Pictures was a screening and discussion, led by a film historian, of short films and movie clips that were shown in Sacramento's early motion picture palaces in the 1920s. Charleston! offered an opportunity for the group Midtown Stomp to provide free dance instruction.

Similar programming took place in 2012, focused on the 1940s. Through lectures, films, displays, and special events audiences learned about such topics as war industry work, rationing, Japanese internment, and settlement of the suburbs. The most recent series, on the 1950s, involved a partnership with Sacramento Modern, programs on shelters and the beginning of the atomic age, and the screening of a recently restored Chamber of Commerce film.

Capital Decades has been conducted four times, covering the 1920s, 1930s, 1940s, and 1950s. Attendance and media attention have both been high, helping the library achieve its dual goals of attracting new library users and broadening appreciation for Special Collections.

● **CHALLENGES.** Capital Decades is a logistically challenging program, involving coordination between and among numerous partners, scholars, and volunteers. In addition, there is the challenge of customizing the series to reflect each different decade. For example, for the 1920s Capital Decades offered dance instruction, while the program on the 1950s included a panel discussion on the Sights and Stories of 1950s Sacramento involving local residents who had lived through the decade.

● **FUTURE PLANS.** The library plans to continue the series in 2015 with the 1960s, for which they will add a music program with a live band. Looking ahead, organizers may continue to the 1970s or move back in time to the 1910s and start the sequence again.

FORGOTTEN
The Arkansas Center Korean War Project
Butler Center for Arkansas Studies, Central Arkansas Library System

OVERVIEW: Forgotten: The Arkansas Center Korean War Project (Korean War Project) is an initiative of the Butler Center for Arkansas Studies (Butler Center) that documents and interprets the Korean War and its impact on Arkansans. The Korean War Project is ambitious, with multiple elements, one of them being a national conference that brought together many veterans, scholars, educators, and other stakeholders. The project and the conference have resulted in a unique collection of documentary evidence provided by veterans and their families and greater public consciousness of the impact of the Korean War in Arkansas.

Much of the history of the Korean War exists only in the memories and mementos of its veterans. We want to ensure that these materials are preserved for educators, researchers, and family members to help future generations understand more about the war and our veterans' experiences in it.

—Brian Robertson and Stephanie Bayliss, Coordinators, Forgotten: The Arkansas Center Korean War Project, Butler Center for Arkansas Studies

The Korean War Project is a special project of the Butler Center, the special collections unit of the Central Arkansas Library System (CALS), the mission of which is to promote greater understanding and appreciation of Arkansas history, literature, art, and culture. The Center has widely varied holdings, including manuscripts, maps, photographs, oral histories, and Arkansas art and music, and carries out numerous exhibitions, educational initiatives, and documentation activities.

In 2008, Butler Center staff recognized that the Korean War had been relatively overlooked by members of the general public and was not well represented in the Center's collections. To address these issues they first surveyed Arkansas veterans about their wartime experiences and started to record their memories. They also started to identify and build a collection of documentary evidence about the war. These activities revealed the importance of the war for Arkansas and the need to expand public awareness of this critical period in the nation's history. Accordingly, the Butler Center has carried out the following activities.

CONFERENCE. In 2010 the Butler Center hosted a one-day conference, Forgotten: The Arkansas Center Korean War Project, which examined the Korean War and its significance across the state. As an extension of the Korean War Project, this national conference featured five sessions highlighting aspects of the war. The keynote speaker was historian Dr. James I. Matray of California State University at Chico. The program included a panel discussion with local veterans.

DOCUMENTARY. *Uncle Sam Desired Our Presence: Arkansas in the Korean War*, a 60-minute documentary produced by the Butler Center, was a key component of the Korean War Project. The film featured photographs, documents, and selected oral history interviews as well as video footage from the National Records and Archives Administration. It complements a lesson plan of the same title (see below).

KOREAN WAR COLLECTION. One of the most important components of the Korean War Project is a collection of archival materials documenting Korean veterans' and their families' experiences in the war. The growing collection includes family papers, artifacts, photographs, and journals.

LESSON PLANS. *Uncle Sam Desired Our Presence: Arkansas in the Korean War* is one of the lesson plans developed by Butler Center staff to enrich high school teaching using primary materials in the Butler Center Collections.

LECTURES. The Butler Center's Legacies and Lunch monthly lecture series featured the Korean War project in 2010.

STATE CAPITAL EXHIBITION. In July 2013, the Butler Center mounted Arkansas Remembers: The Forgotten War, an exhibition of Korean War photographs and other memorabilia that commemorated the sixtieth anniversary of the signing of the armistice. A ceremony featuring the governor of Arkansas and the Korean Consulate helped marked the occasion.

The national conference and related activities reinforced one another and helped to build momentum for the collection development that is ongoing. Together, they demonstrate how archival projects that include collecting, preserving, educating, and fostering dialogue can help address a neglected public issue or event.

❍ **CHALLENGES.** The primary challenge in carrying out the Korean War Project involved collection development: locating veterans and nurses, working with out-of-state veterans, and convincing veterans to donate materials.

❍ **FUTURE PLANS.** Butler Center staff is continuing to document Korean War veterans and present programs that promote understanding of the war and build the Korean War Collection.

HACKLEY AFTER DARK LECTURE SERIES
Detroit Public Library

OVERVIEW: The Hackley After Dark Lecture Series, developed by Romie Minor, curator of Detroit Public Library's (DPL) E. Azalia Hackley Collection of African Americans in the Performing Arts (Hackley Collection), started in 2008 as a single series intended to "promote the collection as well as present an historical perspective on African American Performing Arts themes and subjects." The series has continued and grown, along with public awareness of the collections. The preeminence of the collection, the quality of Minor's research, and his effort to draw people in and make connections with the material have all helped build a constituency for the series and attracted donations to the Hackley Collection.

> For the first program in 2008 there were about 10 people. These days, for lectures on Michael Jackson, there can be 75 people or more. Sometimes we have to move out of the Hackley Collection Room to a larger space.
>
> —Romie Minor, Assistant Manager, Special Collections and Curator, Hackley Collection

The Hackley Collection is one of five special collections that were brought together in 2006 to comprise DPL's Special Collections Department. Other components are the Burton Historical Collection, which focuses on the history of Detroit, the state of Michigan and the Old Northwest; the Ernie Harwell Sports Collection; the National Automotive History Collection; and a Rare Book Collection, including first editions, fine bindings, illuminated manuscripts, and incunabula.

The Hackley Collection, the first collection to focus on African American music, was established in 1943 through a donation of original materials from the Detroit Musicians Association. Holdings include rare books, manuscripts, archives of performing artists, and organizational records of the Motown Recording Company, among others. Photographs and prints in the collection date from the nineteenth century to the present, including many images of prominent black performers by the American writer and photographer Carl van Vechten. There is a Recorded Sound Collection documenting music either performed or composed by black musicians, with recordings of ragtime and African chant, opera, jazz, and rhythm and blues. There are also collections of sheet music, contemporary "popular music," and a Detroit Electronic Music Archive, the most recent addition to the Department. Hackley Collection materials are gradually being digitized and added to the library's digital collection for wider public access.

The impetus for the Hackley After Dark Lecture Series came from Special Collections Librarian Romie Minor. "When I was first hired by the library as an archivist in 2006, I was assigned to the Hackley Collection. It was, and still is, in a room closed to the public. I was amazed at what was in the collection and the fact that so many people did not know about it. I decided to do a series of lectures that would expand people's understanding of what is here."

The series that Minor designed started in 2008 with four lectures a year and has expanded to six or eight lectures a year. Each year Minor focuses on different themes and performers. The first series was titled History of Detroit Sound. In 2009 the lectures included According to the Gospel, which examined the roots of gospel music and its lasting influence in African American culture, and in 2010 Minor examined the history of Hip Hop, the music of Michael Jackson, and the phenomenon of disco music. Subsequent topics have included Southern Soul, Jazz Giants: The Life and Times of Duke Ellington, Whitney Houston, and the Movies of Spike Lee.

In organizing the lectures Minor draws on his in-depth knowledge of the Hackley Collection, employing music, images, and video clips to bring his subjects alive. Some audience members attend the lectures on a regular basis, take notes, and regard the series as a form of continuing education. Some come for particular topics. Others come for the dialogue that follows each lecture, in which local residents often elaborate on the topic with personal reminiscences about a musician or a performer, or debate stylistic approaches and the relative quality of different performances. The lectures have proven highly effective in broadening appreciation of the scope and value of the Hackley Collection and building connections between the collection and Detroit residents.

Aside from the Hackley After Dark Lecture Series, there is an annual Hackley Lecture by a specialist on African American music or performing arts history. The Hackley Collection also has an annual Open House, during DPL's participation in Noel Night in Detroit's Cultural Center, which draws 300 to 500 people to learn about the collection.

● **CHALLENGES.** Staffing shortages at DPL have reduced Special Collection's capacity to carry out more programs.

● **FUTURE PLANS.** Hackley Collection staff hopes to record the Hackley After Dark Series to expand public access.

HISTORY DETECTIVES
Grand Rapids (MI) Public Library

OVERVIEW: Each year the History and Special Collections Department (Special Collections) of the Grand Rapids Public Library (GRPL) collaborates with six other local history organizations to present History Detectives, a daylong event featuring talks by six local researchers, some of whom are scholars and some of whom are local individuals with expertise in a particular topic. Started in 2007, the event has grown to attract more than 1,200 people, and has had a positive impact on the library in terms of increased public knowledge of the history collections and how they can be used by scholars and others.

History Detectives is an opportunity for all our local history groups to work together to sponsor local researchers so that they can share their projects with the public. For the Library, "History Detectives" helps showcase ways that researchers use our collections.

—Timothy Gleisner, Manager, Grand Rapids History and Special Collections

History Detectives is one of a number of public programs—exhibitions, outreach, lectures, tours—organized by GRPL to expand awareness and use of its large and varied Special Collections. Holdings include manuscripts, family records, yearbooks, city directories, newspapers, maps, and more than a million photographs documenting the development of Grand Rapids, Kent County, and the surrounding areas of Michigan and the Old Northwest. Many items are available online through GRPL's Digital Collection.

Special Collections works closely with a committee of representatives from all the cooperating organizations to plan and produce History Detectives. The library takes the lead by handling program logistics and communications. Collaborating groups include the Grand Rapids Civil War Roundtable, the Greater Grand Rapids Women's History Council, and the Grand Rapids Public Museum. Each sponsor selects its own researcher/presenter; their diversity helps ensure a variety of topical presentations. Some presenters are local residents with deep interest in a topic represented in one of the sponsor organization's collections and others are academic scholars carrying out their own research or overseeing community documentation projects. A selection of program topics offered during the 2013 and 2014 History Detectives symposia reflects the diversity of sponsor groups' collections and local researchers' interests:

- Women in World War II
- The Mystery of West Michigan's Sunken Canoes
- Building a Case: Grand Rapids as an Important Suffrage Center
- Early Timekeeping and the Development of Time Zones in Michigan

History Detectives has proven successful on several counts. It has enabled the sponsoring groups to showcase research based on their collections; it has encouraged new research by members of the general public as well as formal scholars; and, it has expanded the audience for local history. When the program began in 2007 it drew 90 attendees, while the 2013 event drew 1,200.

◉ **CHALLENGES.** As a collaborative program History Detectives requires careful coordination, taking into account differing sponsors' perspectives on program topics and logistics. In addition, as the program has grown it has been necessary to coordinate a growing number of volunteers.

◉ **FUTURE PLANS.** Special Collections staff is committed to continuing History Detectives as an important signature program that fosters awareness and use of the local history collections.

KRUG RARE BOOKS ROOM EDUCATIONAL SERIES

Milwaukee (WI) Public Library

OVERVIEW: The Richard E. and Lucile Krug Rare Books Room (Krug Rare Books Room) of the Milwaukee Public Library (MPL) houses some of the library's greatest treasures. Rare Books Room staff organizes an annual Krug Rare Books Room Educational Series to share these with the public and to build understanding of their significance. The lectures feature scholars with in-depth knowledge of particular items in the collection, such as Japanese Prints or the Bible. As a well-branded series that attracts a variety of audience members, both specialists and generalists, the Krug Lectures demonstrate the value of the Rare Books Room as a destination and a source of learning.

> **We do programs to help bring our collections to the attention of the public. Every program in the Krug series highlights something in the Rare Books Room and helps people make a special connection with that item.**
>
> —Patricia DeFrain, Rare Books Librarian, Krug Rare Books Room

M PL's special collections exist in several locations: the Krug Rare Books Room; the Humanities and Archives Departments; the Wisconsin Architectural Archives; and the Art, Music and Recreation Department. The collections are wide ranging, from the City of Milwaukee Archives, a Genealogy Collection, and the Great Lakes Marine Collection to works by Wisconsin artists and a Historic Photos

Collection. Many items are digitized and there are ongoing digitization projects, such as the Great Lakes Ships Project, which make formerly inaccessible collections available as searchable online databases.

The Krug Rare Books Room houses an array of aesthetically and historically significant items. Some, such as a Folio of prints by John James Audubon, are well-known; others, such as a book with 2,300 autographs from prominent Americans from the 1890s, are less well-known. According to Rare Books Room Librarian Patricia DeFrain, "It is an eclectic collection that merits interpretation for the public."

The donors who supported renovation of the Rare Book Room also provided funds for an ongoing lecture series "to increase appreciation and enjoyment of the collections in the Rare Books Room." The Krug Educational Series was launched in 2006 with a lecture by Max Yela of the University of Wisconsin at Milwaukee on "Why Rare Books? A Discussion of the Continued Importance of Rare Books in a Digital Age." Since inception of the series, Rare Books Room staff has been offering five to eight programs a year. Each lecture focuses on a particular theme rooted in the collection. For each lecture library staff mounts a display of the item or items under discussion. Lecture topics reflect the scope of the collections: The WPA Milwaukee Handicrafts Project; Treasures of Illustration; and 19th-Century Travel Narratives in Indian Country. Staff promotes the Series on social media, through the library's blog, and through print media.

● **CHALLENGES.** One challenge associated with the Krug Educational Series is informing potential attendees beyond regular library patrons. The use of social media such as Facebook and Twitter has helped build attendance, especially when reinforced by e-mail blasts to interested library patrons and creative distribution of flyers.

● **FUTURE PLANS.** Program plans for 2015 and 2016 include presentations on the history of magic, the 25th Infantry Bicycle Corps of the early 1900s, Wisconsin artist Gerald Geerlings and his involvement with World War II mapmaking, and the building of the historic Library-Museum building that the library now occupies.

L.A. IN FOCUS
Los Angeles Public Library

OVERVIEW: Los Angeles Public Library's (LAPL) Photo Collection is one of the richest visual resources available on the development of Los Angeles and Southern California. It is also a rich resource on the history of photography. The Photo collection and its Photo Friends support group offer a public program series, L.A. in Focus, which spotlight aspects of the collection and bring alive unique stories of Los Angeles's cultural history. This long-running series fosters awareness of the library's photograph collections and helps build a community of interest around the photography in Los Angeles.

> **Our photograph collection is incredibly significant, with examples of nineteenth century family portraits and the first uses of 35 mm film, to images that trace the evolution of photojournalism and today's digital photography. Through digitization, social media, and programming we are beginning to raise public consciousness about the importance of the collection.**
>
> —Christina Rice, Curator, Los Angeles Public Library Photo Collection

LAPL's Photo Collection is the largest of the library's special collections, numbering more than 3 million items. It is also one of the most comprehensive visual resources available on the history of Los Angeles, Southern California, and California. The collection was started by the Public Library's History Department before World War II. In 1981, on the occasion of the city's 200th anniversary, the Security National Bank and other entities donated significant collections that have subsequently been expanded, offering image sources for scholars, students, and anyone interested in the development of the city of Los Angeles. In both format and content, the collection also offers an overview of the history of photography, from early glass plate negatives and some of the earlier examples of photos shot with 35 mm cameras by newspaper photographers, to images that reflect the evolution of photojournalism and digital photography.

To stimulate public appreciation and use of the Photo Collection, staff organize exhibitions and programs, digitize collections for online access, and employ social media. One recent exhibition featured the works of photographer Herman Schultheis, How We Worked, How We Played: Herman Schultheis and Los Angeles in the 1930s. Another drew from the library's extensive holdings of newspaper photos to explore: Local News: Tabloid Photographs from the *Los Angeles Herald Express*. More than 90,000 images have been digitized and the online collection is constantly growing.

With assistance from Photo Friends the Photo Collection offers an ongoing series of lectures, L.A. in Focus, that features individual photographers talking about their work or specialists who explore aspects of the Photo Collection. The series started out as a way to highlight LAPL photos, but has evolved to include discussion of photography more generally as it relates to Los Angeles history. Lecture topics vary widely, from a 2012 presentation examining Olympic photography by David Davis, author of a book on the 1908 Olympic Marathon, to a 2013 lecture by Kathy Kobayashi, co-developer of the Shades of L.A. Project in the 1990s, which resulted in 10,000 photos donated to the library from diverse Southern California families. The lectures foster appreciation of the Photo Collection while contributing to wider understanding of photography and its relationship to the history of Los Angeles.

In 2014 the L.A. in Focus series featured a conversation between Gary Leonard, who has photographed the streets and neighborhoods of Los Angeles for decades, and critic Kevin Roderick of LAObserved.com. This program, like others in the series, drew many people who represent a growing constituency for photographs and historical photography. By offering the series, Photo Friends and the Photo Collection are helping build a community of interest around the library's collection and its importance to the history of Los Angeles.

Most of the L.A. in Focus presentations have been videotaped and are available for remote use by individual researchers or in classrooms and study groups.

❯ **CHALLENGES.** According to Photo Collection Curator Christina Rice there is inadequate public recognition of the depth and significance of the Photo Collection. Without targeted resources for marketing, staff must rely on social media and programming to generate awareness and use. The attention generated by public programs such as L.A. in Focus helps to build Photo Collection patrons and supporters.

❯ **FUTURE PLANS.** The Photo Collection and Photo Friends intend to continue L.A. in Focus as an important component of their efforts to expose and explore aspects of the library's rich Photo Collection.

❯ **RELATED PROGRAM.** The Photo Collection has strong connections to local photographers and supports their work in many ways including a regular lunchtime program, the Photographer's Eye, which provides an opportunity for local photographers to discuss their work in an informal setting.

LOCAL & FAMILY HISTORY LECTURE SERIES
Boston Public Library

OVERVIEW: In January 2014, the Boston Public Library (BPL) started its 11th year of providing a free lecture series on Local & Family History. The series theme for the spring, Boston's Changing Neighborhoods: History and Genealogy, provided a framework for 13 distinct programs plus a culminating Speaker's Roundtable on the evolution of Boston's immigrant gateways and neighborhood development. With distinguished speakers, including specialists from the library's research departments, a variety of topics and historical perspectives, opportunities for hands-on learning and exposure to special collections, and thematic coordination with special collections exhibitions, the series offered a model for public history lectures in a library setting.

Boston Public Library's Local & Family History Lecture Series shares information about the history of Boston and its neighborhoods along with tips and guides for those beginning their own family research.

—Boston Public Library website

Boston Public Library is known as one of the leading libraries of America. According to the library's website it is "the first publicly supported municipal library in America, the first public library to lend books, the first to have a branch library and the first to have a children's room." It is also the first to coordinate its special collections exhibitions and programs around the concept of Collections of Distinction, as discussed in chapter 4. These are collections that represent "the most outstanding, expansive and renowned of the library's holdings."

BPL's Local and Family History collection has been designated as one of the library's initial 18 Collections of Distinction. Local and Family History contains family and local history records from Massachusetts and most of New England, with more than 30,000 wide-ranging materials from the seventeenth through the twenty-first centuries. It is fitting, therefore, that one of the library's signature programs—the long-running Local & Family History Lecture Series—provides a vehicle for bringing the local history records to life in the form of varied presentations on aspects of local, regional, and family history.

Each year BPL program organizers select a different theme around which to organize the Local & Family History Lectures. The themes are generally linked to a major exhibition based on BPL Special Collections with complementary programs that explore aspects of the exhibition topic. In 2013, for instance, the tenth year of the series, the presentations were organized around Boston's neighborhoods and the people who make up these local communities. The series was coordinated with and part of the library's ongoing Building Boston initiative that celebrates the city's public spaces. All Local & Family History Series lectures take place in the Commonwealth Salon at the Central Library in Copley Square.

Speakers in the spring 2013 series included: author James Madden speaking about how people, place, and planning have interacted throughout history to create contemporary Boston; two curators from the West End Museum who traced the development of the West End neighborhood from the seventeenth century to the present; researcher Tunney Lee speaking about the evolution of Boston's Chinatown; and archivist Joanne Robert discussing Community Archiving Projects at the University of Massachusetts. The fall 2013 series focused on Colonial and Revolutionary Boston, with presentations that examined pre-Revolutionary War newspapers, rebellious brides, and early battles in and around Boston.

For the 2014 Local & Family History Lectures the focus was again on Boston's ethnic neighborhoods. The series explored how "old enclaves and predictable patterns are changing as Boston becomes a more diverse city." Talks focused on three diverse neighborhoods: East Boston, Mattapan, and Allston Brighton. The series linked to BPL's Norman B. Leventhal Map Center exhibition City of Neighborhoods: The Changing Face of Boston, which provided a visual and intellectual backdrop for the lectures. The exhibition featured maps of Boston's immigrant population based on the 2010 census as well as historic, modern, and digitized maps. Among other presenters, Evan Thornberry and Jonathan Wyss of the Leventhal Map Center spoke on "Tools for Mapping Neighborhood and Stories in the Digital Age."

❯ **CHALLENGES.** It is always a challenge for program organizers to identify an appropriate mix of experts—authors, curators, scholar-historians, archivists, and related professionals—who can address the range of topics that come into play in a diverse city like Boston.

❯ **FUTURE PLANS.** The Local & Family History Lecture Series will continue as a part of the library's collection-related programming, and will also continue to relate thematically to special collections exhibition topics.

THE MEMPHIS ROOM

Memphis (TN) Public Library and Information Center

OVERVIEW: The Memphis and Shelby County Room (Memphis Room), a section of the History and Social Sciences Department of the Memphis Public Library and Information Center (MPLIC), produces a regular television program, the Memphis Room from the Memphis Public Library and Information Center (the Memphis

Room), which is broadcast monthly on WYPL, the library's station. Since the program was launched in 2012, fourteen episodes have been produced on topics ranging from local architecture to civil rights. The Memphis Room has also worked with WYPL to create documentaries on key aspects of Memphis history. The television program, the documentaries, a digital archive—Dig Memphis—and blog posts all help expand the audience for Memphis history and culture. The emphasis on broadcast outreach is unusual for a public library, illustrating the possibilities for using television to generate interest in history and special collections.

> **In all our programming we try to give people meat and substance, not just window dressing. Our role is not to just slap a few things up on the Internet but to give in-depth information.**
>
> —Wayne Dowdy, Manager, Memphis and Shelby County Room

The Memphis Room is a key component of the MPLIC, with a strong collection of Memphis-related materials: family records, rare books, business and organization records, maps, photographs, music, architecture, and a growing collection of films and videos. Dig Memphis is the digital archive of the Memphis Room, showcasing a range of collections from the papers of the Civil Rights Activist Benjamin Hooks to a collection of classroom and school images. Archival staff aims to acquire and preserve the history of "ordinary people . . . not just the rich or wealthy or well-connected," through oral history projects and through television program interviews conducted on the Memphis Room. According to Wayne Dowdy, historian and manager of the Memphis Room:

> We collect as broadly as we can—anything that tells the story of Memphis. Our approach is to be a little more interdisciplinary and eclectic, to bring in music and art and, more recently, films and videos.

MPLIC is one of a handful of public libraries to have a radio and a television channel, along with production studios, offering opportunities for the Memphis Room to develop history content. Currently the library channel features library and community-related topics ranging from education and music to community planning and Memphis history. WYPL may be reached from the library's web page.

When the Memphis Room first launched in 2012, the goals were to contribute substantive programming to the library's television channel and to focus attention on the library's rich history collections. Those goals continue today, along with two additional goals: (1) to foster deeper public engagement with history through visits to the special collections and/or interactions via online media; and (2) to add "the voices of Memphis citizens" to the collections. Staff sees the broadcasts as a form of outreach, a vehicle for collection development, and a means of encouraging deeper connections between the library and the community.

The Memphis Room is organized around interviews between Dowdy and individuals who have expertise or a point of view about an event or issue in Memphis history or contemporary life. Recent episodes featured Happy Jones, a human rights activist and founder of the Memphis Community Relations Council, and Father Don Mowery, an Episcopal priest and former executive director of the nationally known Youth Service USA. The dialogues between Dowdy and the interviewees reveal an array of perspectives on aspects of Memphis life that collectively constitute a unique historical record. Memphis Room staff share these episodes on Dig Memphis and they are posted on Vimeo. Each episode is highlighted on the *Memphis and Shelby County Room* blog.

The Memphis Room complements other programming, including topical displays from the collections, regular local history talks, presentations at schools and colleges, and tours of the collections tailored to special interest groups and students.

◉ **CHALLENGES.** Memphis Room staff has the expertise and material to create more Memphis history programming but is limited as to the amount of time available for educational projects and public programs. As with so many public library special collections, the Memphis Room has a relatively small staff who must share a range of duties: public desk, process manuscript collections, and maintain Dig Memphis. Similarly, WYPL is short-staffed. Because of these limitations neither department can create as many films as they would like.

◉ **FUTURE PLANS.** Dowdy would like to expand collections-based television programming, seeing that as a valuable channel for stimulating viewer's interest in local history and a means of developing content to enrich the department's on-line offerings. He expects to keep improving the digital versions of the Memphis Room by including more visual material along with full transcripts. In addition, Dowdy plans to continue building a collection of moving images. He envisions a "first class film archive" of life and culture in Memphis complementing current audiovisual archives and preserving historical footage and contemporary recordings in multiple formats.

◉ **RELATED PROGRAMS.** In addition to the television program Memphis Room staff has worked with WYPL staff to create four documentary films using items in the history collections. Topics include the Orpheum Theatre and the integration of the University of Memphis. In a special project with the library's radio station, Memphis Room staff produced an audio dramatization of the 1878 yellow fever epidemic starring a group of high school students. Memphis Room staff has also worked with the local PBS station WKNO in the production of *Memphis Memoirs,* a series of historical films that use Memphis Room staff and collections.

PIKES PEAK REGIONAL HISTORY SYMPOSIUM AND BROADCAST PROGRAMS
Pikes Peak (CO) Library District

OVERVIEW: The Special Collections division of the Pikes Peak Library District (PPLD) organizes an annual Pikes Peak Regional History Symposium (History Symposium) that attracts a regional and national audience of more than 200 people each year. The daylong event, involving multiple presentations, has become a signature program that reflects the division's leadership in bringing together institutions, historians, and members of the general public to deepen understanding of the history of southern Colorado and the Mountain West. Symposium themes inform other Special Collections programs and products such as books, exhibitions, and films.

Special Collections also develops content for PPLD TV, PPLD's cable channel, including History Symposium presentations, original films, such as *Frozen to Death on Pikes Peak: A Cold Case Investigation,* and videos related to its collections or community documentation projects. The History Symposium and history programming on PPLD TV demonstrate Special Collections' dedication to using multiple program formats and venues to build public interest in local and regional history.

The annual history symposium gives everyone a chance to be a public historian, avocational historians as well as academics. It fulfills our goals of educating and exciting the public regarding local history while also providing topics that become the basis for other programs and services.

—Tim Blevins, Division Head, Special Collections

P PLD, which serves 598,000 people in El Paso County, in southern Colorado, has an exceptionally active Special Collections Department. Also known as the Regional History and Genealogy Department, Special Collections contains maps, oral histories, photographs, books and manuscripts, pamphlets, government records, genealogical sources, films, and ephemera that illuminate the history of the Pikes Peak region, the state of Colorado and the Rocky Mountains.

The Pikes Peak Regional History Symposium started in 2004 as a one-time event to commemorate the 1904 Cripple Creek Labor Wars. In a statement for the Urban Libraries Council Innovation Award in 2013, Tim Blevins, special collections division head, explained the library's rationale for starting the symposium.

> The record of our community's history was at risk of stagnation due to diminishing new published local history resources, limited accessibility to unpublished resources, and inadequate incentives to encourage new historical research. Uncoordinated local history organizations appealed to small groups with periodic presentations and newsletters, however, the larger regional community, with many new and short-term residents, was seldom engaged.

The 2004 History Symposium proved so successful in addressing these issues that Special Collections leaders decided to try it a second and then a third year. The program has steadily gathered interest and momentum, leading to long-term plans for topics through 2021. The daylong Symposium is held annually during early June. A different topic is selected for each Symposium and a national Call for Proposals solicits presentations for the event and papers for potential publication. Proposals come from amateurs and academics alike; they are carefully evaluated for their scholarly merit.

The range of Symposium topics addressed since 2004 suggests the variety of presenters, audiences, and local interests, from Bigwigs and Benefactors of the Pikes Peak Region (2014) and Massacres of the Mountain West (2013), to Film and Photography on the Front Range (2011). Each year there are new audiences with interest in the current topic. Sometimes the selected topics relate to other Special Collections programs; more often, other programs, such as exhibitions and publications, are generated by Symposium topics.

Approximately 12 speakers are invited to present at the event; all presentations are recorded and also broadcast live on PPLD TV cable channel 17 and via PPLD's online Ustream channel. Edited videos of Symposium presentations are available online on Vimeo and YouTube, and/or on DVD for library check-out. Audio downloads of the symposia are available on OverDrive. Additional distribution of Symposium content occurs through the Regional History Series publication program carried out by Special Collections. Books relate to Symposium topics, containing selected presentations, reprinted primary documents that add to the topic, and related illustrations.

The Pikes Peak Regional History Symposium brings visibility to Special Collections and helps link interested amateurs and scholars with one another and with the collections. The longevity and the scope of the Symposia are unusual in the public library community.

Broadcast programs are another special feature of PPLD's Special Collections programming. Using the library's video production studio, content is produced by library staff, including short pieces and full-length shows for the station and for other local channels. Paula Miller, library executive director, notes:

> In an era when effective communication requires multimedia, our library district is fortunate to have a professional-quality video studio with public broadcasting capability—along with a cadre of talented staff who visualize, act in, and produce really cool productions for our community.

Special Collections is a major contributor of content to PPLD TV, benefiting from the chance to produce videos and films on topics related to its collections and/or current documentation projects. The broadcast programs help extend Special Collections' reach beyond the immediate service area. *Frozen to Death on Pikes Peak: A Cold Case Investigation,* a 30-minute film produced by the Special Collections division and PPLD's Video Production Center in 2011, is one example of the broadcast programs developed by Special Collections. The macabre story behind the film stimulated wide public interest. Nearly 300 people attended the film premiere and it has been broadcast repeatedly on PPLD TV and is available on the Library Channel on Vimeo, and the Special Collections home page. To promote educational use of the video the library shipped 207 DVDs to schools across Colorado, and provided more than 80 copies to educators working with students on National History Day projects.

◉ **CHALLENGES.** Marketing the History Symposia is challenging. Although a core audience always attends, the different topics involve outreach to different audiences each year. The logistics of handling large audiences for a daylong event can also be challenging, although library staff have become adept at event management. With respect to broadcast programming, the primary challenge is the amount of time required for staff to research topics, write scripts, and take part in the production process. A 30-minute film can take months to create from beginning to end, as staff must fit the work in between regular assignments and reference duties.

◉ **FUTURE PLANS.** The History Symposium will continue as a signature program. New broadcast projects under consideration include a film titled *Phantoms in the Archives: Unlocking a Manitou Springs Mystery,* and Tasting History, a video series on historic recipes.

EIGHT

NATIONAL AND INTERNATIONAL PROGRAMS

Blending online and off-line engagement provides new avenues
for librarians and archivists to connect with their communities
for shared preservation projects like that of Queens Memory
Project and Historypin.

—Metropolitan New York Library Council, Sourcing Community-Driven Archival Content:
Lessons from the Queens Memory-Historypin Project, June 30, 2014

Public library archives and special collections regularly take advantage of national programs, including those based on digital tools, to showcase relevant items in their collections, organize special events, start new projects, or involve residents in exploring an aspect of local culture or history as it relates to a national commemoration. These activities complement other programming and build new constituencies for special collections.

Many public libraries take part in nationally recognized days such as Home Movie Day or month long celebrations such as Women's History Month. The number of such national/local programs is enormous and could fill an entire volume of examples. Unfortunately, in some cases libraries routinize these events and carry out relatively predictable programs that do not deepen public engagement with special collections nor reflect the quality of their other programs. In many other cases, however, libraries leverage the visibility of the national initiatives to create meaningful activities that add new dimensions to their usual programming. The following examples of local participation in seven national and international programs and commemorations suggest the many ways that creative archivists and special collections librarians are using these activities for public benefit.

AMERICAN ARCHIVES MONTH

American Archives Month, held in October, is a cooperative effort by archivists, special collections librarians, and others responsible for archival materials to "highlight the importance of records of enduring value." The Society of American Archivists sponsors American Archives Month and provides libraries with supporting material such as press kits and ideas for activities that can draw attention to local archives and the archival profession. Many kinds of libraries and archives participate, from museum libraries and special libraries to municipal archives and public libraries, often as part of citywide or regional collaborations. These complementary activities offer varied approaches to building public understanding of archives.

▶ AUSTIN HISTORY CENTER, AUSTIN (TX) PUBLIC LIBRARY

The Austin History Center, a part of the Austin Public Library, offers an annual Archives Clinic during American Archives Month in which participants can obtain professional advice on "topics ranging from organization to preservation of papers, photographs, scrapbooks, home video and audio recordings, electronic records and other documents." Students and faculty from the University of Texas School of Information work with archivists from the Austin History Center to help assess materials and provide preservation advice.

▶ HARTFORD HISTORY CENTER, HARTFORD (CT) PUBLIC LIBRARY

In 2013, over the course of American Archives Month, the Hartford History Center provided online visitors with a four-part "virtual tour" of the History Center. Using the History Center's blog, each week staff reviewed a different aspect of the collections and how to use it. The four installments gave readers a road map for visiting the collections and using them for study, formal research, enjoyment, or curiosity.

▶ MONMOUTH COUNTY ARCHIVES, MONMOUTH COUNTY (NJ) LIBRARY

Monmouth County Library's Archives (the Archives) has participated in American Archives Month for 12 years. On October 13, 2013, the Archives presented its 12th Annual Archives and History Day with a featured lecture, a seminar on archival consulting, a Video Room screening of selections from its TV 34 News Video collection, a tour of the Archives, and exhibition tables with displays from more than 60 New Jersey historical agencies and organizations. During Archives Month the Archives also presented the Jersey Shore in Monmouth County: An Exhibition of Documents and Photographs, accompanied by the New Jersey History Game in which attendees answer a quiz based on the exhibition.

NEW YORK ARCHIVES WEEK

Archivists throughout New York City area collaborate once a year on Archives Week as part of American Archives Month. Sponsored by the Archivists Roundtable of Metropolitan New York, events include lectures, repository tours, and symposia "designed to raise the public's awareness of the importance of preserving and making accessible our documentary heritage." New York Archives Week typically offers more than 50 events at libraries, archives, and other cultural institutions and is attended by hundreds of New York City residents each year.

▶ SCHOMBURG CENTER FOR RESEARCH ON BLACK CULTURE, NEW YORK (NY) PUBLIC LIBRARY

In 2013, the Schomburg Center for Research on Black Culture participated in New York Archives Week with displays, workshops, and special events. Each of the Center's five divisions offered activities designed to familiarize attendees with the Center's history, purposes, and collections. Events included: displays of collection highlights; a genealogy consultation; a film on Arthur Schomburg and the origins of the Center; workshops on how to organize personal records; and a special presentation by the national organization StoryCorps on their Griot Initiative.

HISTORYPIN

Historypin is an online history and map site. It offers the opportunity for people from different places and backgrounds to share digital images of the past—"pieces of history"—and in so doing to promote wider understanding of one another and the world. The images are usually pinned on a map of the city, neighborhood, or other region for easy orientation. Created by a not-for-profit company, We Are What We Do, in partnership with Google, the site has become a vehicle for local history programming and an open history archive used by individuals and institutions. Many public libraries have taken advantage of the site to place historical photographs online and to build awareness and use of those collections and the wider collections of which they are a part. Historypin is currently working with the Queens (NY) Library through its Queens Memory Project and the Metropolitan New York Library Council to test the feasibility of using the site to expand community archiving within libraries.

▶ DENVER PUBLIC LIBRARY

Denver Public Library's Western History and Genealogy Department uses Historypin to supplement presentation of historical photographs on its own Digital Collections site and to focus public attention on Denver buildings, neighborhoods, and people. Department staff has found that many individuals who would not otherwise have known about the library's photographic collections have encountered them on Historypin and, as a consequence, have pursued further personal or professional research using the collections.

▶ HENNEPIN COUNTY (MN) LIBRARY

The Special Collections Department of the Hennepin County Library has created tours of certain areas of Minneapolis by using both Historypin and Tumblr. Visitors can see historic images of the city along with contemporary street scenes; they can browse through the images or use them to take a tour. Related posts provide context for individual images and collections. Staff has found that Historypin helps Special Collections connect with audiences that are not regular library visitors.

▶ KANSAS CITY (MO) PUBLIC LIBRARY

Kansas City Public Library's Missouri Valley Special Collection (MVSC) has used Historypin to pin nearly 100 images from the more than 16,000 images in the MVSC Collection. Many are overlaid to the present street view. Visitors are encouraged to check out the "stories" for more information about the images. There is also an interactive Google map with images from MVSC.

▶ WEST HARTFORD (CT) PUBLIC LIBRARY

The Local History Room of the Noah Webster Library in West Hartford uses Historypin as a community archive. Staff invites residents to "share your old photographs and slides of West Hartford homes, public buildings, parks, schools, streets, and events as part a collaborative online visual history of our town." Members of the public with items to contribute bring those photos, slides, or negatives to the library to be scanned and pinned, along with their brief descriptions, to the West Hartford Places and Faces channel on Historypin.

HOME MOVIE DAY

Home Movie Day is a national and international celebration of amateur films and filmmaking held annually at venues such as libraries, universities, and art centers. The event was started in 2002 by the not-for-profit Center for Home Movies (CHM), whose founders were concerned about the trend for people to transfer their personal film to videotape or DVD under the mistaken assumption that digital copies will last longer and will retain their original quality. CHM's mission is to raise awareness of the value of home movies and encourage their preservation as forms of cultural heritage. Home Movie Day, which usually takes place in October, involves many public libraries, some of which collect home movies as part of their special collections. Archives and special collections are using the annual event to discover and showcase amateur films and to assist their owners with preservation.

▶ MADISON (WI) PUBLIC LIBRARY

Madison Public Library invites people to bring in their 8 mm and 16 mm home movies for free on-site film inspections by experts and for screenings. The daylong event is a partnership with the Wisconsin Center for Film and Theater Research and the Wisconsin Historical Society.

▶ NEW ALBANY-FLOYD COUNTY (IN) PUBLIC LIBRARY

The library's Indiana Room partnered with the Southern Indiana Arts Council to offer its first Home Movie Day in October 2013 as a part of New Albany's Bicentennial

Film Festival. Attendees were invited to bring their original home movies for consideration for screening and also for consultation on their preservation. The Indiana Room used the occasion to announce its interest in collecting movies shot in and around New Albany and Floyd County.

▶ URBANA (IL) FREE LIBRARY

In 2008 the Champaign County Historical Archives, part of the Urbana Free Library, partnered with the University of Illinois at Urbana-Champaign to offer a combination film festival and film clinic. Experts were available to assess the condition of older films, clean them, and provide information on how to care for family films and videos. Continuous screening of home movies from personal collections enabled those without home equipment to view their old films, while offering audience members fresh views of community history. The Champaign County Historical Archives used the occasion to inform residents about its collection of local films produced in the Urbana-Champaign area in the 1940s and 1950s.

NATIONAL HISTORY DAY

National History Day (NHD) is a worldwide academic enrichment program for students in grades 6–12 that aims to "promote the study of history in schools by offering a creative forum in which students can express their scholarship." Created by history faculty at Case Western University in Cleveland, Ohio, in 1974, NHD has grown to include over 700,000 students annually. Students participating in NHD carry out history research projects organized around an annual theme. The theme for 2014 was Rights and Responsibilities; for 2015 it is Leadership and Legacy in History. Students are expected to use primary sources and to create their own approach to presenting the results of their inquiry. Competitors present their research to panels of experts at the school or regional level. There are subsequent competitions at one of 57 Winners Affiliate competitions and at an international contest held at the University of Maryland.

Students taking part in NHD are encouraged to use local history resources and institutions. Many public library archivists and special collections librarians see this as an opportunity to strengthen their connections with educators and to help build students' understanding of primary sources and research skills. Some offer workshops for teachers; some provide staff assistance, even one-to-one assistance, to NHD students; and others, such as the Monterey (CA) Public Library and the Duluth (MN) Public Library, create online NHD Resource guides that bring together primary materials or other references to support students' exploration of the annual theme.

▶ DENVER PUBLIC LIBRARY

The library's Reference Department offers NHD students the opportunity to make appointments for personalized research assistance, while the Western History/Genealogy Department supports students carrying out research on primary sources in special collections. The two departments collaborate to offer workshops for groups of NHD students that teach them about different kinds of historical sources, how to use newspaper archives, and how to conduct biographical research or searches for images.

▶ HENNEPIN COUNTY (MN) PUBLIC LIBRARY

Each year Hennepin County Public Library sponsors a daylong History Day Hullabaloo—a "research open house"—to help students and their teachers prepare for NHD. Carried out in collaboration with the Minnesota Historical Society, this is a large event that fills the library and involves many departments including Special Collections. Participants may conduct primary and secondary research, view sample projects, tour Special Collections, and attend mini-lessons on different aspects of research and presentation. Special Collections takes particular responsibilities for helping students who are working on projects related to Minneapolis or Minnesota history. Other Minnesota public libraries that offer History Day Hullabaloos include the Eden Prairie Public Library and the Rochester Public Library. The Minnesota program has been adapted by libraries outside Minnesota. The Boulder Public Library in Colorado, for instance, is offering two National History Day Open Houses.

▶ LA CROSSE (WI) PUBLIC LIBRARY

Starting in 2007, the Archives and Local History Department of the La Crosse Public Library has offered Washburn Awards for Excellence in Research to middle school students for quality research projects prepared for National History Day. Students submit their National History Day projects for exhibition at the library. In May 2014, six area middle school students received awards totaling $1,200. The library's Archives also provides research services for students working on NHD projects and in 2013 partnered with the University of Wisconsin–La Crosse Murphy Library to produce a resource page, La Crosse History Unbound, which introduced teachers and students to local topics relevant to the NHD competition.

NATIONAL POETRY MONTH

National Poetry Month is a distributed celebration of poetry developed by the American Academy of Poets in 1996 as a way to "increase awareness and appreciation of poetry in the United States." It occurs every April in the United States and, since 1999, also in Canada. A wide variety of institutions and entities participate in National Poetry Month, each one carrying out their own program or programs, often featuring local poets. According to the Portland (ME) Public Library, National Poetry Month is "a time to celebrate poets and poetry, the beauty of language, and the richness of poetry in Portland."

Many public library archives and special collections participate in National Poetry Month. They may contribute one element, such as an exhibition, to their library's overall celebration, or they may take the lead in focusing attention on the poets and poems in their collections and in their communities.

▶ BOSTON PUBLIC LIBRARY

The library celebrated National Poetry Month in 2014 with a variety of activities planned to "bring out the creativity and inner poet in people of all ages," including a Shakespeare Sonnet-thon and poetry workshops for teens. Special Collections mounted a complementary exhibition, Public Women, Private Lives, which contained books and manuscripts illustrating the public and private lives of well-known writers, many of whom were poets, such as Emily Dickinson, Louisa May Alcott, and Julia Ward Howe.

▶ NEWARK (NJ) PUBLIC LIBRARY

The Newark (NJ) Public Library's James Brown African American Room, with the Frances E. W. Harper Literary Society of the Newark Public Library, celebrated National Poetry Month in April 2015 with a Community Poetry Read that included readings from works by Amiri Baraka, Maya Angelou, and Louis Reyes Rivera.

▶ PORTLAND (ME) PUBLIC LIBRARY

In honor of National Poetry Month in 2014 the Portland Public Library's Portland Room organized a display of books by Maine poets including Elizabeth Coatsworth, Martin Steingesser, Nathaniel Parker Willis, and Betsy Sholl. The display formed part of the library's larger celebration involving "poetry you can carry in your pocket, poetry you can see on the bus, and poetry that you can say out loud."

STORYCORPS

StoryCorps, a nonprofit organization, was founded in 2003 by documentary producer David Isay with the goal of "providing Americans of all backgrounds and beliefs with the opportunity to record, preserve, and share their stories." Through interviews with people throughout the country, in urban centers, rural markets, shopping malls, homeless shelters, railroad stations, and libraries, StoryCorps has collected interviews from more than 60,000 Americans in all 50 states. The Story-Corps "Collection" is one of the largest collections of American voices in existence, and is continually growing.

All StoryCorps interviews are archived at the American Folklife Center at the Library of Congress in Washington, D.C. In addition, there are ten Community Collections at partner institutions throughout the country, including Nashville (TN) Public Library, Milwaukee (WI) Public Library, and Carnegie Library in Pittsburgh (PA).

StoryCorps has created several Special Initiative Archives, such as the StoryCorps Griot Initiative that gathers and preserves the life stories of African American families. The Auburn Avenue Research Library of the Atlanta-Fulton (GA) Library System participated in the initiative, conducting interviews at the library and at the Griot booth set up nearby at the Martin Luther King Library. The interviews are deposited with the Smithsonian Institution's National Museum of African American History and Culture.

STORYCORPS @ YOUR LIBRARY

StoryCorps @ your library (SCL) was a two-year Libraries Initiative carried out during 2007–2008 in partnership with the American Library Association's Public Programming Office, supported by funding from the Institute for Museum and Library Services. The Initiative was designed "to encourage multi-format public programming on broad themes of oral narrative and local history that may be tailored to specific locales, holidays, or heritage months." Ten pilot sites were selected to participate through a competitive process. The following three examples suggest the diverse ways that public libraries and their archives built community participation through storytelling at the libraries.

▶ HILLSBOROUGH COUNTY (FL) PUBLIC LIBRARY

Hillsborough County Public Library created the Our Lives, Our Legacies: The Black Experience in Hillsborough Project as part of its participation in the national SCL program in 2008. The project engaged members of the local African American community by recording and preserving their stories as part of the library's local history collections.

▶ NASHVILLE (TN) PUBLIC LIBRARY

Nashville Public Library's Special Collections Division, nationally known for its Civil Rights Oral History Project, hosted StoryCorps at the central library from September 2007 to September 2008. During that period nearly 500 interviews were conducted at the Nashville StoryBooth in the Nashville Room. Each interview is approximately 40 minutes long and was conducted by family members and friends of the interviewees with the assistance of a trained facilitator. Many interviews are accompanied by digital color photographs of the participants taken at the time of the interview.

▶ SOMERVILLE (MA) PUBLIC LIBRARY

Somerville Public Library's Local History Collection, in partnerships with its new Teen Center, hosted SCL. With more than 53 languages spoken in Somerville, organizers aimed to document as many people as possible from diverse cultural backgrounds. There was an emphasis on collecting stories from teens and their families. The library trained volunteers in the use of StoryCorps, including learning how to use media equipment, storyboards, and animation. The Local History Collection maintains an archive of the interviews and recordings were provided to participants.

VETERANS HISTORY PROJECT

The Veterans History Project is a national initiative of the American Folklife Center, a department of the Library of Congress. The purpose is to "collect, preserve, and make accessible the personal accounts of American war veterans so that future generations may hear directly from veterans and better understand the realities of war." The initiative is carried out through partnerships with institutions and organizations that create their own local collections, which are in turn provided to the American Folklife Center to become part of its national database. Today the Folklife Center has more than 68,000 collections that are available at the Library of Congress; more than 7,000 are digitized and accessible online.

Many public libraries have partnered with the American Folklife Center to organize local recording projects. Some focus on veterans of a particular war, while others are more general, recording the memories of all veterans and support personnel who took part in any armed conflict. Some libraries solicit donations of correspondence, memorabilia, photographs, and other records associated with the interviewee's service in order to build a collection that provides context for the audio or visual interviews. Libraries often train volunteers to carry out the interviews. Depending on a library's resources the interviews are transcribed, digitized, and incorporated into the library's online collections.

Veterans Oral History Projects are mentioned in several profiles in this publication; the following two projects provide additional evidence of the trend for public library archives to reach out to veterans to preserve and share their stories.

▶ CINCINNATI AND HAMILTON COUNTY (OH) PUBLIC LIBRARY

Cincinnati's Genealogy and Local History Department has a Veterans History Project (VHP) that is "creating a lasting legacy of recorded audio and video interviews from those who served in the armed forces, beginning with World War II." The project is regional, including military and support personnel from outside the area who have a local connection. As part of the project, staff has created a special collection with videotaped copies of the interviews and related documentary material and a VHP website. The website currently features a database of recorded interviews, selected images and documents, and video streamed versions of selected interviews. The library trains volunteers to carry out the interviews, providing them with guidelines and a conversation outline. Library staff coordinates the volunteers, preserves the interviews and related documentary material, and provides access to taped copies at the library and on the project website. On occasion local groups or classes that have carried out veterans oral history projects donate their tapes, enlarging the overall collection.

▶ NASHVILLE (TN) PUBLIC LIBRARY

Nashville's Special Collections Department has been a partner in the national Veterans History Project since 2001. The department has carried out successive phases of interviewing, recording the voices and memories of veterans of all armed conflicts covered in the national project starting with World War I and ending with the most recent conflicts. The current phase of the oral history project concentrates on veterans of Operation Enduring Freedom and Operation Iraqi Freedom. Focusing on veterans from Nashville and Davidson Counties, interviewees are invited to participate through public announcements or outreach to local veterans organizations. They are also encouraged to donate letters and e-mails, unit histories, maps, journals, and other items associated with their service in the military to add to the library's Veterans History Project collection.

NINE

ORAL HISTORY AND COMMUNITY DOCUMENTATION PROJECTS

It is so important to build relationships with our communities through oral history and collecting. If we don't have the primary sources it is hard to talk about the past or the future. Gathering evidence on our different cultures and experiences is important for all of us.

—Esther Chung, Community Archivist with the Asian-American Community, Austin (TX) History Center

D igital memory projects, social archives, photovoice exhibitions, community albums, virtual scrapbooks, neighborhood history programs, and oral history projects—these suggest the myriad approaches to community documentation in public libraries nationwide. They reflect trends to fill gaps in archives and special collections—especially with respect to the history of minority and immigrant communities—to use new tools for collecting and sharing local history, and to build participation in community history on-site and online. Natalie Milbrodt, manager of the Queens (NY) Public Library's Queens Memory Project states that such programs are "... a great way to democratize archives and to make the public library the place that gathers and presents community memories."

Evidence of these trends is visible in libraries of differing sizes, with differing internal structures and varied history collections. The Houston Public Library's Houston Metropolitan Research Center, a premier research center, is expanding its oral history activities to carry out interviews of Latino residents and members of the LGBT community; Allen County (IN) Public Library's Local History and Genealogy Division, long known for an emphasis on genealogy, is considering starting an oral history program and has led development of the Allen County Community Album; the Portsmouth (NH) Public Library is working with families who were displaced by Urban Renewal on the North End House History Project; and Boulder (CO) Public Library's Maria Rogers Oral History Program is a source for exhibitions and civic discussions.

Community documentation projects are proliferating, some building on prior oral history activities, and some conceived in response to social and demographic changes in their communities. Each has different elements, technical approaches and emphases, but all are focused on capturing, preserving, and sharing the experiences and memories of local residents. The number of such projects represents a critical mass that is shifting the very meaning of "local history" to be as much about community participation as it is about traditional collection development and preservation. This new landscape of community documentation is distinguished by several features that suggest the depth and range of new approaches.

RENEWING LOCAL HISTORY COLLECTIONS

Many of the newer community documentation projects are the result of an internal consensus that existing collections do not equally represent the experiences of all community residents. For some archivists, including but not limited to younger professionals, existing collections tilt toward the histories of individuals, families, and institutions associated with earlier periods in local history and/or individuals who were educated and privileged enough to have left formal historical records. They acknowledge the need for content that reflects what Irene Wainwright, archivist of the New Orleans (LA) Public Library's Louisiana Division, describes as "ordinary people . . . people who would otherwise be hidden from history."

To address gaps in their collections many libraries are carrying out new documentation projects or revitalizing existing programs. The Pikes Peak (CO) Public Library is working to document the history of the Latino community in the Mountain

West; the Providence (RI) Public Library's Rhode Island Collection is training teens and adults to "make history" by documenting neighborhoods whose residents are not represented in the collections; and the Nashville (TN) Public Library's Special Collections Department, known for its Civil Rights Oral History Program, has started an Immigrant Voices initiative to document the experiences of newcomers settling in Nashville.

As library archivists address the need to make their collections more inclusive, oral history is a preferred means of documentation, augmented, often, by video recordings and digitized images and documents. All across the country there is strong interest in collecting personal stories, from veterans, workers, newcomers, community leaders, and individuals from diverse backgrounds with diverse life experiences and memories. Elizabeth Sargent, assistant director for Special Collections and director of the Houston Metropolitan Research Center, explains: "Oral histories are so powerful because it is often the everyday person that is the source of information, exactly the kind of source that is not usually found in an archival collection."

USING NEW TOOLS AND PARTICIPATORY FORMATS

One of the most visible characteristics of contemporary community documentation is the use of digital tools and social media for collecting, preserving, and sharing individual and community records. These tools augment traditional oral history recordings and enable creation of multimedia collections and online forums where individuals and institutions can share documents, images, metadata, and commentary. The Denver Public Library's Western History and Genealogy Division was a pioneer in the design of a "social archive" that resulted in an interactive Creating Your Communities project. The Hennepin County (MN) Public Library has reached new audiences and gained new knowledge of its collections through the use of social media. Ted Hathaway, manager of the library's Special Collections, explains:

> We are trying more and more to position Special Collections as a community memory repository. This is a good niche for us. . . . Through outreach on Tumblr and other social media channels we are attracting individual visitors and patrons and inviting them to submit comments and additions. In that way we can add value to the digital content that we put up on these sites and we can link people to the history that is meaningful to them. The emphasis is less on building collections and more on interacting with images, events and ideas.

The technicalities and platforms involved in these and other digital initiatives may vary, but they are clearly helping achieve many librarians' goals for increased awareness of and interaction with history collections. Judy Knudson, manager of the new Local History Center in Arlington, Virginia, states: "With digital technologies and new forms of communication we can now be more visible and active and can help people become more personally engaged with family and community history."

Applications of digital tools and use of social media for participatory memory projects is not only increasing but is apparent in public libraries of all sizes and locations. The Queens (NY) Memory Project, serving a population of 2.5 million, is one of the largest and most experimental of the programs. The Columbus (OH) Community Album, a model digital partnership, serves a regional population of 823,000, and the "Catablog" developed by the MacAthur Library in Biddeford, Maine, is a digital history archive for a community of 21,300.

DOCUMENTING LOCAL EVENTS AND LOCAL DISASTERS

The trend to carry out oral history and video documentation of contemporary events, such as street fairs and festivals, and, in particular, to document local disasters, is another feature of the community documentation landscape. Nashville's Flood History Project, Pikes Peak's Waldo Canyon Fire Project, and the Hurricane Sandy documentation projects carried by the Queens (NY) Public Library and the Brooklyn (NY) Public Library are just a few examples of recent efforts to record local catastrophes. These kinds of projects have brought a new immediacy to the work of the archivists involved, several of whom describe themselves as "first responders." Angela Blackman, manager of Special Collections at the Nashville (TN) Public Library, sees her staff functioning as "the eyes and ears of the community during important events."

STORYTELLING

A final trend in community documentation is an emphasis on stories and storytelling. Whether this results from the visibility of the national StoryCorps program discussed in chapter 8 or simply increased recognition that local history is a form of storytelling, it is apparent that some special collections and archives are substituting "storytelling" for "local history" and are finding that members of the public are curious and interested in participating under this rubric. According to Nicholas Butler, historian at the Charleston County (SC) Public library:

People love stories. They come to the public library to check out stories. The Charleston Archive is full of stories, and our programs are vehicles for stimulating people's interest in learning more about these stories in the context of local, regional and national history.

Beyond the four characteristics of current community documentation outlined above there is yet another phenomenon, namely the fact that the process of documentation is not only a means of diversifying collections, and of engaging the public with special collections. It is, in and of itself, a community building process. Many institutions host scanning events, oral history days, or pinning events at local libraries to encourage participation and foster social interaction; many train local volunteers who become outreach arms in the community and help build individual and institutional connections.. Some, like the Austin (TX) History Center, add dedicated outreach personnel to their departments whose jobs involve bringing community members together as a means of generating stronger historical consciousness. In its evaluation of a recent project, Neighborhood Stories, the Queens (NY) Public Library has even highlighted the value of social interaction as a corollary benefit of community-based documentation.

It is clear from the examples discussed below that community documentation and oral history work being carried out today by public library archivists and special collections libraries is in an exciting and dynamic phase of development. It is not only about applying new technologies for community documentation, but it is also about redefining collections, redefining the relationship between community members and official collection keepers, and, even, redefining the roles of local archivists and special collections librarians.

BROOKLYN PUBLIC LIBRARY ORAL HISTORY PROJECTS
Brooklyn (NY) Public Library

OVERVIEW: The Brooklyn Collection, Brooklyn Public Library's (BPL) Special Collections department, is presently involved in three oral history projects that aim to record the experiences and memories of contemporary Brooklynites: Our Streets, Our Stories; the Hurricane Sandy Stories Oral History Project; and the Veterans Oral History Project. While each project is organized differently, all three aim to engage diverse patrons with the Brooklyn Collection and to expand opportunities for future generations to better understand life in Brooklyn in the twentieth and twenty-first centuries.

Everyone's experience is valuable for understanding the changes that have taken place in a neighborhood. By capturing many different stories we can make a richer whole.

—Judy Kamilhor, Director, Older Adult Services,
Department of Outreach Services

The Brooklyn Collection is a rich repository of Brooklyn-related records including maps, photographs, architectural drawings, posters, ephemera, postcards, maps, and a full run of the *Brooklyn Daily Eagle* (1841–1955). The department is deeply committed to educational use of its collections. Staff work intensively with selected schools on the Brooklyn Connections program and offer monthly lectures and topical displays that help engage members of the public. Special collections staff also use social media extensively, with a widely read blog, *Brooklynology*, images on Tumblr, a Twitter account, and regular contributions to the library's Facebook page.

Recognizing the importance of recording the diverse experiences of Brooklyn residents and documenting the changes taking place in Brooklyn today the Brooklyn Collection is carrying out the following projects.

BROOKLYN COLLECTION HURRICANE SANDY ORAL HISTORY PROJECT. Hurricane Sandy, which devastated the New York area coastline in October 2012, was a catastrophic event for some areas of Brooklyn and will have lasting effects. In early 2013 the Brooklyn Collection started a project to document the hurricane's long-term impact on residents, workers, and organizations, particularly in coastline neighborhoods. To recruit interview participants, staff members reach out to groups such as senior citizens and neighborhood organizations. Interviews are conducted on-site in branch locations and at local businesses affected by the storm, mainly in the Red Hook and Coney Island neighborhoods. According to Project Coordinator June Koffi, "People are still trying to rebuild their lives. . . . they have a lot to say about what's happened."

VETERANS ORAL HISTORY PROJECT. Starting in 2008, the Brooklyn Public Library began collecting oral histories from the borough's many veterans. The project is part of the national Veterans Oral History Project, an initiative of the Library of

Congress, Channel 13, and numerous other institutions. The project was revived in 2014, under the auspices of the new Department of Outreach Services (Outreach Services), which focuses on specific underserved communities in Brooklyn, including veterans involved in military combat from World War II to the present day. Outreach Services connects with veterans clubs and invites anyone who has served to share their story. Recordings of the interviews are being archived at the Brooklyn Collection and the Library of Congress; excerpts from selected interviews are available on YouTube.

OUR STREETS, OUR STORIES. The most recent project undertaken by the Brooklyn Collection is a pilot initiative launched in the spring of 2014 to "capture the history of our ever-changing neighborhoods through the voices of those who have lived there." A partnership with the library's Services to Older Adults program (a component of Outreach Services) and three branch libraries, the project is focusing initially on the Williamsburg, Sheepshead Bay, and Flatbush neighborhoods.

The Our Streets, Our Stories project aims to teach local volunteers of all ages interviewing techniques and technology skills necessary to carry out the project. The trainings and interviews are conducted in three neighborhood libraries to increase engagement with volunteers and interviewees where they live. The recorded interviews are being archived at the Brooklyn Collection and will also "lay the foundation for community-produced local history archives at each participating branch." Eventually, the goal is to establish the branch libraries as destinations for people interested in Brooklyn history, and as outreach sites for the Brooklyn Collection. This interdepartmental collaboration aims to create a model for recording the experiences of older adults that can be used by other libraries in the borough and the city.

The collection of new oral histories is a recent initiative for the library, and is still in an experimental phase, with the goal of evaluating the different models presented by these three projects and ultimately developing a more clearly defined oral history program. Issues under discussion include different approaches to engaging targeted communities, the need for a unified cross-department workflow for collecting and preserving oral histories, and the need for consistent metadata.

◉ CHALLENGES. Recruitment of interview participants with distinctive stories to tell is always a challenge. By working with Outreach Services, local organizations and branch librarians, the Brooklyn Collection is able to reach diverse individuals appropriate for each of the oral history project archives. Because the model for Our Streets, Our Stories is community-driven, it is crucial to find motivated volunteers and interviewees who can keep the project momentum going.

❯ FUTURE PLANS. As the Brooklyn Collection works with Outreach Services to continue and expand oral history projects, staff intends to build up the web presence for each project by making more of the interviews available online. For the Hurricane Sandy Oral History Project, for instance, staff aims to create a project website with an interactive map that will enable access to stories pertaining to specific neighborhoods. Long-term, the Our Streets, Our Stories project aims to engage branch libraries as outreach arms for the Brooklyn Collection and as community-based collections reflect the experiences of local residents.

COMMUNITY DOCUMENTATION PROJECTS
Pikes Peak (CO) Library District

OVERVIEW: Pikes Peak (CO) Library District's (PPLD) Special Collections Division is attentive to the need to fill collection gaps, document the traditions and experiences of newcomers, and capture community responses to significant events. Two community documentation projects, the Waldo Canyon Fire Collection (2012–2013) and ¿De Dónde Eres?: Cultural Origins of the Latino/Hispanic Experience in Southern Colorado (2003–2006), have expanded collections in the form of visual and written materials and oral history recordings. Through these projects Special Collections was able to build relationships with community members whose experiences and voices were not yet represented in the collections. In addition, contributors and others associated with the projects built new connections with one another.

> The goal of the Waldo Canyon Fire Collection project was to acquire and preserve information for future research on the fire and the recovery. The unanticipated impact of the project was the near immediate sharing of personal stories and documentary evidence that positively contributed to the healing of a community that loudly declared "Community Does Not Burn."
>
> —Tim Blevins, Special Collections Division Head

PPLD, which serves Colorado Springs and El Paso County in Southern Colorado, has an unusually active Special Collections division that organizes varied programs to engage the public with local history. These range from exhibitions and publications to educational initiatives with local schools and an annual Pikes Peak Regional History Symposium. At the same time the department works on filling gaps in the collection by documenting previously neglected aspects of local history and/or major events that have shaped contemporary life.

WALDO CANYON FIRE COLLECTION. In June 2012 there was a major fire in the Waldo Canyon, on the outskirts of Colorado Springs. This was one of the most devastating fires in Colorado's history, resulting in two deaths and the loss of 347 homes. Before the fire was under complete control PPLD's Special Collections staff recognized the importance of capturing the ephemeral evidence of the destructive event before it was lost. Working with the Colorado Springs Pioneers Museum, PPLD undertook the collection of documents, photographs, oral history interviews, and websites related to the fire.

The documentation process involved recruiting volunteer photographers, some professional and some amateur, to respectfully capture photographs of the lost homes and rebuilding efforts. The resulting images were provided to Special Collections for public use, exhibition, and future access from the library's online Digital Collections. Simultaneously, Special Collections staff conducted video-recorded interviews of 28 people directly impacted by the fire by evacuation or home loss, and of the firefighters and police officers involved in managing the blaze. The library's video production studio helped Special Collections staff create a documentary film, *In Our Own Backyard: Reflections on the Waldo Canyon Fire.*

Additional outreach extended the project beyond the immediate aftermath of the fire. Bulletin boards with blank note cards were hung at all PPLD community libraries in order to collect community members' responses to the devastating event. The note card responses form a part of the permanent Waldo Canyon Fire Collection.

Started as a simple documentation project to be carried out with another cultural institution, the initiative evolved into an ongoing dialogue and community rebuilding process. The initiative included the following products: a major collaborative exhibition of artifacts, images, and interviews at the Colorado Springs Pioneers Museum; photography exhibitions at various PPLD libraries showing the impacts on the Mountain Shadows neighborhood where so many homes were lost; a public exhibition talk by the volunteer photographers who contributed their images to the library collection; and the documentary film which was included in the exhibition and broadcast on the library's cable television channel. By extending the Waldo Canyon project over time and by organizing a wide array of interpretive activities, Special Collections provided an infrastructure for ongoing reflection, dialogue, and planning.

¿De Dónde Eres?: Cultural Origins of the Latino/Hispanic Experience in Southern Colorado was a documentation project intended to expand the library's collections to reflect the diverse heritage of the residents in its service area, in particular Latino-Hispanic residents. In carrying out ¿De Dónde Eres? Special Collections formed an advisory committee of local community activists, historians, and scholars with knowledge of the community who could give input and help promote the project. The Committee determined the need to reach out to the Hispanic community and to ask them to share their history through interviews and donations of diaries, photographs, business records, and letters.

As a result of ¿De Dónde Eres? the library has gained a set of oral histories with Latino/Hispanic residents as well as written and visual materials that they and others donated during the interview process. Special Collections is currently transcribing the interviews. In addition, using its video production studio, staff created two edited documentary-style videos based on the interviews that were broadcast on the library's local cable channel, PPLD TC; they are also available on DVD and OverDrive download.

❯ CHALLENGES. Virtually all of the photographs, videos, reports, and other records acquired for the Waldo Canyon Fire Collection were created and came to the library in digital formats. Prior to this project, Special Collections was hesitant to collect electronic records and had no established procedures or technical infrastructure in place to ensure their long-term preservation. According to Tim Blevins, Special Collections Division Head, "The fire essentially pushed Special Collections into the twenty-first century and forced us to establish procedures to maintain and provide access to the collection in digital form."

With respect to the ¿De dónde eres? initiative, while it captured the stories of some of the region's Latino/Hispanic leaders, it was not as successful in reaching many other segments of the Hispanic community such as recent immigrants and agricultural workers. More outreach will be required to build a more representative collection of stories from Latino residents.

❯ FUTURE PLANS. Following the 2012 Waldo Canyon fire, another fire in the Black Forest in northern El Paso County destroyed 486 homes and killed two people in June 2013. Also in 2013, severe flooding occurred in Manitou Springs, west of Colorado Springs, as a consequence of the Waldo Canyon fire burn scar. Efforts to document both of these disasters follow the model developed for the Waldo Canyon Fire Collection. A documentary film is planned from the interviews conducted with individuals impacted by the flooding.

FLOOD HISTORY PROJECT

Nashville (TN) Public Library

OVERVIEW: In 2010 a major flood devastated large sections of the City of Nashville. Within weeks, staff of the Nashville Public Library's (NPL) Special Collections had initiated the Flood History Project to document the effects of the flood on the residents and landscape of Nashville and to create a digital portal as a repository for researchers and community members. Functioning as "first responders," staff trained volunteers to help residents record their memories and recovery stories. Within a year there was enough material to create an anniversary exhibition that traveled to former disaster relief centers and provided the basis for anniversary events. The project continues, as staff and volunteers document the long-term effects of the flood on the city's residents.

> It is the mission of the library to preserve and share across generations the wisdom, culture, and history of our community. This Flood 2010 Digital Project will be the historical record of what happened, as told by the people who lived through it.
>
> —Donna Nicely, Former Director

O ral History Projects, including the Flood History Project, are part of NPL's Special Collections Division, which documents the history of Nashville and Middle Tennessee. NPL has a strong tradition of oral history work, including its nationally recognized Civil Rights Oral History Program. Other active projects are the Veterans Oral History Project and the Nashville Business Leaders Project. A partnership with StoryCorps has also resulted in the beginnings of a collection of Immigrant Voices. These projects have all involved extensive outreach and community participation. Materials collected can be accessed at the library through transcripts and/or listening stations, and through NPL's Digital Collection. On occasion, Special Collections organizes local programs and exhibitions to widen public awareness of these collections.

The Flood History Project was developed shortly after the City of Nashville experienced an enormous flood, in May 2010, which devastated large portions of the city and surrounding Davidson County. During the following months city leaders agreed on the need to document the flood's impact on the infrastructure of the city and its residents. NPL's Special Collections Division took the lead in creating a citywide digital history project to serve as the definitive historical record of the Flood of 2010. Within a few weeks of the flood, staff had started to record residents' reactions to the crisis. After the flood waters receded, staff began to partner with local institutions, community organizations, and metropolitan area agencies to create a plan for collecting and organizing individual accounts, photographs, videos, mementos, and other materials associated with the flood.

The plan for documentation called for volunteers to be recruited and trained to assist with outreach and interviewing. It also called for the resulting collection to be made available through a web portal housed and maintained by NPL so that scholars, historians, *and* residents would have permanent access to the information.

> After several weeks of announcing the project and putting out a call for volunteers, their numbers exceeded expectations. These community-based members have been essential to the project, helping spread word about the project and helping capture the immediate experiences of residents affected by the flood. According to Special Collections Division Manager Andrea Blackman, one value of the Flood History Project was: "to assist residents in the process of recovery. The devastation occurred on so many levels—physical, emotional, organizational—that it was important to listen and capture the responses in real time."

As the process of collecting moved forward, project organizers provided regular reports to the community. In the first six months of the project, NPL had collaborated with 16 different organizations and agencies; led 5 oral history trainings; set up more than 10 recording stations in community locations; and conducted more than 25 interviews at the Main Library's Special Collections Center. By mid-2014 the collection had grown to include 200 interviews and 900 images. The Flood History Project is now an ongoing program, part of Special Collections and its oral history initiatives, which are coordinated by the Special Collections Center.

❯ **CHALLENGES.** The Flood History Project could not have been accomplished without multiple partners. Special Collections had to quickly develop working relationships with various institutions that provided space for recording interviewees and helped recruit interviewees. Among the partners were Lipscumb University, the Mayor's Office, Bellevue YMCA, and United Way of Middle Tennessee.

❯ **FUTURE PLANS.** The library is continuing to add to the Flood History portal, providing documentation on the city's recovery over time. Staff and volunteers are also embarking on a special initiative to record the experiences of children whose lives were, and still are, affected by the flood.

Library staff sees the Flood History Project as a prototype of future outreach work. By documenting landmark events and making residents' responses readily accessible online, Special Collections functions not only as a historical repository but also a gateway to the contemporary life of the city.

---

40 FAMILIES PROJECT

Palos Verdes (CA) Library District

OVERVIEW: The Palos Verdes Library District (PVLD) has created a community documentation project based on a group portrait of Japanese and Japanese-American families that hung in the Local History Room (LHR) for many years. The 40 Families Project aims to identify and document the families in the picture, all of whom had been farmers and residents of the Palos Verdes Peninsula before being interned during World War II. There has been strong community response to the project, reflecting the power of one galvanizing image or document to spark interest in recovering forgotten history.

> **With the 40 Families Project we have been able to demonstrate how to preserve the memory of the community, how a document or photo provided by one person builds on other information and points to more clues that fill in the larger historical puzzle.**
>
> —Monique Sugimoto, Archivist and Local History Librarian

PVLD is a special library district that serves four cities in the Palos Verdes Peninsula of Southern California. The LHR collections document the social, economic, and physical development of the Peninsula, providing "a panorama of what was important in the Peninsula's past, as well as what might be meaningful to future generations."

The 40 Families Project started in 2005 when the Local History Librarian, Marjeanne Blinn, became interested in a large photograph hanging in the LHR, then located at the Malaga Cover Library. Dated 1923, the photo documented approximately 40 first-generation Japanese families at a ceremony marking completion of a community building on the coast not far from Palos Verdes. Blinn was not the only one who was curious about the picture. Visitors often asked about the identities of the individuals, the location of the image, and how it fit into the history of the Peninsula. Blinn and a small group of interested community members started the project with one goal: to identify all the families in the picture. It was not long before they added another goal: to identify each individual.

When the project was launched LHR held a reception and invited people they had already been able to identify. Those individuals led them to others. Eventually, they encountered actual relatives of people in the picture—children or grandchildren—and one couple in particular who were enthusiastic about the project and willing to support an exhibition and some of the research. Richard Kawasaki, one of the volunteers, became a project leader and has been a critical element in the success of the project. He assumed responsibility for writing up the family biographies and became so familiar with each family that he could make connections that lead to other identifications and discoveries.

In 2012, Monique Sugimoto, a trained archivist, was hired as Local History Librarian. She continued the project, working with a group of dedicated volunteers to research the stories behind the photograph in as many ways as possible: interviews with relatives of family members; outreach to local groups to uncover names and contacts; and research in census records, FBI/Alien Act documents, internment camp records, the National Archives, yearbooks, photos, and obituaries. By 2014 they had identified 60 percent of the people in the photograph as well as many descendants and relatives. The process was like "solving a giant puzzle" with each piece leading the group further along a journey of discovery. The Peninsula Friends of the Library helped by purchasing equipment and sustaining project activities.

Sugimoto reports that volunteer involvement has been essential to the 40 Families Project and other documentation initiatives:

> Our volunteers are making history work happen here. They have built up knowledge of the different communities in our service area and want to participate in creating the documentary heritage of the Peninsula.

As the 40 Families Project evolved Sugimoto and project volunteers created "family files." They are now working to flesh out information on the past and current lives of all the individuals associated with the 40 Families. Most of the families in the picture had been farmers on the Peninsula coast, on land that is now the site of a golf club and Trump resort. Only two families returned to Palos Verdes after their internment during the war. Others created entirely different lives in different parts of California or the Western states.

The original mission of the 40 Families Project was "to preserve the soon-to-be-forgotten history of the Peninsula's Japanese-American settlement to educate future generations." The mission is an ongoing one, as the project continues to uncover and collect stories, pictures, memories, and documents about midcentury Palos Verdes, its Japanese American farmers and how their lives and the local community changed as a result of World War II. The 40 Families Collection has grown to include books, videos, oral histories, maps, family files, and microfilm, all related to the Peninsula families in particular and the Japanese-American experience in general.

The 40 Families Project illustrates how a single image and a relatively small local history department can illuminate significant events in the history of one community. The 1923 photograph has become a portal to the stories of many individuals whose lives and businesses were profoundly changed by World War II. LHR staff and volunteers intend to continue following the stories and using them to engage people in the broader history of Palos Verdes.

● **CHALLENGES.** Sugimoto identifies three primary challenges in implementing the 40 Families Project. The first is the fact that few individuals pictured in the photograph have survived. With timing so acute, there is the need to pursue stories and collections as quickly as possible. The second challenge is the natural tendency of Nisei—Japanese Americans—to be circumspect about their lives and hardships. It has been essential to have a volunteer project leader, Richard Kawasaki, who could help people see the value of documenting and remembering their story or stories. The third challenge is the fundamental issue of staff capacity. More professional staff would help to sustain the project and promote it, keep the community informed about its progress, follow up on leads, train and support volunteers, and process items and tapes that are collected.

● **FUTURE PLANS.** In addition to the ongoing 40 Families Project LHR is carrying out other participatory projects. One, which also relies on volunteers, is an Oral History Project documenting the local Aero Space industry. Volunteers involved in this project have participated in a one-day oral history training at UCLA and are starting to interview engineers, their families, and other workers formerly associated with Aero Space work.

HOUSTON ORAL HISTORY PROJECT
Houston Metropolitan Research Center, Houston Public Library

OVERVIEW: The Houston Public Library's (HPL) Houston Oral History Project, carried out by the Houston Metropolitan Research Center (HMRC) and the African American Library at the Gregory School (Gregory School) is one of the premier oral history initiatives in a public library. With historical tapes dating back to the 1960s and 1970s, interviews with leading Houstonians concerning the years 1950 to 2007, and more recent interviews taped by HMRC and the Gregory School, the Oral History Project offers a constantly growing audio and visual archive that brings the history of the city alive through the voices of its citizens. Project archives include more than 1,600 interviews and are constantly growing. Through special funding the library has been able to transcribe and to digitize many of the interviews, which are searchable by name or subject on the library's Houston Area Digital Archives website.

> **Oral history documentation is a form of outreach that benefits the whole collection, as people who would not otherwise consider their own lives important for the historical record become aware that their stories or personal records are as important as official records.**
>
> —Elizabeth Sargent, Assistant Director for Special Collections and Director, Houston Metropolitan Research Center

H MRC, a key component of HPL's Special Collections, has a long record of organizing and carrying out oral history projects. Oral histories were being collected and preserved even before HPL had established HMRC or Special Collections. When HMRC was formed in 1976 the early oral histories were integrated with the library's other local history collections. Under the direction of the first HMC archivist, Dr. Marchiafava, more than 800 oral histories were produced on such topics as law enforcement and judiciary, religion, ethnic and racial groups, culture (including the Houston Jazz Collection), labor, sports, and prominent Houstonians. His leadership set the tone for HMRC, which has sustained oral history documentation as a priority.

The goal of the Houston Oral History Project is to "record and preserve the dynamic history of Houston through the stories and experiences of its residents." Depending on special collection development initiatives, partnerships, and funding, specific projects have been undertaken at different times. Funding sources include the Texas State Library and Archives Commission, which provided a TexTreasures grant to digitize the earliest oral history tapes in the collection, the City of Houston, and the Friends of the Texas Room.

MAYOR BILL WHITE COLLECTION. Former Houston Mayor White had a keen interest in documenting the experiences of political, business, and civic leaders and key witnesses to the major events that shaped the city during the 1950s to the end of the twentieth century. He supported a project to conduct 100 video interviews of prominent Houstonians. This initiative, carried out from 2007–2008, benefited from the advice of historians from the University of Houston, Texas Southern University, and Rice University. In some cases well-known community members and local volunteers acted as interviewers. HMRC made transcriptions of each interview. During a subsequent phase of the project all the interviews were entered into the Houston Area Digital Archives, where users can browse interviews by subjects such as the oil and gas industry, legislators, conservation, and government.

NEIGHBORHOOD VOICES is an ongoing effort to document Houston's many neighborhoods. The project started in 2008, when Houston residents were invited to library locations throughout the city to briefly record their own recollections of life in Houston. Many of those who participated in the original interviews subsequently took part in longer and more structured interviews. The project has been continued through interviews at community events, during Hispanic Heritage Month, or during "Scanning Days" and "Oral History Days" at local libraries.

HMRC Director Sargent states that Neighborhood Voices has enabled the library to demonstrate its interest in filling in gaps in its collection by recording the experiences of particular groups or neighborhoods:

> So many of the people we interviewed would not otherwise have considered their own stories important for the historical record . . . After being interviewed they would come forward with family documents or memorabilia that are so important for rounding out the stories of our families and communities.

GREGORY SCHOOL INTERVIEWS. In 2009 Houston Public Library opened the Gregory School, Houston's first public school for African Americans, which is a repository and educational center that carries out documentation projects, including oral history interviews. Staff and trained volunteers "record the personal experience of men and women who helped shape the African American history of Houston and the surrounding areas." As part of the Houston Area Digital Archive these interviews are an important and growing resource. In 2014 the Texas Oral History Association awarded its Mary Faye Barnes Award for Community Oral History to the Gregory School.

In addition to these discrete projects, much oral documentation takes place in combination with outreach to various communities, such as the Indo-American community, the LGBT community, and, in particular, the Hispanic community. HMRC's recent appointment of a Hispanic Collections archivist reflects expanded efforts to document the experiences of Houston's Hispanic residents, including their personal and professional stories.

With the diversity and number of stories that have been taped, and the fact that transcripts are available for so many, the Houston Oral History Project is a portal to life in the city of Houston from the 1950s to the present day. The project complements other elements of the HMRC and the Gregory School and it demonstrates how a public library can help bring alive the history of a city though citizens' voices.

❯ **CHALLENGES.** In sustaining its tradition of oral history documentation HMRC faces the ongoing challenge of freeing up staff for outreach and interviews. Other challenges include the need to transcribe the interviews and to find and train qualified volunteers to help with the oral history work.

❯ **FUTURE PLANS.** HMRC and the Gregory School expect to continue their oral history work. Aside from its expanded outreach to the Hispanic community, HMRC has several communities targeted for interviews, including members of the LGBT community.

MARIA ROGERS ORAL HISTORY PROGRAM
Boulder (CO) Public Library

OVERVIEW: Boulder Public Library's (BPL) Maria Rogers Oral History Program (MROHP) is a long-standing program that has evolved from a traditional collection of audio-taped interviews, available for review at the library, to a dynamic multimedia resource accessible through a rich online archive. The MROHP collection consists of 1,900 interviews that reflect the lives of Boulder residents in the twentieth and early twenty-first century. With part-time management and a cadre of dedicated volunteers MROHP has emphasized outreach and collaboration, which have helped to continuously expand the collection and ensure its utility beyond the scholarly community. In its efforts to make certain that the program is visible, relevant, and useful, MROHP is an excellent example for other institutions.

Oral history in a public library is really important. It brings the voices of the community right into the library's collection in a way that few other things do. Oral history also gives people ways to interact with one another and with their community's history. And, oral history gets people listening to each other and understanding each other in ways they hadn't beforehand.

—Susan Becker, Program Manager, Maria Rogers Oral History Program

M ROHP is a component of BPL's Local History Collection (LHC), which focuses on the history of the City of Boulder and Boulder County. Holdings include photographs, documents, maps, books, periodicals, and ephemera. MROHP was started in the late 1970s by librarian Maria Rogers, after whom it is named. Since that time the collecting effort has been consistently sustained, adding 50 to 80 interviews each year. The interviews cover all aspects of life in Boulder, from city planning and the Rocky Flats nuclear weapons plant to the changes in mining, agriculture, business, and education that have reshaped life in the region over time. The interviews record the memories and experiences of diverse residents—settlers and homesteaders, cattlemen, farmers, housewives, university professors, activists, attorneys, physicians, teachers, artists, and coal miners—as well as covering key events in the community's history.

In its early years the MROHP collection consisted of a relatively small number of audiotapes that were infrequently accessed. Today, the large and growing collection is used for filmmaking, historical research, local planning, performances and exhibitions, family history, and as prompts for community conversations on contemporary issues. Volunteers have been important in implementing the program, carrying out interviews and transcription work under the direction of a part-time program manager. Partnerships with local organizations have also been important, helping to recruit volunteers and interviewees and widening the impact of the collections. An endowment from the family of Maria Rogers supports the part-time program manager position, and occasional grants support specific projects.

While many of the oral history interviews have been available online for some years, the MROHP recently launched a new digital archive that makes the interviews more accessible to search, hear, and view. In its first six months the new archive has nearly doubled online usage. Among its features are the capacity to listen to full interviews, read full transcripts and, in many cases, watch online videos; the addition of photos and other supplementary documents to provide context for many of the interviews; and the capacity to browse by name, topic, or collection.

To ensure that the MROHP is widely visible online and known to as many potential users as possible, Program Manager Susan Becker employs a variety of outreach and marketing strategies.

- The interviews are accessible at three different levels: (1) "History in a Minute" modules that distill the most accessible or interesting insight; (2) "Shorts" of up to 20 minutes; and (3) the full interview, which can last up to two hours. The shorter versions can be used in a variety of settings to attract viewers and users.
- All three levels of videos are posted on the library's YouTube Channel.
- *Listen to This*, the program blog, includes regular posts about special projects and new elements available for on-site or digital users.
- The interviews are integrated into the library's catalog, with each interview having its own cataloging record and a link to its online archive location.
- Staff has created podcasts of some of the interviews which are available through iTunes; there is a playlist for these items.
- The library's Facebook page includes posts about MROHP and links to specific interviews.
- The robust online archive allows for searching by name, subject, or collection.

Beyond marketing the collection and ongoing archival work, MROHP staff carries out special projects that expand the collection, increase its visibility, and expand its potential uses.

LATINO HISTORY, a collaboration with the Boulder County Latino History Project, is an initiative to document the experiences of Latino residents. Before interviewing individuals the partners convened stakeholders in the Latino community to identify potential interviewers. MROHP staff train the interviewers and groups of high school and college students who participate as videographers.

THE ROCKY FLATS PROJECT consists of interviews that were collected over a period of twelve years to document the 50-year history of this controversial Cold War nuclear weapons plant from the point of view of workers, managers, government regulators, union leaders, sick workers, affected community members, and protesters. The interviews have been used for community presentations that stimulated dialog among diverse populations and recently were used as part of an exhibition—Rocky Flats Then and Now: 25 Years after the Raid—and for a comprehensive weekend symposium on the issues embodied by the plant's history.

In the Rocky Flats exhibition, which was held at the Arveda Center near Boulder, selections from the library's MROHP interviews were integrated with exhibition artifacts and photographs at three levels: (1) as stand-alone panels, with one-sentence quotes relevant to adjacent artifacts; (2) integrated into larger explanatory panels in which the interpretive text was augmented by a quote; and (3) as audio clips provided via a dial-in system whereby visitors could retrieve sound bites on their cell phone. For the audio clips, of which there were 20, a small label on the wall prompted visitors to punch in a certain number to hear the corresponding clip. The clips ranged in length from 30 to 60 seconds. Exhibition developer Larry Borowsky worked closely with Becker to select the quotes for the exhibition. In explaining his use of the oral interviews, Borowsky states:

> The exhibit was meant as the context for discussion about a particularly controversial and complex part of local history. The quotes were excellent vehicles to reflect the multitude of points of view about Rocky Flats. Without an interpretive authority, or a "correct" historical narrative, the voices of people told the story in a way that nothing else could. They helped bring the story to life.

BOULDER ACTION FOR SOVIET JEWRY PROJECT documented the experiences of members of a local group that helped Soviet Jews immigrate to Boulder as a result of religious and political turmoil in the late 1980s and early 1990s. The Boulder group was notable for its success in guiding immigrants through the resettlement process. In fact, a key interview question was directed at understanding the group's methods in order to provide lessons about immigrant settlement. In one case, the interviews resulted in a request from two interviewees, who had been ideological opponents, asking to be reinterviewed in dialog with each other as they talked for the first time in 24 years.

FLOOD OF 2013 is an initiative to document the reactions of people and organizations to a major local flood. Interviews were planned to cover the event from as many perspectives as possible, recording flood damage, recovery efforts, government responses and individual experiences. Recognizing that such events have long-term consequences, MROHP staff plans to reinterview many of the same people in 10 or 15 years.

MROHP is unusual for its scope, visibility, and content uses. The rich array of interviews, their accessibility in different formats, the extent of complementary materials beyond the interviews, the emphasis on thematic projects, and the efforts of the library staff to ensure the visibility and usefulness of the interview collection—all these are hallmarks of an exceptional program that offers a model for other libraries committed to documenting the voices and experiences of its residents.

● **CHALLENGES.** Program Manager Becker identifies two challenges. One is the need to carry out archival work in pace with the amount of interviews being done so that a backlog doesn't accumulate. This can be difficult when there are long interviews that must be transcribed, tagged, integrated into the catalog, edited for "shorts," and so on. The second challenge is keeping up with technological change. To fulfill the program's commitment to make content accessible at all times, it is necessary to constantly migrate content to the most up-to-date formats. The new online archive, based on a WordPress platform, is not only low cost but also flexible and adaptable, which is intended to help with continual upgrading.

● **FUTURE PLANS.** Having recently achieved a new level of operations, with a new Online Archive, a variety of Special Projects and project partners, a presence on multiple social media channels and a growing audience—both local and beyond—MROHP leaders are focused on maximizing exposure and use of the new site and on updating equipment.

NORTH END HOUSE HISTORY PROJECT
Portsmouth (NH) Public Library

OVERVIEW: The North End House History Project (the Project) is a digital archive and community history project developed by the Special Collections Department (Special Collections) of the Portsmouth Public Library (PPL) that documents the nearly 170 buildings demolished during the Urban Renewal movement following World War II. Drawing on a collection of appraisal booklets and related photographs of the buildings that were destroyed, Special Collections staff has established a dynamic online archive that has helped former North End residents recover an important part of the history of Portsmouth. The project reflects the trend toward community archiving by public library special collections across the country. It also demonstrates the galvanizing effect of a community archive in bringing together residents who might not otherwise find common ground.

> This kind of project is a natural for us—we have the infrastructure, the public space and the skills to help people to recover their history. It is important for an overall understanding of the development of our city.
>
> —Nicole Cloutier, Special Collections Librarian

PPL's Special Collections, focused on local history, art, and genealogy, reflect the history of the city of Portsmouth, as well as other towns in Rockingham County and Strafford County, New Hampshire, and adjacent York County in Maine. Holdings include city documents, vital records, maps, historical newspapers, photographs, World War II records, and the works of several local artists. In order to expand access to these materials, Special Collections staff has begun to digitize discrete categories, starting with local history records. According to Special Collections Librarian Nicole Cloutier, "Our hope is to create a dialogue with the Portsmouth community about our shared local history."

The North End House History Project is based on a set of 170 "Appraisal Report and Valuation Analysis" booklets in the library's city records, each documenting a property in the North End District of Portsmouth that no longer exists. There are also photographs of many of the buildings at the time of their destruction. The North End, primarily an Italian neighborhood, was then a viable and cohesive community with active businesses, residences, and historic structures. The records of the neighborhood are valuable historical resources, especially for the families of the residents and business owners who were displaced during Urban Renewal. Family members visit Special Collections "to reminisce and gather images of their childhood neighborhood." Today, the North End is undergoing commercial and retail development, creating somewhat of a local controversy and reminding some people of what was lost in the 1950s.

Recognizing the contemporary relevance of the North End building records, Special Collections staff decided to digitize the documents, make them available to remote users, and also use them to attract other records that provide context for the collection. The project web page states: "Our hope is to foster a community history project, including a way for the public to contribute memories, more photographs, and perhaps oral history for each property . . ."

To encourage donations and community participation the library reached out to the families of former North End property owners, asking them to identify other families and alert them about the project. At the same time, staff worked with volunteers to scan the survey booklets for all 170 buildings and put them online along with related photographs. The response has been far greater than the library had anticipated. Many family members have donated images and family records and helped to create interest in the project across the community. Cloutier reports that "It is amazing how the static images we put online elicited such personal reactions and memories."

When Special Collections launched the project they held introductory meetings to stimulate community interest. Staff explained the goals of the project and made an effort "to let them know that we want to tell their stories . . . that over the years their stories have been told by others . . . that this project is about the human side from their perspective." Staff also discussed the kinds of donations they sought to build out the Collection: family anecdotes, factual details about the residences, businesses, neighborhood, and information on the people who lived in the buildings. Community response to the project, and community participation, have grown steadily from the outset. In fact, some community members have created a cohesive team whose members enjoy working together. Foot traffic has increased in Special Collections, while statistics for online visitation to the Project website have "skyrocketed." Cloutier states:

> The (North End House History) Project validates focused archival work and community partnerships. People have been touched that a public institution was interested in their history. The more we put online the more people are coming in and wanting to help scan images and become involved. Other neighborhood groups want us to help them create a digital archive.

Several factors have contributed to the success of the project. Internally, the project aligns well with PPL institutional goals to expand community partnerships and promote the library as a community gathering space. Externally, the project coincided with efforts by Italian Americans in Portsmouth to recover their identity and history after decades of feeling sidelined and somewhat invisible. As a city agency, PPL activities are instrumental in helping preserve Italian American culture in the city.

One result of the project has been requests from other community groups for assistance in documenting and archiving their stories and histories. Special Collections is providing advice and training to one of these groups, from the Haven School Neighborhood, enabling volunteers to carry out their own research and interviews and start the process of developing an online community archive.

❯ **CHALLENGES.** In implementing the North End House History Project the primary challenge was working with Omeka open source software and a Linux server; ultimately library staff had to seek the help of an Omeka developer to build the site. Another challenge was finding the time to continue "feeding" the digital collections. Despite the fortunate involvement of interns from the Simmons College School of Information, and the commitment of trained volunteers, there are insufficient hands to fulfill the project's potential.

❯ **FUTURE PLANS.** Special Collections staff is continuing to gather materials for the North End digital collection. In addition, the library is working with other history institutions in Portsmouth on a portal project, a central site "that those researching

Portsmouth history can come to in order to discover what digital collections exist in each institution."

ORLANDO MEMORY
Orange County (FL) Library System

OVERVIEW: The Orange County Library System (OCLS) launched Orlando Memory in 2008, with the goal of capturing, preserving, and helping people explore the history of Orlando through the memories and images of current and former residents. Today, the interactive site includes thousands of photographs, videos, documents, audio files, and web links and more than 600 registered users. Many residents and community organizations have contributed content that attracts and assists people from throughout the United States and beyond.

> **Orlando Memory helps residents understand where their stories fit in and why they are important. It also is a capsule of history and memory that preserves our community heritage for future generations.**
>
> —Donna Bachowski, Manager, Orlando Memory Project

In 2007 Mary Anne Hodel, OCLS library director/CEO, learned about new software that would allow library staff and community members to create a digital community history scrapbook. At the time OCLS, especially its flagship library, the Orlando Public Library (OPL) was known for its genealogical collection, one of the largest in the Southeast, and its Florida collections. Hodel and other library staff were searching for ways to document and preserve more of Orlando's local history, especially the history of the community before the advent of Disney World. They envisioned an interactive digital collection as a vehicle for finding, preserving, and sharing images and documents of value to longtime and recent residents. According to Hodel, "We wanted to explore and honor the rich and unique history of the area and also provide our community with a vehicle to bind it together."

Orlando Memory launched in 2008, an early example of a virtual community archive. Using open source KETE software, OCPLS staff populated the initial site with images and documents in four broad categories: places, persons, events, and organizations. They then conducted outreach to invite diverse members of the community to add to the site. Speaking to organizations, public leaders, educators, and special interest groups, they encouraged people to share their personal and community stories in whatever form they might take: written accounts of events and people, personal documents, organizational records, ephemera, photographs, and audio interviews. Within three years of launching the site, Orlando Memory included 3,500 images, 400 documents, and 500 registered users.

Outreach has been essential for the growth of Orlando Memory. Project Manager Donna Bachowski reports that staff has an "educational project to do," first, in helping people to see the historical value in their own stories and documents and second, in helping people learn how to use the site. OCPLS staff has had to build trust with people unused to sharing memories or memorabilia. They have also had to find ways to reach individuals and groups that do not usually use the library.

Scanning events at branch libraries have been particularly helpful in growing Orlando Memory. The neighborhood events are publicized in advance, inviting people to bring their personal historical materials and stories to the library for copying or recording. OCPLS staff scan items and interview the donors to gather as much detail about them as possible. They also conduct oral history interviews on-site or arrange a follow-up visit. In addition to scanning events, interviews with public officials have proven to be a useful means of outreach. The interviews engage these leaders with the project and use their involvement as a demonstration for others in the community.

Since launching Orlando Memory, OCPLS staff has continued to populate the site with historic items from the library collections. They have also worked to improve site usability. In 2013 they worked with designers to redo the site, using the Drupal content management system. Since then usage and additions have grown.

In order to keep expanding community participation, project staff work continuously to broaden awareness. They have created posters and a library display about the project and worked with local organizations to publicize the site to their members and constituents. As a result of a recent outreach event at the West Oaks Branch Library, staff added a series of interviews about growing up in central Florida titled "I Love Ocoee." Another recent addition is a collection of materials relating to the history of the Orlando Negro Chamber of Commerce. And, working with the Holocaust Memorial Resource and Education Center of Central Florida, which was commemorating the 75th anniversary of Kristallnacht, staff documented a series of lectures on the Holocaust and placed the videos on the Orlando Memory site. Each body of materials attracts different groups of residents, who then join discussions about shared experiences.

Library leaders see Orlando Memory not only as a service for the community but also a public relations vehicle. The site has made the library more visible within and beyond Orlando and has helped to draw in organizations and audiences that might not otherwise feel a part of the library. In addition, OCPLS staff is enthusiastic about the preservation value of the project. They note that many items contributed to the site would never have ended up in the library's collection and most would never have been digitized or shared with the community. According to Bachowski, Orlando Memory "adds a completely new dimension to our work and our collections." Orlando Memory was recognized by the Urban Libraries Council as an Outstanding Project in 2010.

❷ **CHALLENGES.** OCPLS staff cites two primary challenges in their work on Orlando Memory: the ongoing need for public awareness and the need to reorganize some Special Collections tasks to give staff time to conduct outreach and help people contribute to Orlando Memory.

❷ **FUTURE PLANS.** Orlando Memory leaders intend to sustain the project as a means of preserving the stories of "everybody" in the community. The project website states:

> Together, we can create a knowledge basket that contains the social and economic history of central Florida. With your help, Orlando Memory will become a mosaic of collections that evolves from our local heritage and traditions.

QUEENS MEMORY PROJECT
Queens (NY) Public Library

OVERVIEW: The Queens Memory Project (Queens Memory), a digital archive, is a Queens Library program that aims to gather and present the stories of people living in Queens whose lives are not represented in the current archival collections, while also connecting online users to the library's archives and the rich history of the borough. The development of Queens Memory offers an instructive example of how a traditional archive can absorb an interactive community archive, including working with other library departments to ensure its technological development. Queens Memory also demonstrates how community outreach and digital communications can expand archival content and transform the relationship between an archive and its constituents.

The Queens Memory Project is community-directed . . . instead of archivists imposing values and deciding what is most important, the community decides what is most important to record.

—Natalie Milbrodt, Director

Queens Memory is a special program of the Queens Library Archives (the Archives), which specializes in the history of Queens and Brooklyn, as well as Nassau and Suffolk counties. Holdings include manuscripts, business and organizational records, nineteenth- and twentieth-century newspapers, family papers, more than 100,000 historic photographs, and maps and atlases covering the years 1639 to the present. Queens Library also maintains featured collections, or Special Collections, that are distributed in varied branches and departments, including the Black Heritage Reference Center at the Langston Hughes Library and Cultural Center.

Queens Memory started in 2011 as a grant-funded collaboration between the Archives and Queens College Libraries' Department of Special Collections and Archives, with the goal of recording the personal histories of underrepresented community members. The project was subsequently taken over by the Archives with the Queens College Library as a continuing collaborator. In absorbing Queens Memory, Queens Library sought to expand the Archives' capacity for outreach and collection development, while applying digital technologies to deliver and build historical content.

Since 2011, Queens Memory has grown considerably as evidenced by its extensive documentation activities and community partnerships, the number of interviews carried out by staff and volunteers, the amount and variety of content made available online, the design and operability of the website, and the extent to which Queens residents have become involved in the project as contributors, volunteers, and beneficiaries. These activities have all been in service of the primary project goals: "to record borough history as it happens and empower residents from all ethnicities and walks of life to document their lives in the borough."

During this time of growth the project has become institutionalized within the library. Officially a part of the Archives, the program is now operated through the Library's Technical Services Department, specifically, its Metadata Services Division, with assistance from the Information Technology Department. The project's internal position reflects the evolution of the library's digital team and the formation of a Metadata Services Division with responsibility for digitizing the library's archival and special collections and creating metadata for all physical and electronic holdings.

Working with the Archives, Metadata Services coordinates long-term preservation and access to the digital collections, as well as perpetuating Queens Memory through partnerships, public events, and varied collecting and processing activities.

DOCUMENTATION ACTIVITIES. While the face of Queens Memory is its website, the core work involves documentation and presentation of individual life histories or topical stories using a combination of historical and contemporary photographs, maps, news clippings, and oral history interviews. These records and interviews are preserved in the Archives and excerpts are created for the website. Donors and interviewees are recruited by community organizations, educational institutions, or community libraries. Milbrodt explains the effort to be inclusive: "With 2.2 million people living in Queens, there are innumerable possibilities for enriching the picture of the borough and its people. We always try to reflect the huge variety of ethnic and cultural backgrounds here, and we are working hard to bring in material in non-English languages."

The size and diversity of the Queens population has necessitated a variety of approaches to collecting. One method is to invite individuals in a neighborhood to a "Story Sharing Event" at a local community center or library, where Queens Memory staff or volunteers interview people on-site or schedule follow-up interviews. Another means of collecting is through collaboration with educational institutions, including graduate classes as well as middle schools. Class projects and individual interview assignments have resulted in new archival records and uncovered topics for future exploration. The website, which is designed to foster interaction and content contributions, offers yet another method for collection development.

DIGITAL COLLECTIONS. The Queens Memory website features selections from the growing collection of digitized oral histories and related documents along with relevant selections from the Archives collections. Construction of the site is a major project in itself, one that is constantly evolving in relation to the interactions of users and the dynamic environment of the World Wide Web. The current website is divided into two major sections: Browse (People, Places, Events, Year) and Gallery (featured collections or topics). The content reflects past and current documentation projects, including the following.

HURRICANE SANDY. In the immediate aftermath of Hurricane Sandy, Queens Memory and Archives staff worked with librarians at community libraries in Broad Channel and the Rockaways to advise people on how to preserve their historical documents and to record immediate reactions to the storm. Project personnel also collaborated with *Jamaica Bay Lives,* a documentary film in production when the hurricane struck; the film crew conducted filmed interviews with residents during and after the storm and donated the footage to the Archives.

IMMIGRATION. English and Social Studies teachers at the Metropolitan Expeditionary Learning School in Forest Hills have engaged 8th graders in a yearlong oral history project on immigrant stories in Queens. Queens Memory staff trained the students in oral history interviewing; the students then conducted interviews with elder relatives about their immigration experiences and wrote up the interviews in the speaker's voice. The students' work is based on research guidelines and other free resources that the project makes available for teachers and students. The students' essays have been compiled as a book and their interviews form the core of the Immigration section on the website.

CULINARY TRADITIONS OF QUEENS. In 2012, Milbrodt collaborated with Queens College Sociology professor Dr. Anahi Viladrich, to develop an oral history project on the culinary traditions in Queens' immigrant communities. The project created experiential learning opportunities for students who generated interviews, photos, and other evidence of culinary traditions in Queens immigrant communities. Six student projects were featured in an exhibition titled Embracing Nostalgia: Retracing Queens' Culinary Traditions through Immigrants' Voices, which was shown in Long Island City, Queens.

QUEENS: NEIGHBORHOOD STORIES is a current experiment in crowdsourcing that tests approaches to community archiving within libraries. Through a collaboration with Historypin and the Metropolitan New York Library Council (METRO), Neighborhood Stories extends the scope of Queens Memory with digital tools and programming that engage local residents in creating interactive maps that express the history of their neighborhood. To carry out this pilot project Queens Memory staff identified several Queens neighborhoods where the Archives has relatively little historical information. Initial sites were St. Albans in southeast Queens and the Bayside community. Project staff organized local "pinning" events and worked with residents of these communities to engage them in local archiving and storytelling sessions. Residents have contributed their own photos, videos, and other materials to create interactive historical maps of their neighborhoods.

Queens: Neighborhood Stories has significance beyond Queens. As a national Historypin project, focusing on feasibility of community archiving in libraries in general, and as a collaboration with METRO, the findings from Neighborhood Stories will inform archivists and librarians throughout the region and the country. Queens Memory, Historypin, and METRO intend to create five videos to train future librarians, archivists, and community volunteers—videos that will help spread community archiving to other libraries.

Given the scope and depth of Queens Memory activities, and the project's impact on organizations and individuals throughout Queens and beyond, it is not surprising that Queens Memory received the Educational Use of Archives Award from the Archivists Round Table of Metropolitan New York in 2014 and an Outstanding Collaboration Citation in 2012 by the Association for Library Collections and Technical Services, a division of the American Library Association.

> **CHALLENGES.** Development of the Queens Memory website involved a massive software design process involving all the Queens Library departments that support the Project: Metadata Services, Archives, and IT. Specialists from these departments have assisted with cataloging, standards for metadata, software design, site construction, site analytics, and other technical matters. With an ongoing need for personnel, the project has benefited from a relationship with Queens College whereby students are assigned to assist with technical aspects as well as curatorial work.

> **FUTURE PLANS.** An important aspect of the program's future is improvement of its technical infrastructure. Staff is designing a new front-end interface that will serve as a curated space, enabling project staff and public users to select groups of records and publish them in galleries with relevant narratives. Users will also be able to upload their own digital photos and audio. The goal is to distinguish more clearly between Queens Memory as the site of user-generated content while maintaining the Queens Library's digital archives site as a comprehensive research tool.

> **RELATED PROGRAM.** Queens Memory/Queens Public Library are partners with the Santa Ana (CA) Public Library and Historypin, in a federally funded Institute for Museum and Library Services National Leadership/Demonstration Grant project to conduct library-based community memory programs that build community connections and cultural heritage collections through sharing stories of migration in America. The project aims to "outline the practices necessary to make libraries an anchor of intergenerational and intercultural discussions on a local and national level." Among other deliverables, the project will produce training guidelines and create a "getting started guide" for librarians.

SUMMIT MEMORY

Akron-Summit County (OH) Public Library

OVERVIEW: Summit Memory is a virtual community archive containing historical images and documents from institutions, organizations, and individuals in Summit County, Ohio. Developed by the Special Collections Division (Special Collections) of the Akron-Summit County Public Library (ASCPL) and launched in 2007, Summit Memory has revealed strong community interest in sharing records that would otherwise not be available online. It is an example of the national trend in public library special collections, including those that focus on genealogy, to use digital tools for aggregating, preserving, and sharing community history materials from multiple sources.

> **As the role of the library changes local content will become more and more important. People are interested in local history and while they will be able to get information on rain forests easily, information on something local may be less easy to obtain.**
>
> —Judy James, Special Collections Division Manager

ASCPL's Special Collections houses local history resources pertaining to Summit County and one of the most extensive genealogical collections in the area. Historical materials include organizational records, photographs, vertical files, postcards, and high school yearbooks. Special Collections has digitized some resources for online access. Public programs, such as exhibitions, lectures, and workshops, help draw attention to local history and the library's collections.

The concept for Summit Memory was prompted by the Robert W. Little Foundation, which approached ASCPL regarding the possibility of a multiyear grant for a major new project. Judy James, Special Collections Division Manager, was aware of the many small organizations, libraries, and institutions in Summit County whose historical records were not available in digital format. She was also aware of Ohio Memory, a statewide project involving multiple institutions with unique records and its success in helping to preserve them digitally and make them available online. James and her colleagues devised a plan for a similar collaborative effort in Summit County, which would aggregate and share digital collections for educational, research, or personal use.

In developing Summit Memory, the library identified collections within its holding that would be appropriate for the community scrapbook and would complement other organizations' holdings. Staff also conducted outreach to other institutions to encourage them to take part. In working with the Barberton Public Library, the Summit Historical Society, and other organizational donors, the library has assumed responsibility for digitizing the selected materials and creating the associated metadata. Donors provide the initial descriptions. For small historical societies and local organizations, such as the local nurses alumni association, this process has been tremendously helpful. Without Summit Memory they would not have the capacity to share records that are important for a holistic understanding of Summit County, past and present.

Special Collections staff has been gratified and surprised by the positive community response to the project. According to James: "We knew at the beginning that a community scrapbook was important but we did not anticipate how important. It has brought about new and positive relationships across organizations and we are getting almost 50,000 views a month."

To date, ASCPL Summit Memory has worked with about 15 organizations or other partners. The process of creating Summit Memory has, in and of itself, been a collaborative and community-building exercise, with benefit to organizational and individual donors alike. ASCPL pays for the licensing fees, software, and other equipment, and supports one librarian who works part-time on the project. Students from the Kent State School of Information assist on occasion in organizing materials for digital exhibitions.

Summit Memory demonstrates the value of bringing together a growing collection that is a unique resource for individuals, educators, organizations, and scholars. James states: "People want to identify with a place and a community. The popularity of Summit Memory is a testament to how a library can bring people together to share memories and experiences that are meaningful."

❯ **CHALLENGES.** Summit Memory staff finds that some organizations are reticent about sharing their records and images. As a consequence they sometimes have to educate potential donors about the value of sharing historical materials for educational and public use.

❯ **FUTURE PLANS.** As Summit Memory continues to grow, staff aims to engage more institutional and organizational partners. A recent upgrade to CONTENTdm software will facilitate expansion. In another initiative, started in late 2014, Special Collections has begun to digitize a large portion of the *Akron Beacon Journal*'s photo collection to place on Summit Memory.

❯ **RELATED PROGRAMS.** Special Collections has from time to time conducted oral history projects, some of which are now accessible on Summit Memory. One of these is a project carried out in 2008, The Times They Were A-Changin': Akron Remembers 1968, which documented the riots in Akron. Another is the Neighborhood History Project, an ongoing initiative to document the experiences of individuals in specific communities.

TEEN TECH SQUAD
Providence (RI) Public Library

OVERVIEW: The Rhode Island Collection (RI Collection) of the Providence Public Library (PPL) is well-known for its rich historical collections pertaining to the eighteenth through the early twentieth century. However, the RI Collection is less strong on the late twentieth and early twenty-first centuries and, in particular, the histories of the diverse neighborhoods that make up contemporary Providence. To address this issue the library has organized a program that engages teenagers as "volunteer historians" to help build the collections. Offered during the summer, Teen Tech Squad participants take part in a history seminar that includes creating digital profiles of Providence neighborhoods for inclusion on the library's website. This out-of-school learning experience benefits the youth participants while helping expand the Rhode Island Collection.

> We are located in a city where a number of other institutions are serving academics, private collectors and specialists. As a public library we reach a slightly different audience, which includes these researchers but also includes members of the general public. In developing our collections and programs we need to consider our broad public mission.
>
> —Kate Wells, Manager, Rhode Island Collection

The RI Collection is a major component of PPL's Special Collections, including more than 16,000 printed books and pamphlets, more than 9,000 images of peoples, places and buildings, maps, clippings, the *Providence Journal* newspaper, manuscripts and ephemera, and a Genealogy Collection. The collection is heavily used by scholars and genealogists interested in the history of Rhode Island and/or New England. In order to reach beyond scholars to members of the general public, the RI Collection offers lectures, exhibitions, and workshops. In fall 2014, for instance, the RI Collection mounted an exhibition titled Protecting Providence: Three Centuries of Providence's Police Department. The Collection's *Rhode Island Red Blog* provides an opportunity to highlight items from the collection and to provide context for other library events.

In another effort to serve public audiences, while also filling gaps in its collections, RI Collection Manager Kate Wells designed Teen Tech Squad, a project that engaged young people in community documentation and collection development. The program was a collaboration with the Brown University Center for Public Humanities, the Rhode Island Historical Society, the Providence Preservation Society, and the Providence Youth Center.

Launched in the summer of 2014, Teen Tech Squad involved a seminar for teenagers on the use of digital technologies for historical documentation. With the assistance of staff from the library's technology training program, participants learned how to work with digital tools to carry out digital photography, videography, and aural recording for research and presentations. The teens were provided with iPads and encouraged to conduct oral history interviews, create documentary videos, design digital exhibitions, and collect ephemera reflecting their own neighborhoods. Participants also received an introduction to the concepts of public history and primary source documentation, and were encouraged to think critically about how to present neighborhood history for future researchers.

Over the course of the program Teen Tech Squad members created nine digital Neighborhood Profiles which were introduced at a Special Gallery Night at the RI Historical Society's John Brown House Museum. Topics ranged from Providence's Castle Theatre and North Burial Ground Cemetery to the Carrie Tower at Brown University. The Neighborhood Profiles are now part of the library's digital collections and provide the basis for future neighborhood histories by staff and/or volunteer historians. The program received a federal grant from the Institute for Museum and Library Services, administered by the State Library of Rhode Island.

❯ **CHALLENGES.** With only one full-time professional working on the RI Collection, Wells juggles many activities, from reference assistance and equipment maintenance to fundraising and planning for digitization. Teen Tech Squad and similar innovative programs are important additions to the department's agenda but, for now, they are carried out over and above routine archival duties.

❯ **FUTURE PLANS.** Plans for the immediate future include increased oral history work to continue expanding the RI Collection's documentation of twentieth- and twenty-first-century life in Providence neighborhoods.

❯ **RELATED PROGRAM.** In order to expand participation in its community documentation efforts the RI Collection has designed a Family History Workshop Series. The Series aims to introduce varied audiences and age groups to the excitement of family and community history, expose these groups to the RI Collection, and build a cadre of "volunteer historians" able to augment staff in carrying out future oral history projects. The series is cumulative, with "each workshop building upon the last." One session is led by a public humanities specialist from Brown University who provides in-depth training on interviewing, using a digital audio recorder, saving files, and transcribing interviews. The library lends audio recorders to all workshop participants and encourages them to pursue their own interviews and donate them to the RI Collection.

TEN

TOURS, COMMEMORATIONS, AND SPECIAL EVENTS

We are taking a fresh look at our Special Collections, looking for the stories behind the items, and finding ways to communicate those stories to different audiences.

—Michael Johnson, Special Collections Manager,
Enoch Pratt Free Library (Baltimore, MD)

Tours, commemorations, and special events are not a new phenomenon in special collections and archives. Quite the opposite. Along with exhibitions and lectures, these have been, and still are, among the most common archival programming formats.

Tours, in particular, are ubiquitous. Nearly every special collection has at one time or another hosted a group of teachers, donors, school children, or visiting professionals for one or another form of tour. These might be pro forma "show and tell" public tours, hands-on tours, behind-the-scenes tours, or topical tours connected to a special occasion. In the larger institutions, tours or special events take on special importance in the context of fundraising and marketing.

Similarly, commemorations are common in library archives and special collections. What better reason to mount an exhibition or organize a lecture than the birthday of a writer whose works are in the collection or a historical event that is relevant to the community? Despite their usefulness, these programming hooks can become routinized, and all too often provide the framework for a predicable program agenda.

The examples of tours, commemorations, and special events in the following pages demonstrate that some institutions are experimenting with new approaches— approaches that are different in scale, content, and even location. There are tours that do not take place within the library but outside of it, benefitting from the guidance of archivists, information drawn from the collection, and the use of digital tools for communicating and sharing information. There are commemorations that are not limited to one program format and one occasion, but are the catalyst for multiple activities at multiple venues with widespread participation. And there are events that do not simply occur once but are recorded and disseminated electronically to reach broader audiences.

Among the new approaches are discernible trends. With respect to tours, some archivists such as Michael Johnson, Special Collections manager at the Enoch Pratt Free Library in Baltimore (MD), are experimenting with scripted "experiential" tours. Other archivists are creating apps for self-guided walks of historic neighborhoods. Special Collections staff at the La Crosse (WI) Public Library is finding a large audience for its Footsteps Tours that involve costumed interpreters and dramatizations of local history stories. These efforts and others suggest the range of current experimentation. Whether they are redesigning on-site tours, creating off-site experiences, or developing virtual tours, archivists and librarians are reinventing an old program format.

Commemorations are changing as well, reflecting more varied content, expanded scale, and local partnerships. It is no longer enough to commemorate a key national or local event with one public program or plaque. Nor is it adequate to celebrate the birthday of a major author or political figure with one celebration, reading, or lecture. Commemorations are being extended from one-time, one-place events to multiday celebrations with multiple partners and multiple venues.

Two initiatives in Philadelphia exemplify this trend. The Rosenbach of the Free Library of Philadelphia has extended its renowned Bloomsday event from one day to one week, encompassing readings of *Ulysses,* exhibitions, performances, a pub crawl, and special tours. The Free Library of Philadelphia has developed an even more ambitious approach to commemorating major authors represented in Special

Collections. Using as a centerpiece a major exhibition mounted in the library's Rare Books Room, the Free Library organized a Year of Dickens (2013) and a Year of the Bard (2014), both of which involved collaborations with numerous partners across the city to expand the scope and diversity of the commemoration. Similarly, Boston Public Library's commemoration of the 150th Anniversary of the Civil War offered exhibitions, lectures, tours, and performances over the course of a nine-month period. The programs, which explored multiple aspects of the Civil War, demonstrated how special collections can stimulate learning and discussion through varied program formats.

Coordinated thematic programming is another characteristic of changes in approaches to commemorations such as Black History Month or Hispanic Heritage Month. The Newark (NJ) Public Library's 2014 exhibition Edible History: How Latin American Food Evolved and Transformed the World was the central focus for an in-depth monthlong "examination of the history and cultures of Latin America through the lens of food." Other institutions are carrying out similar thematic programs to enrich long-standing monthly commemorations.

Some commemorations have particular local significance, and archivists and special collections librarians are exploring new methods for bringing that significance to wider public attention. The reenactment of the 1939 Alexandria (VA) Library Sit-in, for example, focused attention on the historical importance of the sit-in while bringing to life items in the library's collection. Special Collection Librarian George Combs observed: "It was exciting to see so many people assembled to commemorate a nationally significant event that took place just 10 feet off the library entrance. People realized, some for the first time, the importance and the relevance of their own community history."

On a larger scale, the Birmingham (AL) Public Library coordinated a worldwide event to commemorate the anniversary of Martin Luther King Jr.'s "Letter from Birmingham Jail." Conceived by Jim Baggett, manager of Special Collections, this event took hold in remarkably diverse venues, from courthouses to street corners to libraries, successfully extending Birmingham's commemoration of King beyond an annual Memorial Lecture. The global response to the commemoration demonstrates the impact that one special collections unit can have on how the public understands, and engages with, an iconic document.

The following examples are only a small sampling of the creative ways that public library archivists and special collections librarians are revitalizing tours, commemorations, and special events.

BLOOMSDAY

The Rosenbach of the Free Library of Philadelphia

OVERVIEW: For two decades the Rosenbach of the Free Library of Philadelphia (The Rosenbach) has celebrated James Joyce's *Ulysses* with Bloomsday, a daylong festival on June 16, commemorating Leopold Bloom's walk through Dublin on June 16, 1904. In 2014 the festival was expanded to a week of events including walks through Philadelphia, readings from *Ulysses* by prominent Philadelphians, lectures, tours, a *Ulysses*-themed pub quiz, a major exhibition, and an author event at its sister institution, the Free Library of Philadelphia. Bloomsday demonstrates how a public research library can create events that are both informative and entertaining, and can use one special item to promote awareness of the overall institution.

> **Reading [*Ulysses*] is like trying to read a crossword puzzle. But listening to it, the linguistic fireworks come alive.**
>
> —John C. Haas, Director

Ulysses is one of the best known of the many treasures in the collections of the Rosenbach of the Free Library of Philadelphia, formerly the Rosenbach Museum and Library. The collection was founded in 1954 by A.S.W. and Philip Rosenbach, dealers in manuscripts, fine art, and books. Housed in an 1860s townhouse, the collections include paintings, sculpture, decorative arts, 30,000 rare books and more than 130,000 manuscripts. James Joyce's manuscript for *Ulysses* is one of the highlights of the Rosenbach's extensive collections of American and English literature. Other Joyce holdings are rare editions of all Joyce's works, including four copies of the rare first edition of *Ulysses*.

The Rosenbach's annual Bloomsday event involves an "open-air festival" that includes readings of excerpts from *Ulysses* at locations across Philadelphia and a tour through the city to commemorate Leopold Bloom's fictional odyssey through Dublin. Each year readers perform from the steps of the Rosenbach at Delancey Place, many of them prominent Philadelphians, Joyce specialists, and individuals representing the 20 Zip codes in the metropolitan area. Featured readers in recent years included BBC host, writer, and Joyce specialist Frank Delaney and H. E. Michael Collins, Ambassador of Ireland to the United States. Related activities in 2013 included an exhibition of Joyce materials—Exile Among Expats: James Joyce in Paris—an evening program with Irish author Jamie O'Neill, Bloomsday 101—a crash course on *Ulysses*—and hands-on tours of the Rosenbach's collections of works by Irish authors.

In 2014, the Rosenbach expanded Bloomsday to a six-day citywide festival. The extended commemoration was due, in part, to the Rosenbach's recent merger with the Free Library of Philadelphia. The celebration began with readings at Parkway Central of the Free Library, following which there was a tour through the city and final readings at the Rosenbach. Throughout the week of June 16–20 there were programs on different aspects of Joyce, his works, and the city of Dublin. Joyce's *The Dubliners* was the focus of special readings and programming one day. Activities included a *Ulysses*-themed pub quiz, an author event at the Free Library, and a tour of Rosenbach collections titled James Joyce and Irish Authors. In addition, the Rosenbach's 2014 Bloomsday exhibition I'll Make A Ghost of Him: Joyce Haunted by Shakespeare, linked the Rosenbach's Joyce and Shakespeare collections to the Free Library of Philadelphia's yearlong celebration "Year of the Bard."

❯ **CHALLENGES.** In carrying out Bloomsday, the Rosenbach endeavors to make *Ulysses* meaningful to varied audiences. Emily Parker, director of education, states: "The challenge is always to make *Ulysses* accessible to broad audiences. It's an intimidating book. Not only is it literature, it's modernist literature. But we've made great strides towards making it more approachable by reading it aloud, outside, in a public place, where passers-by can just happen upon the reading."

❯ **FUTURE PLANS.** For Bloomsday 2015 the Rosenbach plans to include new festival programs and additional reading locations.

EDGAR ALLAN POE EXPERIENTIAL TOUR
Enoch Pratt Free Library (Baltimore, MD)

OVERVIEW: The Special Collections Department (Special Collections) of the Enoch Pratt Free Library (Pratt Library) in Baltimore, Maryland, is experimenting with nontraditional approaches to creating connections between public audiences and research collections. A new type of introductory tour to its famed Poe Collection is one such experiment, and is also part of a citywide effort to promote Poe sites and collections. As a first for Special Collections, the Edgar Allan Poe Experiential Tour provides an opportunity to reconsider its traditional guided tours. Focusing on certain moments in Poe's life in Baltimore, and using letters, images, and other personal memorabilia, the tour aims to provide a meaningful experience for visitors beyond the usual "show and tell." Public responses to the tour will inform planning for other interpretive activities.

> **We have to be more creative and flexible today in order to attract people to focus on rare books or explore a topic in depth.**
>
> —Michael Johnson, Special Collections Manager

Pratt Library opened its doors in 1886, making it one of the oldest library systems in the United States. A major collection of papers and works by Edgar Allan Poe, presented in the Poe Room, form one part of the library's Special Collections, which also includes rare maps, paintings, prints, drawings and photographs, war posters, bookplates, African American rare books, and works by H. L. Mencken. In 1934 Joseph L. Wheeler, director of the Pratt Library, opened the Edgar Allan Poe Room to the public with the statement: "Our idea was to make it [the Poe Room] a living memorial to the great genius who stimulated American literature."

To fulfill Wheeler's vision, and to expand appreciation and use of the Poe Collection, Special Collections is developing an "experiential tour" of the Poe Room. The Room itself provides an engaging setting for the tour, which will feature the letters, memorabilia, images, and printed books that illuminate Poe's life and works, especially his personal relationships and his time in Baltimore. The tour will be one of several destinations on a citywide tour, organized by the local tourist agency Visit Baltimore, that is designed to link together Baltimore's various Poe-related sites and collections for visitors.

Drawing on letters from Poe to his wife, aunt, and other relatives, the department is developing and testing several tour scripts designed to help visitors gain insight into key moments in Poe's life. One script focuses on the circumstances of Poe's death, taking advantage of documents relating to the mystery surrounding his death. Another approach features Poe's impact on mystery fiction, especially through his stories *Murders in the Rue Morgue*. A third approach is organized around Poe's communications with his aunt and her daughter, Virginia, who was to become Poe's wife. Based on public responses different tour narratives will be refined and tailored for particular audiences such as students, scholars, and general visitors.

❯ **CHALLENGES.** A major challenge for Special Collections is finding ways to connect with patrons who of necessity are focused on economic issues rather than cultural enrichment. Another challenge for the department is determining the best means of promoting collections and programs. Special Collections staff prepares blog posts on the library's *Pratt Chat* blog, offering stories of items in the collection or information on acquisitions and upcoming events. Similarly, staff provides information for the library's Facebook page and Twitter account. Library staff are finding that these kinds of messages are proving as effective as longer blog posts in building audiences.

◉ **FUTURE PLANS.** If the narrative tour–approach works well with test groups, Special Collections plans to train a cadre of docents to help bring the Poe Collection alive with visitors.

◉ **RELATED PROGRAMS.** Exhibitions are an important part of the library's outreach to the general public. To enhance its exhibition program, Special Collections is experimenting with new kinds of exhibitions including one-day commemorative displays using single items from the collections. In September 2014, for instance, when the library carried out a series of events commemorating the War of 1812, Special Collections displayed its rare copy of the first periodical to publish the "Star-Spangled Banner." According to Johnson, "Brief displays and impromptu exhibitions can sometimes be as important in building visitors' connections to Special Collection as bigger and splashier programs. For us, as a public library with such a wide variety of audiences, we need to do both."

EDIBLE HISTORY
How Latin American Food Evolved
and Transformed the World
Newark (NJ) Public Library

OVERVIEW: Edible History: How Latin American Food Evolved and Transformed the World (Edible History) was a 2014 exhibition mounted at the Newark Public Library (NPL) that examined the history and cultures of Latin America "through the lens of food." The exhibition drew from various research collections, including Special Collections and the New Jersey History Research and Information Center (NJHRIC). With an array of accompanying programs involving Latin American chefs, writers, historians, performers, restaurant owners, and museum professionals, the exhibition provided a unique framework for the library's commemoration of Hispanic Heritage

Month. In addition, the Edible History exhibition initiative demonstrated how a public library can draw on its collections to enhance routine commemorations and to move beyond celebration to intellectual and cultural exploration.

So many of the world's favorite and most important food crops came from Latin America. Can you imagine a world without chocolate?

—Ingrid Betancourt, Project Director, New Jersey History Research and Information Center

NPL is the largest municipal library in New Jersey, with a collection of more than 1.5 million books, audio and visual materials, a renowned Special Collections Department, and other research level collections. NPL is also recognized nationally as a leader in services to Latino communities. Through its NJHRIC, which is made up of La Sala Hispanoamericana, a Hispanic Reference Collection and a Puerto Rican Community Archive, the library has developed an institutional structure for collection development, research, public services, education, and cultural programming that advances understanding of Hispanic history and culture and aids longtime Latino residents and newcomers alike. Throughout the year, under the leadership of Ingrid Betancourt, NJHRIC mounts public exhibitions and programs on Hispanic culture; NJHRIC also organizes the library's annual Hispanic Heritage Month activities. The commemorative programs, which may involve different library divisions, are organized around themes that illuminate important aspects of Hispanic culture, such as the 2011 theme exploring the African Spirit in Latin America.

For the 2014 Hispanic Heritage Month, NJHRIC staff selected food as the overarching theme for an exhibition and related programs. Edible History, a three-month exhibition on the "vast culinary landscape of the Latin world," featured diverse food products and food traditions originating in Latin America that have influenced cuisines around the world. It looked at the origins of different Latin American cuisines, and the worldwide economic, cultural, and political impacts of major foodstuff such as peanuts, corn, potatoes, and cacao. It also examined ways that Latin American food has influenced cuisine in the United States. As an interdisciplinary exhibition, Edible History included documents and images drawn from various library collections, with prints from the library's Special Collections. The exhibition also provided contemporary artistic responses to Latin American foodways in New Jersey through original works by painter Fernando Mariscal and photographic essays by reporter Gerry Vereau.

Public programs extended the themes of Edible History. Using diverse formats—lectures, cooking demonstrations and tastings, musical performances, and films—organizers encouraged members of the public to explore such subjects as Pre-Columbian food, Novo-Andean Cuisine, the connections between food and musical traditions in Latin America, fusion cooking versus maintenance of distinct culinary traditions, and the role of food in immigrant or expatriate Latino communities.

Edible History was supported by a variety of public agencies and involved cooperation with numerous organizations across New Jersey. The breadth of the program and its success in attracting diverse audiences helped expand recognition of NPL as a leading resource on Latin American history and culture.

⦿ CHALLENGES. During the last six years NPL has faced millions of dollars in budget cuts and has had to execute major reductions in staff and services. This has affected every aspect of the library's work, making it increasingly challenging for staff to continue offering the same level of cultural and educational public programs.

⦿ FUTURE PLANS. NPL's Hispanic Heritage Month in 2015 will focus on the history of Cubans in New Jersey; through an exhibition and public programs NJHRIC will examine why Cubans were drawn to the Garden State during the second half of the twentieth century, building vibrant communities, and how they transformed the culture and economies of many towns in northern New Jersey.

HISTORY TOURS
La Crosse (WI) Public Library

OVERVIEW: The La Crosse Public Library (LPL) Archives and Local History Department (Archives) have created a series of History Tours of La Crosse neighborhoods and buildings that use varied formats for "bringing the facts alive." Scripted walking tours, a stage production enlivened by costumed interpreters, self-guided online tours, and trolley tours led by a narrator are examples of Archives' experimentation with tours. There has been strong response to the tours' initiatives, which has also prompted new awareness and increased use of LPL's Archives.

One of the goals of our Archives Department is to do more public programs, especially programs that attract middle-aged and younger audiences.

—Anita Taylor Doering, Manager, La Crosse Public Library Archives

LPL's History Tours began in 2009, when the library met with other community organizations to discuss ways to implement a grant from the Wisconsin Historical Society to the La Crosse community in conjunction with a Wisconsin Public Television documentary production titled *Wisconsin Hometown Stories—La Crosse.* The groups decided to create a website devoted to the city's architectural and historical sites. The Archives, as the primary repository of historical materials related to the city of La Crosse, agreed to coordinate the project.

Archives staff worked with an architectural historian to develop content for what was to become the Footsteps of La Crosse website, announced as an opportunity to "Experience the development and beauty of La Crosse from the boomtown riverboat days to today through the evolution of building styles and details." The website consists of four self-guided tours with audio narration on the significance and highlights of a particular neighborhood and an interactive map offering details on landmarks. The website tours were also the basis for walking tours conducted by the specialist. As the website and tours were rolled out it was clear that the tours helped promote the website, and vice versa.

When the architectural specialist was no longer available, Archives took over leadership of the tours and shifted the focus to neighborhood history. Staff created a new set of tours that explore four historic neighborhoods through the lens of social, economic, and political history. Tour content draws on Archives' collections: maps, photographs, city records, organizational documents, scrapbooks, newspapers, family papers, cemetery records, yearbooks, and local histories. Led by Archivist Scott Brouwer, the walking tours include the use of tablets with which participants can examine relevant photos and documents from the library's collections. These tours have proven to be so popular that the library now offers the series in both spring and fall. Their success also led the library to examine other tour approaches.

The next tour experiment was Dark La Crosse, developed by Archives staff with a local writer and storyteller, that focused on "downtown La Crosse's macabre past . . . the red light district, Prohibition, small town politics and vigilante justice in a young and restless river town bordered by the sleepless Mississippi River." When these tours were introduced in October 2013 four events were scheduled. However, media attention and word of mouth led to long waiting lists. Additional tours were added then and in each subsequent season. The tours now fill up quickly with both residents and visitors. The tours give Archives staff the opportunity to talk about their collections and the many ways they could be used not only by scholars but anyone living in the community with curiosity about local history.

The success of these History Tours prompted Archives staff to consider how they could repurpose tour content for different audiences, including tourists and young children. To enliven the tours they tried including minimally costumed actors; people added a first-person twist on events to bring them to life. The dramatized tours were highly popular with audiences; they are now standard offerings. To address accessibility, Archives staff has arranged for trolley tours, led by a narrator, in conjunction with the La Crosse Area Convention and Visitors Bureau.

As the History Tours initiative has evolved Archives staff has noted the increasing number of younger adults and family groups taking the tours. It is clear that the tours are helping to fulfill Archives' mission to "develop and promote a vital historical connection within the community between the past, the present and the future . . ."

⊙ **CHALLENGES.** Archives staff has faced two primary challenges in implementing the History Tours. The first is finding the right balance between regular archival duties and emerging functions such as the History Tours and related digital projects. The second challenge is promotion. While social media channels are especially effective in promoting the History Tours, along with print and broadcast media, it is difficult for Archives staff to do both programming and related marketing.

⊙ **FUTURE PLANS.** With support from the Wisconsin Humanities Council, Archives staff is planning to further repurpose the best of the tour content by adding new stories to the scripts and creating an old-fashioned "radio show." Through collaboration with the Pump House Regional Arts Center, Archives will bring together a group of actors to enact stories linked to places on the tours. Live music and historical images projected behind the actors will help establish time and place. The radio format will extend the tour content to those who are not mobile and unable to take part in other types of tours. Beyond the History Tours, La Crosse Archives intends to carry out more interpretive programs such as "Sense of Place" neighborhood history presentations for local association meetings or community-led walks.

HISTORY TOURS
Sacramento (CA) Public Library

OVERVIEW: In recent years Sacramento Public Library's (SPL) Special Collections, known as the Sacramento Room, has developed history-themed programs that are proving effective in attracting new visitors to the library and new interest in the archival collections. History Tours have been especially effective: the Haunted Stacks Tour of the Sacramento Room; the annual Archives Crawl; and sacQR, an app for mobile devices that is used to explore the architectural and social history of Sacramento's K Street. In combination with other new programs these varied approaches to traditional tours are increasing public involvement with Special Collections.

> We want to expand, to reach a broader audience, including young people who would not normally visit special collections in a public library. We're working on developing fun activities that get them interested in the collections.
>
> —Amanda Graham, Archivist

Sacramento's History Tours grew out of the efforts of the library's first full-time archivist, Amanda Graham, who was appointed in 2010 with the understanding that outreach and programming would be key components of her position. Until 2010, Special Collections were used primarily for research, and programming was limited. Many Sacramento residents were not aware of the Sacramento Room holdings, which range from the history of Northern California to Printing and Book Arts, nor the Sacramento Collection, which includes maps, photographs, ephemera, rare books, yearbooks, and biographical documents. Since assuming her position Graham has worked with colleagues to experiment with programming designed to attract non-researchers and stimulate their interest in Special Collections. They have developed three tour types, all of which are proving successful in drawing new users and enhancing their understanding of special collections. Other library departments have helped the tours' initiative by assisting with communications and technology.

Haunted Stacks is an annual Halloween after-hours tour that attracts adults and young adults alike. Each year the tour is organized around a different time period and theme. The program starts with a classic film screening, followed by a behind-the-scenes tour of the Sacramento Room. Characters selected from the city's Old City Cemetery index are portrayed by staff in costume; they emerge at points during the tour to share their story in two to three minute sketches. Living characters pop out from different locations to speak to and sometimes interact with the audience and with one another. The tour changes each year—the theme, the movie, the characters being portrayed, and the route around the room. The program has been very popular, especially with younger adults, and has started to transform the image of the Sacramento Room to what Graham terms "a fun place."

Sacramento Archives Crawl is an annual fall event carried out by the Sacramento Room in conjunction with three other local archives. Participants are given the opportunity to view treasures from the collections, meet special collections librarians and archivists, and have behind-the-scenes tours of each archive. They receive "stamps" in an archival passport that is used for admission to the tour sites. In addition to an introduction to the content of the various collections, participants learn about preservation and storage issues and other aspects of archival work. With a free shuttle bus and special door prizes, this event has drawn 400 to 500 people a year into the Sacramento Room. Some participants return later to volunteer, do research, or to read and explore.

In addition to tours of the Sacramento Room during the Archives Crawl, staff has used the library's Tsakopoulos Library Galleria space to host other archives and vendors at the central library. In 2013 they celebrated that year's Archives Crawl theme, "A Passion to Preserve," by hosting a large preservation fair in the Galleria, with experts and demonstrations on preserving film, photographs, art, and more. This component significantly enriched the annual event.

SacQR is an app for mobile devices that enables users to take a self-guided tour of downtown K Street. Users can walk along K Street while reading descriptions of buildings and specific locations, viewing historic photographs of highlighted locations, and listening to audio narration. Special Collections staff created the content for sacQR, selected images and text descriptions for each site, and recorded the audio portion. Staff also persuaded local businesses to post QR codes in their windows so that people using the app could scan those locations. This is an experimental initiative, aimed primarily at young people who are used to using mobile devices for everyday functions.

Collections staff attribute the success of their History Tours to several factors. One is the involvement of staff in other departments. According to Graham, "by informing other staff about the program or getting them involved in program planning they become allies who spread the word to their patrons." Another factor is the equal emphasis on fun and on education. Both components have proven important in attracting attendees and users. A third reason for their success is extensive use of social media. By using a variety of online channels including Facebook, Twitter, Pinterest, and Instagram, program organizers reach audiences who might otherwise be unaware of the library, much less its historical and cultural treasures. In addition, Archivist Graham's role in helping create alt+library, an innovative group of twenties and thirties librarians who seek to get together and post information on what they are doing, has helped build visibility for the history tours.

● **CHALLENGES.** One of the biggest challenges in attracting people to the new tours has been overcoming the previous perception of the Sacramento Room as a place where collections are preserved rather than shared. The new programs have been designed to change this perception and to create a sense of excitement about local history and special collections.

● **FUTURE PLANS.** Sacramento Room staff is concentrating on strengthening the tour programs, each of which now has its own identity and track record, and broadening the audiences for those programs through social media and improved marketing. They also hope to create more formal tours that can draw in people with connections to particular neighborhoods or locations. As they create more mobile apps these can complement the tours, and vice versa.

JFK
A Lasting Impression
Fort Worth (TX) Library

OVERVIEW: JFK: A Lasting Impression was a major project undertaken by the Genealogy, Local History, and Archives Department (Local History and Archives) of the Fort Worth Library (FWL) in 2013 to mark the 50th anniversary of President Kennedy's 1963 Texas visit. The project included an opening event with the journalist Bob Schieffer and others who remembered Kennedy in Fort Worth. The commemoration helped draw attention to the library as a destination for history education and built staff capacity for public programming.

> The public response to our JFK exhibit was overwhelmingly positive. We did tours for public and school groups for 3 months.
>
> —Betty Shankle, Manager, Genealogy, Local History and Archives Department

JFK: A Lasting Impression was the largest and most visible of the exhibitions undertaken to date by Local History and Archives. The Department's collections offer multiple topics for exhibitions, covering the settlement and growth of Fort Worth, its social and family history, and its businesses, cultural traditions, architecture, and organizations. For Local History and Archives the 50th anniversary of President and Mrs. Kennedy's visit to Fort Worth was an appropriate occasion to showcase materials from its collections and to develop related programs exploring the significance of the event.

JFK: A Lasting Impression focused on two Kennedy visits to Fort Worth, one during the 1960 presidential campaign, and one on the day before his trip to Dallas.

For the latter trip, images and documents recorded the Kennedys' arrival in Fort Worth, their stay in the Hotel Texas, the president's informal remarks to local crowds, and his breakfast meeting with city leaders and citizens, where he delivered his last public speech. The exhibition also examined connections between Lee Harvey Oswald and the city of Fort Worth, and it documented the city's efforts to create the JFK Tribute in General Worth Square. Many of the photographs, items, and artifacts on display were from History and Archives; others were loaned by members of the JFK Resources Consortium, a group of North Texas institutions with collections pertaining to John F. Kennedy and his Texas connections.

In conjunction with the exhibition opening, the library organized a major event that featured Bob Schieffer, host of *Face the Nation*. Local CBS affiliate anchor Tracy Kornet interviewed Schieffer about the day the president was assassinated and how the tragedy continues to affect the nation. A video of that broadcast is available on the library's website along with audio recordings of Kennedy's two last speeches, both given in Fort Worth. Through extensive student and public tours, History and Archives staff and local historians worked to expand visitors' understanding of the significance of Kennedy's visit to Fort Worth.

◉ CHALLENGES. The size and significance of JFK in Fort Worth: A Lasting Impression, and the strong public response to the exhibition and opening events, presented library staff with logistical challenges such as crowd control, security, and the staffing of tours.

◉ FUTURE PLANS. Looking ahead, Betty Shankle, Manager of Local History and Archives, sees the need and the potential for a new building that would hold the growing collections and allow for more substantial exhibitions, such as the JFK exhibition, on an ongoing basis.

LETTER FROM BIRMINGHAM JAIL BY MARTIN LUTHER KING JR.
Birmingham (AL) Public Library

OVERVIEW: On April 16, 2013, readings of Martin Luther King Jr.'s "Letter from Birmingham Jail" occurred in more than 250 locations worldwide commemorating the 50th anniversary of its creation. Led by the Birmingham Public Library's (BPL) Department of Archives and Manuscripts (Archives) this first-time world celebration resulted in widespread public reflection on the significance of the letter, which was written while King was incarcerated in an isolation cell in Birmingham, Alabama. The large global response to the anniversary reading affirms the value of the library's efforts to use archival collections for education and inspiration and illustrates the power of public library archivists who are willing to stretch beyond their usual programmatic boundaries.

> **It is my humble honor to join with the Birmingham Public Library and so many voices around the world in reading an excerpt from Dr. King's letter on the floor of the House of Representatives.**
>
> —U.S. Congresswoman Terri A. Sewell reading from the House floor in Washington, D.C. April 16, 2013

BPL's Archives contain more than 400,000 photographs and 30,000,000 documents, including government and business records, maps, letters, diaries, scrapbooks, and architectural drawings. The Archives also includes the most comprehensive collection of research materials relating to the civil rights movement in Birmingham in existence. Among the items in the Civil Rights Collections are images of Dr. King and other protest leaders marching in Birmingham on the day that he was jailed. The library also owns the original copy of King's remarkable "Letter from Birmingham Jail" as well as two of the earliest printed editions. The famous letter, which had to be smuggled out of the prison on scraps of paper, encouraged King's fellow demonstrators to continue to press forward and explained "why we find it difficult to wait." King's status as one of the leading voices for human rights in the twentieth century makes the letter a moral, political, and spiritual touchstone for people worldwide.

For many years the BPL Archives celebrated Martin Luther King Jr. through exhibitions, book talks, family events, and programs for scholars. Starting in 2003 the Archives sponsored an Annual Martin Luther King Jr. Memorial Lecture. Over the years Archives staff discussed how they might create an event that would have even greater impact, leading to the concept for public readings of the "Letter from Birmingham Jail." In 2012, anticipating the 50th anniversary of the letter, a group of Archives staff led by Archives Manager Jim Baggett started to organize a one-day event of readings to take place on April 16, 2013.

To implement the program Archives issued an open invitation via the Internet and a press release that encouraged readings by and in institutions of all types. There were no strict guidelines for the readings other than that they be "public." BPL suggested that people read the "Letter from Birmingham Jail" in groups of "two people to hundreds of people" in any setting at any time on April 16. The effort to support, publicize, and document the event grew to include staff throughout BPL. Communications staff helped to make sure there were widespread postings and alerts on various social media sites such as Facebook and Twitter. They also created a database of participants and circulated periodic updates. Archives staff provided advice to individuals and institutions that lacked experience in creating public programs. The library's webmaster and Archives staff provided images and graphics for participants to use on their promotional materials and websites. A Pinterest page was created where participants could share images and video from their readings. Baggett states: "We think this is a good example of how programming can be done by applying imagination and using the staff and tools (in this case the Internet and social media) at hand."

Participation in the reading event far exceeded BPL's original expectations. Reports from local organizers indicated that there were more than 250 readings worldwide, including 33 states and 22 countries. Sites included the City Archives of Iceland, the South Africa Apartheid Museum, the Palmer Research Station in Antarctica, the Hochmeister Platz in Berlin, and the entrance to the Birmingham Jail. Across the United States a wide variety of institutions took part: churches, city halls, colleges and universities, bookstores, high schools, synagogues, and courthouses. Libraries in Tuscaloosa (AL), San Jose (CA), Vergennes (VT), Fayetteville (AR), and New York City are a small selection of the many that participated. Comments from those who read the letter and those who listened to it being read indicate how powerful the document was—and is—as a statement on human rights.

The worldwide reading of BPL's "Letter from Birmingham Jail" was selected by the Library Leadership and Management Association (LLAMA), a division of the American Library Association (ALA), as one of eight libraries to receive the John Cotton Dana Award for outstanding public relations in 2013.

◉ **CHALLENGES.** One of the challenges that BPL staff faced in implementing the worldwide reading was allocating time to communicate with and track participants. Although social media channels were helpful, the appropriate level of communications took a great deal of time.

◉ **FUTURE PLANS.** BPL expects to carry out a similar commemoration at an appropriate anniversary date in the future.

1939 ALEXANDRIA LIBRARY
SIT-IN ANNIVERSARY

Alexandria (VA) Public Library

OVERVIEW: One of the first civil rights sit-ins in the country, and the first to take place in a public library, occurred in 1939 at the Barrett Library, Alexandria's first public library, when five men protested policies that excluded African American residents. In 2009, Alexandria Public Library's (APL) Special Collections Branch (Special Collections), which houses documents relating to the Sit-in, spearheaded a commemoration of the event including a reenactment of the 1939 Sit-in by students. The commemoration attracted a large regional audience, national media attention, and increased awareness of the library's historical collections. In 2014, Special Collections organized an even larger program, including events throughout the year and a special program in August to commemorate the 75th anniversary of the protest.

> Due to the bravery of these men, 75 years later our library is a community hub that supports all individuals by providing equal access to books, technology, culture, and so much more.
>
> —Rose T. Dawson, Director of Libraries

APL's 2009 commemoration of the 1939 Sit-in was a first for the library's Special Collections. With holdings that focus on Alexandria and northern Virginia history, archaeology, business, law, genealogy, the Civil War, and the Confederacy, there are also materials on the history of African Americans in Alexandria. These include records of slaves and free blacks and documents pertaining to the landmark Sit-in.

In 1939, five African American men protested against segregation by attempting to exercise their rights as city residents to register for library cards. Their "Sit-Down" protest challenged library policies that excluded blacks, and they were charged with disorderly conduct. Their right to library services was defended in court by local attorney Samuel Wilbert Tucker. There was no actual settlement of the case. Instead, the library constructed a separate library, the Robert Robinson Library for African Americans, within one year. The outcome disappointed Tucker who did not believe that "separate but equal" was a just doctrine. In fact, one of the library's most import-ant documents is a letter written by Attorney Tucker to the then library director, expressing his outrage at the library's reliance on a separate facility as a means of settling the legal challenge.

In 2009 Rose Dawson, library director; George K. Combs, manager of Special Collections; and Audrey Davis, curator of Alexandria's Black History Museum, joined teachers from the Samuel Tucker Elementary School to create an event that would provide a signal to the larger community regarding the significance of the 1939 Sit-in. The event included a Reenactment of the Sit-in, music by students, and two lectures by specialists in southern history and the civil rights movement. Rele-vant documents from the library's Special Collections were on display. Organizers' expectations for at least 100 people was vastly exceeded, with a much larger audience of a cross section of residents and civic leaders, as well as reporters from the local media, the *Washington Post*, and CSPAN.

The library's commemoration of the Sit-in was expanded in 2014 to include a Civil Disobedience Film Series, book clubs, a "Sounds of Freedom" concert, inter-faith church services, author talks, historical lectures, theatrical presentations, and a bicycle tour of sites associated with the Sit-in. The major event featured speeches by Frank Smith, director of the African American Civil War Museum and Patricia Timmons-Goodson, North Carolina Supreme Court Justice and a Commissioner of the United States Commission on Civil Rights. To extend discussion of the event the library invited the public to share their experiences online.

Both the 2009 and the 2014 commemorations were supported by volunteers and benefited from the involvement of many partner organizations and the library board. As a result of the program Library Director Dawson has established the Samuel W. Tucker Fund to support acquisition and care of materials relating to civil rights and the African American experience, along with programs and lectures.

● **CHALLENGES.** Library staff, especially Special Collections staff, was not accus-tomed to organizing major public events, especially the associated marketing. Nor did they expect the level of media attention that occurred in 2009.

● **FUTURE PLANS.** To follow up on its commemoration of the 1939 Sit-in, APL has applied for a Presidential Medal for Samuel Tucker and plans to petition the US Postal Service for a Samuel Tucker stamp. With support from the new Tucker Fund Special Collections staff plans to digitize and upload more documents relating to the 1939 Sit-in and other aspects of Alexandria's African American history.

TORN IN TWO
The 150th Anniversary of the Civil War
Boston Public Library

OVERVIEW: In 2011 Boston Public Library (BPL) launched a commemoration of the sesquicentennial of the Civil War—"A Citywide Commemoration of History"—that encompassed a wide range of interpretive programs, showcased Collections of Distinction, launched new online collections, and engaged specialist and general audiences through exhibitions and programs at the Central Library and branch libraries. The commemoration, which unfolded over seven months, involved many departments, in particular the Norman B. Leventhal Map Center, Exhibitions and Programming, Special Collections, and Digital Services. With a major exhibition titled Torn in Two: The 150th Anniversary of the Civil War as a centerpiece, the program demonstrated the value of coordinating diverse library assets and programs around a common theme to illuminate an important historical event.

The extraordinary collections of the Boston Public Library allow us to connect modern audiences with actual artifacts in powerful and exciting ways.

—Beth Prindle, Manager, Exhibitions and Programming

BPL Special Collections include some of the most significant artistic, historical, and bibliographic holdings in the United States, from Maps and Prints to Pictorial Archives, Manuscripts, Rare Books, and Local History. With collections dating from its founding in the mid-nineteenth century, BPL offers extraordinary resources for scholarship, education, and inspiration. Starting in 2011 the library has endeavored to identify its most valuable and important materials, "Collections of Distinction," in order to make them more visible to the general public. These materials receive priority in terms of preservation, digitization and interpretation. At the same time, the library is using thematic programming, in multiple formats and at multiple locations, to feature and illuminate the significance of Collections of Distinction and other core collections.

In 2011, the 150th Anniversary of the American Civil War provided an opportunity to demonstrate BPL's dedication to presenting and interpreting key collections. Over the course of the nine-month commemoration, BPL carried out numerous educational and interpretive programs.

EXHIBITIONS. Four simultaneous exhibitions enabled BPL curators to mine their vast collections of prints, maps, photographs, manuscripts, periodicals and letters to "tell the tales of the war."

- Torn in Two: The 150th Anniversary of the Civil War was a focal exhibition that showcased 50 historic maps along with relevant photographs, prints, paintings, cartoons, diaries, music, and press of the period. Organized by the Norman B. Leventhal Map Center, the multimedia display explored the central role geography played in the "causes, conduct, consequences and commemorations of the American Civil War." Using items from across the library's vast Special Collections, the exhibition showcased materials from recently designated Collections of Distinction, including Boston and New England Maps and the Twentieth Massachusetts Regiment Collection. BPL published a catalogue of the exhibition, consisting of essays by scholars. The exhibition subsequently traveled to Ford's Theater in Washington, D.C., and the University of Southern Maine's Osher Map Library and Smith Center for Cartographic Education.
- Home Front: Boston and the Civil War focused on ten notable Bostonians, using artifacts, prints, letters, and other materials to tell "the story of the Civil War through the eyes of those who lived it." Curators also developed a complementary online exhibition of digitized materials and selected content drawn from the physical display.
- Winslow Homer's Illustrations featured the library's exceptional collection of prints by Homer, especially those created for illustrated weeklies between 1858 and 1873. His images reflected the brutality of the Civil War, its impact on rural life, and the changing roles of women. A digital gallery enabled visitors to examine Homer's 120 illustrations for *Harper's Weekly*, and 35 additional Homer prints from the Print Department are now available online.
- Photo by Brady: The Civil War through the Lens of Matthew Brady drew from BPL's collection of 375 Civil War photographs by Matthew Brady and others from the Brady studio. These are part of the Twentieth Massachusetts Regiment Collection, a Collection of Distinction.

PUBLIC PROGRAMS. The four major exhibitions at the McKim building in Copley Square provided the visual and intellectual underpinnings for public programs at the central library and branch libraries. Central library programming included exhibition tours, a Civil War film series, a string band performance, and a lecture on fashions of the Civil War era. In addition, the BPL's two signature series, the Lowell Lecture Series and the Local and Family History Series, both focused on Civil War themes. For the Lowell Lectures, five national experts presented on aspects of the Civil War, such as battlefields and fiction about the period. The Local and Family History Series focused on Massachusetts' involvement with the conflict and featured local regiments each month. In the fall of 2011 a panel of experts from around the country shared their insights on the war in a daylong symposium focusing on maps and cartographic resources of the period.

Branch library programming was highly varied, with performances of music of the Civil War, impersonations of historical figures such as Harriet Tubman and Louisa May Alcott, and an exhibition at the Brighton Branch of the BPL that featured paintings, stamps, and reproductions of Civil War–era newspapers.

ONLINE ACCESS. Boston Public Library's web services team created a dedicated web page for the commemoration, providing details on the programs as well as recommended books and movies. A virtual tour of the Torn in Two exhibition provides ongoing access to the exhibition content and digitized images; The Home Front exhibition is available via the library's exhibition page.

❯ CHALLENGES. This was the first major thematic initiative launched by the library, so defining the scope, participants, content, funding, and parameters all required new procedures and programmatic structures.

❯ FUTURE PLANS. The library continues to catalog and digitize materials exhibited during the commemoration, such as the anti-slavery collection, and to make them available electronically and through the Internet Archive.

YEAR OF THE BARD
Free Library of Philadelphia

OVERVIEW: In 2014 the Rare Books Division of the Free Library of Philadelphia (FLP) mounted a major exhibition on Shakespeare—Shakespeare for All Time—that was the centerpiece of Year of the Bard: Shakespeare at 450, a yearlong multifaceted celebration to commemorate the 450th anniversary of Shakespeare's birth. The program mobilized many library departments and external partners. Following on the prior year's celebration of Charles Dickens, which also featured a rare books exhibition, Year of the Bard demonstrated FLP's commitment to collections-based public programming and its capacity to engage varied ages and audiences through diverse program activities. FLP's system-wide approach to thematic programming based on special collections offers a model for building a critical mass of concentrated activities that can have wide impact on the cultural life of a city.

> It is inspiring to see the impact of a Rare Book Department exhibition, how it is radiating outward from Parkway Central Library and how the material speaks to everyone. This is where book arts and high culture meet popular culture, for public benefit.
>
> —Janine Pollock, Manager, Rare Book Department

FLP's special collections are among the nation's premier public library collections in terms of their depth, breadth, and quality. From the first donation in 1899, the library has benefited from gifts of cuneiform tablets and incunabula, orchestral music and children's literature, drawings by American artists, letters by American presidents, and rare editions of works by Beatrix Potter and Charles Dickens. In all these subject areas, and more, the library is an extraordinary resource for collectors, researchers, and students. In recent years the library has sought to reach beyond these audiences by providing more programs such as tours and classes that "help to open the department's collections to a wider public."

In 2010 the library's approach to programming based on special collections "hit a new vein" with a yearlong Year of Dickens. With an exhibition of Dickens materials as the focal event, the library organized citywide programming that engaged audiences in reading Dickens, discussing Dickens, or watching performances inspired by Dickens. Programs in the neighborhood libraries and at the Parkway Central Library were reinforced by digitization of Dickens' letters and by related blog posts and dialogue about Dickens on social media sites. The Twitter account for Charles Dickens, for instance, captured people's imaginations and became quite popular. The success of the Year of Dickens, with so many people participating in diverse events, prompted the library to consider doing similar celebrations.

Shakespeare for All Time/Year of the Bard: Shakespeare at 450 is a major exhibition by the library's Rare Book Department that commemorated the 450th birthday of the "Bard." This exhibition, mounted in the Rare Book Department's new William B. Dietrich Gallery, was the inspiration for yearlong programming carried out by the library in partnership with the Philadelphia Shakespeare Company and numerous other cultural organizations.

Shakespeare for All Time, which was curated by Janine Pollock, manager of the Rare Books Department, featured Shakespeare's First Folio, published in 1623—one of only 40 complete iterations for the First Folio that is extant. The Second, Third, and Fourth Folios, also from the Rare Book Department, were likewise on display. In addition, the exhibition included portraits, prints, and editions of Shakespeare's plays that have been produced over the course of four centuries, many of them beautifully illustrated. The exhibition explored classical influences on Shakespeare and underscored the continuing influence of his plays, the comedies, histories, and tragedies, which continue to be read, performed, and celebrated today.

Opened in January 2014, at the Parkway Central Library, Shakespeare for All Time kicked off a 12-month exploration of Shakespeare's work and influence at Free Library and locations throughout the City of Philadelphia. The Press Release for the program stated that Year of the Bard would be: ". . . a year packed full of engaging, enlightening and entertaining programs and events designed to celebrate Shakespeare in all his classic and modern incarnations."

Each month throughout 2014 there were numerous activities, including readings, film screenings, an insult contest, radio programs, lectures, a Shakespeare Trivia Contest, craft sessions, and creative writing workshops at neighborhood libraries and other locations. All ages were targeted: a toga party for children, performances of Shakespeare's sonnets for adults, and a birthday party in April for families. The Pennsylvania Ballet offered Shakespeare-related performances and the Philadelphia Shakespeare Company mounted two major productions: *The Tragedy of Julius Caesar* and *Romeo and Juliet*.

The involvement of departments and libraries across the Free Library system was a major feature of the Year of the Bard. The Edwin Fleisher Collection of Orchestral Music, for instance, dedicated an hour-long program on its discoveries from the Fleisher Collections radio series to orchestral works inspired by Shakespeare. Neighborhood library activities ranged from readings from *Twelfth Night* at the Northeast Regional Library to a workshop on mask making at the David Cohen Ogontz Library. In addition, as a result of the library's recent merger with the Rosenbach Museum and Library the Rosenbach took part in the Year of the Bard with tours and talks about its Shakespeare-related materials and a summer 2014 exhibition on Shakespeare's influence on Joyce, titled I'll Make a Ghost of Him: Joyce Haunted by Shakespeare.

The scope and quality of the library's Shakespeare celebration reflect its commitment to expand access to special collections through public programs and to use special collections for cultural enrichment and education.

❯ **CHALLENGES.** For any special collections department there is an ongoing challenge in terms of integrating work on exhibitions and planning for interpretive programs with ongoing cataloging, research services, and digitization projects. With the Rare Book Department's expanded exhibition space this challenge will be highlighted and staff will probably have to spread themselves a little thinner.

❯ **FUTURE PLANS.** The high level of participation in the library's two intensive collection-based celebrations—Dickens and Shakespeare—affirm the value of organizing similar programs in the future. Upcoming plans include a citywide celebration of FLP's Pennsylvania German Fraktur Collection in 2015 as well as a celebration of the 150th anniversary of the publication of *Alice's Adventures in Wonderland* in collaboration with colleagues at the Rosenbach of the Free Library of Philadelphia.

INDEX

CPSIA information can be obtained at www.ICGtesting.com
Printed in the USA
LVOW03s0005150615

442432LV00022BA/655/P

9 780838 913352